ANOTHER MEXICO

Graham Greene

ANOTHER
MEXICO

THE VIKING PRESS

NEW YORK

CONTENTS

Author's Note

This is the personal impression of a small part of Mexico at a particular time, the spring of 1938. Time proved the author wrong in at least one of his conclusions – the religious apathy in Tabasco was more apparent than real. A month after the author left Villahermosa, the capital, peasants tried to put up an altar in a ruined church. Bloodshed and an appeal to the Federal Government followed, with the result that the Bishop of Tabasco was allowed to return to his diocese, the first resident bishop for fourteen years. There remains Chiapas . . .

Note to Third Edition

Eleven years have passed since this book was written, and it may seem now that the author dwells too much on a religious situation liable to change at the expense of more permanent sides of Mexican life. My excuse must be that I was commissioned to write a book on the religious situation, not on folk lore or architecture or the paintings of Rivera.

1950

What made the change? The hills and towers
Stand otherwise than they should stand,
And without fear the lawless roads
Ran wrong through all the land.

EDWIN MUIR

Man's like the earth, his hair like grasse is grown,
His veins the rivers are, his heart the stone.

Wit's Recreations (*1640*)

To consider the world in its length and breadth, its
various history, the many races of man, their starts, their
fortunes, their mutual alienation, their conflicts; and then
their ways, habits, governments, forms of worship; their
enterprise, their aimless courses, their random achievements and requirements, the impotent conclusion of
long-standing facts, the tokens, so faint and broken, of a
superintending design, the blind evolution of what turn
out to be great powers or truth, the progress of things, as
if from unreasoning elements, not towards final causes,
the greatness and littleness of man, his far-reaching aims,
his short duration, the curtain hung over his futurity, the
disappointments of life, the defeat of good, the success of
evil, physical pain, mental anguish, the prevalence and
intensity of sin, the pervading idolatries, the corruptions,
the dreary hopeless irreligion, that condition of the whole
race, so fearfully yet exactly described in the Apostle's
words, 'having no hope, and without God in the world'
– all this is a vision to dizzy and appal; and inflicts upon
the mind the sense of a profound mystery, which is abso-
lutely beyond human solution.

What shall be said to this heart-piercing, reason-
bewildering fact? I can only answer, that either there is
no Creator, or this living society of men is in a true sense
discarded from His presence . . . *if* there be a God,
since there is a God, the human race is implicated in some
terrible aboriginal calamity.

CARDINAL NEWMAN

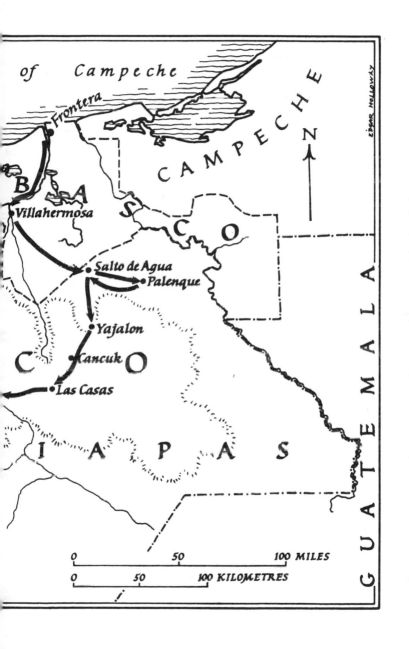

of Campeche

Frontera

CAMPECHE

N

EDGAR HOLLOWAY

B A

Villahermosa

S

C O

Salto de Agua
Palenque

Yajalon

C O
Tancuk

Las Casas

C I A P A S

G U A T E M A L A

0   50   100 MILES

0   50   100 KILOMETRES

ANOTHER MEXICO

PROLOGUE

(1)

THE ANARCHISTS

I was, I suppose, thirteen years old. Otherwise why should I have been there – in secret – on the dark croquet lawn? I could hear the rabbit moving behind me, munching the grass in his hutch; an immense building with small windows, rather like Keble College, bounded the lawn. It was the school; from somewhere behind it, from across the quad, came a faint sound of music: Saturday night, the school orchestra was playing Mendelssohn. I was alone in mournful happiness in the dark.

Two countries just here lay side by side. From the croquet lawn, from the raspberry canes, from the greenhouse and the tennis lawn you could always see – dominatingly – the great square Victorian buildings of garish brick: they looked down like skyscrapers on a small green countryside where the fruit trees grew and the rabbits munched. You had to step carefully: the border was close beside your gravel path. From my mother's bedroom window – where she had borne the youngest of us to the sound of school chatter and the disciplinary bell – you looked straight down into the quad, where the hall and the chapel and the classrooms stood. If you pushed open a green baize door in a passage by my father's study, you entered another passage deceptively similar, but none the less you were on alien ground.

There would be a slight smell of iodine from the matron's room, of damp towels from the changing-rooms, of ink everywhere. Shut the door behind you again, and the world smelt differently: books and fruit and eau-de-Cologne.

I was an inhabitant of both countries: on Saturday and Sunday afternoons of one side of the baize door, the rest of the week of the other. How can life on a border be other than restless? You are pulled by different ties of hate and love. For hate is quite as powerful a tie: it demands allegiance. In the land of the skyscrapers, of stone stairs and cracked bells ringing early, one was aware of fear and hate, a kind of lawlessness – appalling cruelties could be practised without a second thought; one met for the first time characters, adult and adolescent, who bore about them the genuine quality of evil. There was Collifax, who practised torments with dividers; Mr Cranden with three grim chins, a dusty gown, a kind of demoniac sensuality; from these heights evil declined towards Parlow, whose desk was filled with minute photographs – advertisements of art photos. Hell lay about them in their infancy.

There lay the horror and the fascination. I escaped surreptitiously for an hour at a time: unknown to frontier guards, I stood on the wrong side of the border looking back – I should have been listening to Mendelssohn, but instead I heard the rabbit restlessly cropping near the croquet hoops. It was an hour of release – and also an hour of prayer. One became aware of God with an intensity – time hung suspended – music lay on the air; anything might happen before it became necessary to join the crowd across the border. There was no in-evitability anywhere . . . faith was almost great enough

2

to move mountains . . . the great buildings rocked in the darkness.

And so faith came to me – shapelessly, without dogma, a presence about a croquet lawn, something associated with violence, cruelty, evil across the way. I began to believe in heaven because I believed in hell, but for a long while it was only hell I could picture with a certain intimacy – the pitchpine partitions of dormitories where everybody was never quiet at the same time; lavatories without locks: 'There, by reason of the great number of the damned, the prisoners are heaped together in their awful prison . . .'; walks in pairs up the suburban roads; no solitude anywhere, at any time. The Anglican Church could not supply the same intimate symbols for heaven; only a big brass eagle, an organ voluntary, 'Lord, Dismiss Us with Thy Blessing', the quiet croquet lawn where I had no business, the rabbit, and the distant music.

Those were primary symbols; life later altered them; in a midland city, riding on trams in winter past the Gothic hotel, the super-cinema, the sooty newspaper office where I worked at night, passing the single professional prostitute trying to keep the circulation going under the blue and powdered skin, I began slowly, painfully, reluctantly, to populate heaven. The Mother of God took the place of the brass eagle: I began to have a dim conception of the appalling mysteries of love moving through a ravaged world – the Curé d'Ars admitting to his mind all the impurity of a province, Péguy challenging God in the cause of the damned. It remained something one associated with misery, violence, evil, 'all the torments and agonies,' Rilke wrote, 'wrought on scaffolds, in torture chambers, mad-houses, operating

3

theatres, underneath vaults of bridges in late autumn . . .'

Vaults of bridges: I think of a great metal bridge by the railway station of my old home, a sense of grit and the long reverberation of plates as the trains went by overhead and the nursemaids pushed their charges on past the ruined castle, the watercress beds, towards the common, past the shuttered private entrance which the local lord had not used for a generation. It was a place without law – I felt that even then, obscurely: no one really was responsible for anyone else. Only a few walls were left of the castle Chaucer had helped to build; the lord's house had been sold to politicians. I remember the small sunk almshouses by the canal and a man running furiously into one of them – I was with my nurse – he looked angry about something: he was going to cut his throat with a knife if he could get away from his neighbours, 'having no hope, and without God in the world'.

I returned to the little town a while ago – it was Sunday evening and the bells were jangling; small groups of youths hovered round the traffic lights, while the Irish servant girls crept out of back doors in the early dark. They were 'Romans', but they were impertinent to the priest if he met them in the high street away from the small, too new Catholic church in one of the red-brick villaed streets above the valley. They couldn't be kept in at night. They would return with the milk in a stranger's car. The youths with smarmed and scented hair and bitten cigarettes greeted them by the traffic lights with careless roughness. There were so many fish in the sea . . . sexual experience had come to them too early and too easily.

A boy of twenty and a girl of fifteen had been found

headless on the railway line. They had lain down together with their necks on the rails. She was expecting a child – her second. Her first had been born when she was thirteen, and, though that wasn't mentioned at the inquest, her parents had been unable to fix responsibility among fourteen youths. The coroner suggested there was nothing to justify a verdict of 'unsound mind'. That was warranted only where pain and distress had been intense, but here – 'The only suggestion here,' he said, 'is that the girl might have been going to have a baby. It appears to be a case where that stage was reached through sheer lack of courage.'

A juror asked, 'Did the father and mother of the girl make any disturbance at the thought that there was going to be another baby?'

The father, 'No, we spoke to her calmly.'

A juror, 'It had no effect on her?'

The father, 'Yes, she dropped her head and started crying.'

I walked down towards my old home, down the dim drab high street, between the estate agents, the two cinemas, the cafés; there existed still faint signs of the old market town – there was a crusader's helmet in the church. People are made by places, I thought; I called this 'home', and sentiment moved in the winter evening, but it had no real hold. Smoke waved in the sky behind the Tudor Café and showed the 8.52 was in. You couldn't live in a place like this – it was somewhere to which you returned for sleep and rissoles by the 6.50 or the 7.25; people had lived here once and died with their feet crossed to show they had returned from a crusade, but now . . . Yellowing faces peered out of the photographer's window, through the diamonded Elizabethan pane – a genuine pane, but you couldn't believe it because of the Tudor Café across the street. I saw a face I knew in a wedding group, but it had been taken ten years before – there was something *démodé* about the waistcoat. With a train every hour to town there wasn't much reason to be photographed here – except, of course, for passports in a hurry. Well, next month, perhaps Mexico . . . and why Mexico? Did I really expect to find there what I hadn't found here? 'Why, this is hell,' Mephistopheles told Faustus, 'nor am I out of it.'

In the evening paper a woman made a statement to the police, 'I went downstairs. Oh! I had such a funny feeling. I saw the bread-knife. I sharpened it up and thought if I only had the strength I could push it in with one go. I went upstairs. My husband was lying on his back. I pulled back the bedclothes, and holding the knife in both hands I made sure to get him in the right place. I do not know, but it seemed if someone hit my hands down with a mallet. The knife went in as if his body was rotten. He sat up in the bed and hollered out "Hi, hi, hi."' It seemed if someone . . . one was reminded of the unseen companion on Everest to whom Smythe offered food, and of that Antarctic trudge at the limit of strength when there always seemed to Shackleton's companions one more than could be accounted for.

At the newsagents' they were selling a game called 'Monopoly', played with a picture-board and dice and little counters. It was very popular locally: there were 'Monopoly' parties. 'The object,' the rules said, 'of owning property is to collect rent from opponents stopping there. Rentals are greatly increased by the erection of houses and hotels . . . Players falling on an unoccupied square may raise a loan from the bank,

otherwise property will be sold to the highest bidder . . .
Players may land in gaol.'

In a shabby little shop there were second-hand copies
of *London Life* – articles about high heels and corsets
and long hair. And there the great buildings stood – the
chapel, the hall. There were new ones since my time.
On this side of the boundary they are always building:
you go away and come back and there is always something new – *London Life* and the Tudor Café and the
Irish servant girls making their assignations for a ditch.
Up on the hillside – scenes of Sunday walks – the beech
trees were in flamboyant decay; little boxes for litter put
up by the National Trust had a dainty and doily effect;
and in the inn the radio played continuously. You
couldn't escape it: with your soup a dramatised account
of the battle of Mons, and with the roast a Methodist
church service. Four one-armed men dined together,
arranging their seats so that their arms shouldn't clash.

In the morning, mist lay heavy on the Chilterns.
Boards marking desirable building lots dripped on short
grass, and the skeletons of harrows lay unburied on the
wet stubble. With visibility shut down to fifty yards you
got no sense of a world, of simultaneous existences: each
thing was self-contained like an image of private signifi-
cance, standing for something else – Metroland loneliness. The door of the Plough Inn chimed when you
pushed it, ivory balls clicked, and a bystander said,
'They do this at the Crown, Margate' – England's heart
beating out in bagatelle towards her eastern extremity.
In a small front garden before a red villa a young girl
knelt in the damp with an expression abased and secretive while she sawed through the limbs of a bush, the saw
wailing through wet wood, and a woman's angry voice

called, 'Judy, Judy,' and a dog barked in the poultry farm across the way. A cigarette fumed into ash with no one in sight near a little shut red door marked 'Ker Even'.

The cairn terrier farm stood on the crest of the hill. The dogs can never have been quiet; masculine women holding big steel combs strode in tweeds past the kennels. A notice said, 'Mazawattee Tea'. Bungalows were to let. Among the beech woods a brand new house was advertised for sale. It had been built with dignity as if to last, as though it stood for something – if only the pride of ownership. But it had been lived in only a month; the woods and commons were held out precariously by wire. The owner had married in December and had been divorced in August; they had seen one of each season – except for autumn – and neither wanted the house to live in afterwards. A handyman swept up the beech leaves from the paths – a losing fight against the woods – and lamented the waste of it all.

'Four coats of paint in every room . . . I was going to make a pool in the dell down there – another month and I'd have got the kitchen garden straight.'

A few acres of land, a desirable residence for as long as the marriage lasts, the soil exacting no service and no love – no responsibility for the child on the line. 'The object of owning property . . .'

(2)

THE FAITH

In July 1926, Father Miguel Pro landed at Veracruz. He was twenty-five years old and a Jesuit. He came back to his own country from a foreign seminary much as

8

Campion returned to England from Douai. We know how he was dressed when a year and a half later he came out into the prison yard to be shot, and he may well have worn the same disguise when he landed (the equivalent of Campion's doublet and hose): a dark lounge suit, soft collar and tie, a bright cardigan. Most priests wear their mufti with a kind of uneasiness, but Pro was a good actor.

He needed to be. Within two months of Pro's landing, President Calles had begun the fiercest persecution of religion anywhere since the reign of Elizabeth. The churches were closed, Mass had to be said secretly in private houses, to administer the Sacraments was a serious offence. Nevertheless, Pro gave Communion daily to some three hundred people, confessions were heard in half-built houses in darkness, retreats were held in garages. Pro escaped the plain-clothes police again and again. Once he found them at the entrance to a house where he was supposed to say Mass; he posed as a police officer, showing an imaginary badge and remarking, 'There's a cat bagged in here,' and passed into the house and out again with his cassock under his arm. Followed by detectives when he left a Catholic house and with only fifty yards' start, he disappeared altogether from their sight round a corner – the only man they overtook was a lover out with his girl. The prisons were filling up, priests were being shot, yet on three successive first Fridays Pro gave the Sacrament to nine hundred, thirteen hundred, and fifteen hundred people.

They got him, of course, at last (they had got him earlier if only they had known it, but they let him go). This time they made no mistake, or else the biggest mistake of all. Somebody had thrown a bomb at Obregón's car in Chapultepec Park – from another car. The evidence since then points to Government complicity. All the assailants escaped but the driver, who was shot dead. A young Indian called Tirado was passing by, fled at the explosion, and was arrested. He was tortured without effect: he persisted in declaring himself innocent. The police pounced on those they feared most – Pro and his two brothers, Humberto and Roberto, and Luis Segovia Vilchis, a young engineer and Catholic leader. No evidence was brought against them; they were not tried by the courts. The American ambassador thought he could do more good by not intervening and left next day with the President and Will Rogers, the humorist, on a Pullman tour; one South American ambassador intervened and got a reprieve – timed too late to save any but Roberto. Pro was photographed by the official photographer, praying for his enemies by the pitted wall, receiving the *coup de grâce*; the photographs were sent to the Press – to show the firmness of the Government – but within a few weeks it became a penal offence to possess them, for they had had an effect which Calles had not foreseen.

For Mexico remained Catholic; it was only the governing class – politicians and *pistoleros* – which was anti-Catholic. It was a war – they admitted it – for the soul of the Indian, a war in which they could use the army consisting mainly of Indians attracted by a dollar a day. (The individuals who composed the army, too, were Catholic, but it is quite easy to keep an uneducated soldier in ignorance of what he is doing.) By the time I left for Mexico, Calles had been gone some years – flown over into exile by his rival, Cárdenas. The anti-religious

laws were still enforced except in one state, San Luis
Potosí, but the pressure from the Catholic population
was beginning to make itself felt. Churches – now
Government property – were allowed to open in most of
the states, except for the hundreds that had been turned
into cinemas, newspaper offices, garages. A proportion of
priests calculated according to the size of the population
was allowed to serve by the state governments. The ratio
was seldom more favourable than one priest to ten
thousand people, but the law, particularly in the Federal
District of Mexico City, was slackly enforced. But in
some other states the persecution was maintained. In
Veracruz the churches remained closed until the peasants rose when a child was shot, early in 1937, in
Orizaba; in Tabasco, the tropical state of river and
swamp and banana grove, every church was believed to
have been destroyed by the local dictator, Garrido
Canabal, before he fled to Costa Rica – there wasn't a
priest in the state; in Chiapas no church was open for
Mass, the bishop was in exile, and little news came out
of that mountainous untravelled region where the only
railway line runs along the coast to Guatemala. Nowhere
were priests allowed to open schools. Educational programmes everywhere were laid down by the Government
on dusty rationalist lines – nineteenth-century materialism reminiscent of Herbert Spencer and the Thinkers'
Library, alpaca jackets and bookshops on Ludgate
Hill . . .

(3)

The rabbit moved among the croquet hoops and a
clock struck: God was there and might intervene before

the music ended. The great brick buildings rose at the end of the lawn against the sky – like the hotels in the United States, which you can watch from Mexico leaning among the stars, across the international bridge.

1. The Border

The border means more than a customs house, a pass-port officer, a man with a gun. Over there everything is going to be different; life is never going to be quite the same again after your passport has been stamped and you find yourself speechless among the money-changers. The man seeking scenery imagines strange woods and unheard-of mountains; the romantic believes that the women over the border will be more beautiful and complaisant than those at home; the unhappy man imagines at least a different hell; the suicidal traveller expects the death he never finds. The atmosphere of the border – it is like starting over again; there is something about it like a good confession: poised for a few happy moments between sin and sin. When people die on the border they call it 'a happy death'.

The money-changers' booths in Laredo formed a whole street, running downhill to the international bridge; then they ran uphill on the other side into Mexico, just the same but a little shabbier. What makes a tourist choose one money-changer rather than another? The same prices were chalked up all the way down to the slow brown river – '3.50 pesos for a dollar'; '3.50 pesos for a dollar.' Perhaps they look at the faces, but the faces were all the same too – half-caste faces.

I had imagined a steady stream of tourist cars going across from America on this side into Mexico over there, but there wasn't one. Life seemed to pile up like old cans and boots against a breakwater; you were part of the silt yourself. A man in San Antonio had said I'd be sure to find a car going down, and an agent near the bridge-head said that was right – he knew for a fact that there was a Mexican driving down from San Antonio ('in a fine German car') who would give me a seat to Mexico City for a few dollars. I waited and waited and of course he never turned up; I don't think he even existed, though why they should have wanted to keep me on *their* side of the river I don't know. They weren't getting any money out of me.

Every half-hour I walked down to the river bank and looked at Mexico; it looked just the same as where I was – I could see the money-changers' booths running uphill through the heat and a kind of mass of people near the bridge-head – the silt washing up on their side of the breakwater too. I could imagine them saying over there, 'There's an American going from Monterrey to New York in a fine German car. He'll give you a seat for a few dollars'; and people like me were waiting on the other side, staring across the Rio Grande at the money-changers and thinking, 'That's the United States,' waiting for a traveller who didn't exist at all. It was like looking at yourself in a mirror.

Over there – one argued to oneself – were Chichen Itzá and Mitla and Palenque, the enormous tombstones of history, the archaeologists' Mexico; serapes and big hats and Spratling silver from Taxco to delight the tourist; for the historian relics of Cortés and the Conquistadores; for the art critic the Rivera and Orozco frescoes; and for the business man there were the oilfields of Tampico, the silver mines of Pachuca, the coffee farms in Chiapas, and the banana groves of Tabasco. For the priest prison, and for the politician a bullet. You could buy a great deal for your dollar, everyone said.

I walked back up to the plaza and bought a paper. It was my unlucky day. The paper was being edited by the high school students – guest editors and guest reporters; it was full of small-town gossip and what was muttered on the campus. Impatient, revolutionary young men and women? Not a bit of it. The platitudes of age are often the main discoveries of youth. Geneva . . . democracy . . . popular fronts . . . the threat of Fascism. One might as well have been in the Albert Hall. As for Mexico, there wasn't as much news of it here as in New York. In New York there had been stories of fighting across the border from Brownsville – a man called General Rodríguez had organised discontented farmers, who were losing their land to the Indians under the Agrarian Laws, into a Fascist body called the Gold Shirts. The New York papers had sent down special reporters: one of them had taken a taxi from Brownsville to Matamoros and back and reported he'd seen no fighting but a lot of discontent. One pictured the earnest tough face peering through the glass at discontent on the dry plain. Somebody in New York told me General Rodríguez had forty thousand trained men on the Texas border – I'd be missing everything if I missed Rodríguez.

You get used in Mexico to disappointment – a town seems fine at evening and then in daylight the corruption seeps through, a road peters out, a muleteer doesn't turn up, the great man on acquaintance becomes strangely muted, and when you get to the gigantic ruins you are too tired to see them. It was that way with Rodríguez. He came to nothing.

The night before I had been in San Antonio. That's Texas, and Texas seemed to be half Mexico already – and half Will Rogers. In the train from New Orleans a Texan in the car talked continuously in the Will Rogers voice, the commercial drawl, the small-town complacent wisdom. All through the night the proverbs welled out full of fake kindliness and superficial truth – a Metro-Goldwyn philosophy. And a New Mexican with an exotic shirt covered with polka dots and an untrustworthy mestizo face talked back, neither paying attention to the other, all through the night talking at a tangent over the hip flasks.

The brown and convex plains spread out on either side of the car, and oil flared on the horizon like the flames on a sacrificial pyramid, and the New World and the Old World talked in the carriage. That is really the only thing that journeys give you – talk. There is so much weariness and disappointment in travel that people have to open up – in railway trains, over a fire, on the decks of steamers, and in the palm courts of hotels on a rainy day. They have to pass the time somehow, and they can pass it only with themselves. Like the characters of Chekhov they have no reserves – you learn the most intimate secrets. You get an impression of a world peopled by eccentrics, of odd professions, almost incredible stupidities, and, to balance them, amazing endurances.

BIOGRAPHY

While the Texan talked across the car, my neighbour stared out of the window. He had a sensitive sick face, an air of settled melancholy. He looked like a Victorian with religious doubts, somebody like Clough, but he had no side-whiskers and his hands were practical hands – not the pretty useless hands of a writer or a theologian. He said he had been travelling for eight thousand miles, all round the United States by train in a great loop. One more loop and he'd be home, somewhere a hundred miles from San Francisco. It was his first holiday for three years, but he wouldn't be sorry when it was over.

He talked gently, with difficulty, staring moodily out at the Texan plain. It seemed that he hadn't spoken to anyone much for three years. He lived alone and he couldn't see people at his job. Now he was going back for another three years' loneliness. I wondered what his job could be to make him a hermit within a hundred miles of San Francisco. 'You see,' he said, 'you're at it night and day. You can't trust a hired man. The birds are so sensitive they get nervous and sick if a stranger's around.'

It appeared that he bred turkeys, living alone with his flock of eleven hundred. They lived in the fields and he lived in an auto trailer, sleeping wherever his turkeys chose to sleep, bumping after them till they settled at sunset. He had a gun under the pillow and his dogs warned him if there was a thief or a wild dog near. Sometimes he was awakened four times in a night and never knew what he would have to face, an armed hobo or just a skulking dog. The first year or two he'd slept pretty badly. Well, in another three years maybe he'd have saved enough money to go into a business which would allow him to enjoy life, see people, marry (you couldn't expect a girl to live in a trailer alone with him and eleven hundred turkeys).

'What sort of business?'

17

He turned his sad inward-looking eyes away from the dark plain and the flaming oil. 'Breeding chickens. They're stationary.'

SAN ANTONIO

In the day San Antonio is more Mexican than American, not quite genuine Mexican (it is far too clean for that) but picture postcard Mexican. The sermon was preached in Spanish in the Catholic cathedral, while electric fans revolved above statues representing in their pale colours and plaster poses the most noble and fragile sentiments. As for the congregation, they were like pictures in early Victorian albums: the black mantillas and the small vivid pointed faces might have come out of Lady Blessington's *Book of Beauty*. The San Antonio River is wound cunningly through the town like a pattern on a valentine (does it make a heart?) with little waterfalls and ferny banks. Just as when you read a keepsake album –

To me more dear than all their rich perfume
The chaste camellia's pure and spotless bloom –

you have the sensation in San Antonio by day of the world's being deliciously excluded. Original sin under the spell of elegance has lost its meaning. Where, I thought, loitering on a bridge above the little tamed river, was there any sign of that 'terrible aboriginal calamity' which Newman perceived everywhere? This – during the day – was the perfect ivory tower. The horror and the beauty of human life were both absent. It was a passing sensation, for the ivory tower has its own horror: the terrifying egoism of exclusion.

But you had only to open a paper to escape from that vacuum – or to take a bus into the dreary hovels of the Mexican West Side, where the pecan workers live who shell pecan nuts by hand for a few cents a day. Nowhere in Mexico did I see quite so extreme a poverty. In Mexico the standard of living is appallingly low outside the great towns, but here that low standard lay next door to the American standard: the West Side hovels were mocked by the Plaza Hotel soaring yellowly up to scrape against the sky. There are one hundred and forty-seven pecan shelleries lying discreetly out of sight in San Antonio and they shell in a good year twenty-one million pounds of nuts – a fair-sized industry. Wages had been cut recently by a cent a pound, which meant that a pecan worker could earn from thirty cents to a dollar and fifty cents a day at most. With the help of a Mexican priest, Father López, the pecan workers organised a strike, though later Father López retired from the direction of the strike when the Communists took it over.

This strike was the first example I had come across of genuine Catholic Action on a social issue, a real attempt, led by the old, fiery, half-blind Archbishop, to put into force the papal encyclicals which have condemned capitalism quite as strongly as Communism. But the Vatican has been many years ahead of the bishops and the laity – for years the Pope has had to meet a kind of passive resistance from the Church. (He has himself referred to the Catholic employers who in one place succeeded in preventing the reading of the encyclical *Quadragesimo Anno* in the churches.) Spain may have awakened the social conscience, but you cannot expect a perfect technique all at once. There was something a little pathetic about Catholic Action in San Antonio. Father López had been outmanoeuvred, and now the Church was trying to negotiate a settlement between workers and employers on the dubious line that the employers should open their books for the workers' representatives and if those books did not justify a cut, the cut should be restored. There was a meeting in the Mexican Park – a dry drab plain of trampled earth and a few bandstands and benches and a swing or two. An orchestra of young Catholic ladies played cheerful and sedate airs, and then the old Archbishop and Father López spoke. In the audience there were two hundred workers and a few American ladies with the fussed air of energetic slummers. There was bad management with the microphone, so that you couldn't hear much; it was very hot; and the young American girls looked pale and weak and self-conscious before the dark sensual confident faces of the half-castes – who knew instinctively, you felt, all the beauty and the horror of the flesh.

The intention was good, of course, but the performance was deplorable. One compared it mentally with the soap-box orator and the Red Flag and a crowd singing the 'Internationale'. Catholicism, one felt, had to rediscover the technique of revolution – it wasn't practised here among the pale violinists. And these fussy and prosperous women who stood about in little groups segregated from the workers by a few feet of dusty floor and an abyss of the spirit – good souls, I am sure, but a little too anxious that the Archbishop should have a favourable reception and not be over-tired – how would they, one wondered, have reacted to the words of St

James (quoted by Pius XI in one of his last encyclicals), 'Go to now, ye rich men: weep and howl in your miseries which shall come upon you. Your riches are corrupted, and your garments are motheaten. Your gold and silver is cankered; and the rust of them shall be for a testimony against you, and shall eat your flesh like fire . . .' ? Those are the words of revolution – not the dim promise that account books shall be inspected (how can a Mexican worker living on thirty-five cents a day trust an account book ?).

FREAK SHOW

That night I went into a freak show in a little booth near where the West Side begins. America is entrenched around the Plaza and dies slowly out in miniature Broadways, skyscraper lights in the smooth southern sky, towards the pioneering edge of town – wooden houses and raw shows and the brothels in Matamoros Street where the hold-ups happen nightly and the local paper prints a column of them at the weekends – the kind of city to which you picture men returning in the old days with a bag of gold for a rough and quick good time.

One didn't need a bag of gold for the freak show; one got an awful amount for ten cents in the little stuffy booth. I was the only person there; I had a sense that nobody had been for a long while – it couldn't really compete with Matamoros Street – the dry exhibits were dusty with neglect. There were a Siamese sheep – eight legs sticking out like octopus tentacles – and calves with so-called human heads (like those of morons), and dogs created upside down rolling glass eyeballs towards legs that sprouted from somewhere near the backbone, and 'a frog baby born to a lady in Oklahoma'.

But the high points of the exhibition were two dead gangsters – Dutch Kaplan and Oklahoma Jim, his henchman, lying in open coffins, mummified. Jim was dressed in rusty black, with a loose fly button and the jacket open to disclose the brown hollow arch of the breast, and his former leader was naked except for a black cloth across the loins. The showman lifted it to disclose the dry, dusty, furry private parts. He showed the two scars upon the groin through which the taxidermist had removed all that was corruptible and put his fingers there (a terrible parody of St Thomas) and urged me to do the same – it was lucky to touch the body of a criminal. He put his finger in the bullet-hole where the brains had been blasted out and touched the dingy hair. I asked him where they got the bodies from. The question irritated him. 'The Crime Prevention League,' he said, and changed the subject, leading me to a curtain at the booth's end. For another ten cents, he said, I could see examples of abortion, 'very instructive', and a poster challenged me – 'Can You Take It?' I didn't try: I was satisfied with the frog baby.

It isn't really any comfort to tell yourself that these things are probably ingenious fakes (a man with a little tail was a relic of Barnum's show); even so the fact remains that they were created by man to satisfy some horrifying human need for ugliness.

I came out again, and a little way down the flaring street America died into the dark: across waste ground, between the dimly lit saloons, Mexican labourers converged fingering guitars, picking their way across the hewn-up edge-of-town earth. I went into a variety show and saw dancers like guerrilla horses pounding across a plain: a woman stamped and sang, setting a gold-plated crucifix swinging round her neck. All round were advertisements of the next week's film – '*Quién Es la Eterna Mártir*'.

('Whose sad face on the cross sees only this
After the passion of a thousand years.')

LAREDO

So next day I got a seat in a car going to Laredo. Doc Williams drove it, with an unlit cigar stuck in the corner of his mouth, over the plain rolling like an Atlantic swell towards the border, Spanish dagger bursting into bloom at the roadside. A shabby man with a hacking cough sat in the back seat; he had come down from Detroit without luggage and his sister was dying in Laredo. He coughed and coughed and wondered whether his sister would hold out till he arrived. 'Well, you can't do anything about it,' Doc Williams said, chewing his cigar-end.

I asked Doc Williams if he knew anything about Rodríguez. He didn't know the name, but maybe if I asked someone in Laredo – Who? Oh, anyone. And so I came to the border, and began the aimless walking, passing the time, waiting for the car, up to the plaza and down to the river, taking a look at Mexico, back to the agent's office. The third time I began to realise there wasn't a car. I went in and said, 'Well, has it come yet?' and the same man who had always answered me said, 'What come?'

I said, 'The car.'

He said, 'What car?'

It seemed to me then that there couldn't be a car at all.

A mestizo who was joking about something with the agent said, 'You the gentleman who's looking for Rodríguez?'

Doc Williams had told somebody – who had told somebody else.

The agent said to me, 'This gentleman's a friend of Rodríguez.'

But he wasn't what you or I would call a friend. He said it wasn't any good seeing Rodríguez: Rodríguez was no good to me; he was '*iñorant*'; anyway, he wasn't in Laredo – he'd gone to El Paso. I said I always meant to go over the border at El Paso – perhaps I could get a car there. You won't find him, he said; he went to Brownsville. Then Brownsville . . . Oh, he was probably in Los Angeles now.

But what about the fighting, I said, over at Matamoros?

There wasn't any fighting, he said. There was just an explosion somewhere – in a factory – and people thought it was a rebellion. I could see Rodríguez's brother if I liked – he had a house in town – but I mustn't mention him: he didn't want to get mixed up in politics. Somebody would think he was spying and then he might get into a lot of trouble. Rodríguez's brother was watched by the police and by Mexican agents.

He called across the street to the ugliest money-changer of the lot. He'll tell you, he said, if Rodríguez's brother is in town.

Oh, yes, the money-changer said, scowling, he was in town. He came in last night.

I said perhaps he wouldn't want to see me.

Oh, yes, the first man said, he'd want to see me if I

said I'd write a bit about his brother. That's how his brother lived, having fool newspapermen in New York write about him. Then he'd send copies of the papers to landowners right down in the south of Mexico – in Yucatán and Chiapas – and they'd think Rodríguez was doing something for them and they'd send him money.

More people came in and listened; it seemed to me that soon everyone in Laredo would know there was an Englishman who wanted to see Rodríguez's brother. I thought perhaps I'd change my mind and go and look at Mexico instead. Why, if this snowball went on getting any bigger it might stop me from going across the bridge at all. I said I didn't want to see Rodríguez or his brother, it was all a mistake, and went out for another walk.

I went to a cinema and saw William Powell and Annabella in *The Baroness and the Butler* – it wasn't any good; then I went to Pete's bar and had a brandy and Coca Cola highball. Pete was a Greek, and had been in America for thirty-seven years, but he couldn't speak enough English for you to notice it. Germany was a fine country, he said; America was no good at all; Greece wasn't so bad – his opinions puzzled me till I realised that he judged every country by its drink laws I suppose, if you are in the business, that's as good a way as any other. We writers are apt to judge a country by freedom of the Press, and politicians by freedom of speech – it's the same, really.

Then I went down to the river bank again and had a look at Mexico; the lights were coming out on the other side of the Rio Grande; it seemed absurd to wait any longer on *this* side: the side of the freak show and the paper edited by the local high school and the coloured comic supplement – Mr Gump, with the horrible missing jaw and the stuck-out nose, quarrelling with Mrs Gump week by week, year after year; Moon Mullins and Kitty Higgins; Tarzan eternally young and brave and successful; Dick Tracy, the G man, for ever on the track.

I went back to the agent's and got a taxi; he no longer tried to pretend that a fine German car was on the way from San Antonio. We drove slowly between the money-changers to the bridge-head, I deposited five hundred pesos at the customs, and then we drove past the other bridge-head, uphill between the money-changers. This was Mexico, that was the United States. The only difference was dirt and darkness: there weren't so many lights in Mexico. They called this Nuevo Laredo to distinguish it from the town in Texas, but as so often happens the son looked older than the father, more acquainted with the seamy side of life. The streets were dark and unsurfaced, the little plaza stuffy with greenery; all the life there was went on behind the swing doors of the cantinas and billiard parlours. There was a large cockroach dead on the floor of my room and a sour smell from the water-closet. Thunder came rolling up from Texas and rain splashed and dug and churned the unmade roads. I tried to read myself to sleep with *Barchester Towers* ('St Ewold's is not a rich piece of preferment – it is worth some three or four hundred a year at most, and has generally been held by a clergyman attached to the cathedral choir . . .'), but I couldn't concentrate. The world is all of a piece, of course; it is engaged everywhere in the same subterranean struggle, lying like a tiny neutral state, with whom no one ever observes his treaties, between the two eternities of pain and – God knows the opposite of pain, not we. It is a

Belgium fought over by friend and enemy alike. There is no peace anywhere where there is human life, but there are, I told myself, quiet and active sectors of the line. Russia, Spain, Mexico – there's no fraternisation on Christmas morning in those parts. The horror may be the same, it is an intrinsic part of human life in every place: it attacks you in the Strand or the tropics; but where the eagles are gathered together, it is not unnatural to expect to find the Son of Man as well. So many years have passed in England since the war began between faith and anarchy: we live in an ugly indifference. Over here lay the grave of Pro, Tabasco with every church destroyed, and Chiapas, where the Mass was forbidden. The advertisements for aerated waters and patent medicines line the modern highway which leads to the front line and the tourists go back and forth, their cars laden with serapes and big hats, and their minds sprightly with the legend of a happy and picturesque Mexico.

'He was content to be a High Churchman,' I read of Mr Arabin, under the bare globe, on the hard iron bedstead, 'if he could be so on principles of his own, and could strike out a course showing a marked difference from those with whom he consorted.' Trollope's gentle irony, the sense of breakfasts at the archdeacon's, dining-room prayers, and somewhere in the far distance, beyond the Barchester spires, a doubt about everything. A drunken voice sang in Spanish and the rain fell over the dreary Nuevo León plain, and I thought of Father Pro coming into this country in disguise – the badly cut suit and the striped tie and the brown shoes; then the secret Masses, the confessions at street corners, the police hunts and the daring evasions – the long rainy season and afterwards the dry and then the rains again, and, when they cleared, arrest and death, unshaven, crying, 'Hail Christ the King' in the yard of the prison. They had killed Campion, they said, for treason, not for his religion, and they said the same of Pro in 1927. The war doesn't change its character in a few centuries; it moves as slowly as evolution through a thousand years – it takes more than ten centuries to change one muscle – and Pro speaks with the psychology of Thomas of Canterbury, who also was in love with the good death, 'The victims are many; the number of martyrs grows every day. Oh, if only I should draw a winning number.'

The rain came down and the lights went out in the United States and Mr Arabin made his tentative efforts at love in the flower garden.

2. The Rebel State

There was nothing to do all morning but wait around for the man from San Antonio, who I knew would never turn up. The side streets were ankle-deep in mud, and there was nobody to talk to. It was a small town and it sank every way you walked but one into the muddy plain. That one way was the bridge: I was in looking-glass land now, staring back at the United States. The tall Hamilton Hotel stood up clearly above Laredo; I sat in the Mexican plaza and had my shoes cleaned and looked at it. The morning was like a replica of yesterday, only reversed: the walk down to the river and back to the plaza, the morning paper. Several people had been shot by a police chief in a quarrel – that was the regular feature of a Mexican paper; no day passed without somebody's being assassinated somewhere; at the end of the paper there was a page in English for tourists. That never included the shootings, and the tourists, as far as I could see, never read the Spanish pages. They lived in a different world, they lived in a few square inches of American territory; with *Life* and *Time* and coffee at Sanborn's, they were impervious to Mexico.

Lunch was awful, like the food you eat in a dream, tasteless in a positive way, so that the very absence of taste is repellent. All Mexican food is like that: if it isn't hot with sauces, it's nothing at all, just a multitude of plates planked down on the table simultaneously, so that five are getting cold while you eat the sixth; pieces of anonymous meat, a plate of beans, fish from which the taste of the sea has long been squeezed away, rice mixed with what look like grubs – perhaps they are grubs – a salad (dangerous, you are always warned, and for a long while you heed the warning), a little heap of bones and skin they call a chicken – the parade of cooling dishes goes endlessly on to the table edge. After a while your palate loses all discrimination; hunger conquers; you begin in a dim way even to look forward to your meal. I suppose if you live long enough in Mexico you begin to write like Miss Frances Toor – 'Mexican cooking appeals to the eye as well as to the palate.' (It is all a hideous red and yellow, green and brown, like art needlework and the sort of cushions popular among decayed gentle-women in Cotswold tea-shops.) 'The artistic instinct is alive even in the humblest cook.'

In the afternoon I caught a train to Monterrey – I couldn't wait any longer for the car. The melancholy plain lay like lead under the rainclouds; mules in a waste of thorny scrub; mud huts and a few factories and then nothing at all until the seal-grey mountains gathered slowly round, little outcrops of rock like sailing-ships on the horizon.

There was one other tourist on the train – an old gentleman from Wisconsin, the police commissioner in some obscure town; he was armed with a walking-stick and a great many letters, letters from his state senator, from a Mexican consul, from God knows whom. He spoke no Spanish and was immensely inquisitive about inessentials, noting everything down in tiny handwriting in a tiny notebook. He was going to give a talk when he got back. He had no hesitation at all in buttonholing anyone (he buttonholed me in the end): a Mexican officer was travelling with his young wife – he cornered her because she knew a little English; he brought excitement that long afternoon into the lives of several unescorted Mexican women. No one could resent it: he was so pink and old and he had so many introductions. And a police badge under his lapel. He sat himself down opposite me and began to talk. He was a widower and he had never been out of the States before. He had got a round-trip ticket to Mexico City and he'd arranged his side trips, here and there; he was very astute about money and very innocent; he knew exactly what he wanted to see and what he didn't; there was American management in all his hotels. I said, 'I see the police chief in such and such a place has shot some men,' and a safety-curtain dropped over his face. He said he thought he'd feed at Sanborn's. Though he supposed in some parts he'd have to eat strange food.

'You're all right,' he said, 'if you don't eat fish. Or meat. Or vegetables.'

'What's left?'

'Well, there's cereals,' he said.

Outside the window there was the dark coming down, the path to a white shrine far away like a snail shell, and the rain falling. He was a good man – and embarrassing as a child is. He padded up and down the compartment with his walking-stick, inserting himself between husband and wife, between a lover and his girl, saying, 'What's that?' 'What's that?' at trivial things. The dry and prickly desert: the cacti sticking up like pins with an effect of untidiness, and the night deepening. Paths went off into the dark gleaming with wet, going to nowhere one knew of at all.

And suddenly – I can't remember how it happened –
the old, good, pink face disclosed the endless vacancy
behind. You expected somebody of his age – from
Wisconsin – an honorary police commissioner with a
badge – to believe in God – in a kind of way, a vague,
deistic way. I had imagined him saying you could worship God as well in your own home as in a church; I had
taken him already and made a character of him, and I
had got him entirely wrong. He didn't believe in any
God at all – it was like suddenly finding a cruel intelli-
gence in a child. For one can respect an atheist as one
cannot respect a deist: once accept a God and reason
should carry you further, but to accept nothing at all –
that requires some stubbornness, some courage. Three
years ago he'd nearly died; the doctors had given him
up; his children had gathered round the patriarchal bed.
He could remember it all quite clearly; he had known
what it meant, but he had felt quiet, at peace; he hadn't
been scared – he was just going into nothingness. And
then he hadn't died at all, and here he was, across the
border in Mexico – his first trip out of the USA. He had
a clipping in his pocket from a Main Street paper: 'Our
respected fellow-townsman – travelling in Mexico,' and
all the while, behind that pinkness and that goodness,
eternal nothingness working its way through to the
brain.

MONTERREY

It was at Monterrey as though you had been whisked
back across the border into Texas – one of those bad
dreams where you never reach your destination – and
my time was short and my destination, Tabasco and

Chiapas, far away in the south. The hotel was American, the rooms were American, the food and the voices all American: it was less foreign than San Antonio. This was a luxury town run for Americans on the way to Mexico City: I couldn't understand where the old gentleman got his sense of strangeness as we sat in the bright clean restaurant eating American food, and yet he said, 'It's strange, very strange; I guess I'll get on to it in time.'

I made him drink a tequila – the spirit made from agave, a rather inferior schnapps. He became a little more reminiscent, a little daring over the nuts. 'I embarrassed a young lady in a store once by asking for pee-cans. She took it very well.' The small grossness was as unexpected on his tongue as the firm statement of disbelief had been. And all the time you were aware of goodness, a childlike goodness, flowing out of him, the kind of goodness which in reminiscence brings tears to the eyes like certain natural things you remember from many years ago – the smell of a turned field in winter, a hedge going up to a horizon of nettles.

He came tentatively out with his walking-stick to the steps of the hotel. Tequila moved like daring in his veins. I said, 'What do you say to our seeing if there's a cabaret anywhere?'

He hesitated a long while; he said, 'I guess I'll wait till Mexico City.' He protested anxiously when I said I was going for a walk, 'Now be careful. Don't get lost,' staring into the wet, well-lit Monterrey streets as if they were part of the dark wilderness through which we had come.

I walked down a kind of Tottenham Court Road, cantinas and hideous fake modern furniture in shop windows, a florid and impressive statue – the Indian Juárez defying Europe which had so dismally conquered in the street behind – and then most lovely in the dark, across a leafy square, from under a white moony colonnade, the cathedral, bells rising in dark metallic tiers towards the enormous sky, silence and dripping leaves.

I woke next morning to the sound of cheering – I had had a silly dream full of triumph and happiness. There had been a mass religious revolt under the eyes of Stalin. 'You've let the churches be opened. You can't stop us now.' 'From this moment,' he said, 'they are doomed.' I remember taking part in a procession round a small room – the dictator in the middle very stubborn and powerless and *en brosse* – and we sang 'O God, Our Help in Ages Past', but I couldn't remember the second verse. As we turned to go, I saw a little first-class honours scientist – product of night school and a gnawing sense of exclusion – grinning in a corner and we mocked him happily, marching round the room. And then I woke to what must have set all the singing going in my dream – it was five-thirty and the crowd cheered and cheered. They might have been applauding a hero or a politician at the railway station as he passed through; perhaps the President was here. I got out of bed and looked through the window and saw darkness in the sky and the stars still out, lights burning in the flat-roofed town, and dawn like smoke in a level bank above the roofs. The cheers were everywhere, stretching out to the dim mountains: they weren't cheers at all, but the cocks crowing for miles around, an odd Biblical rhapsody at dawn.

I went to eight o'clock Mass in the cathedral. Nearly all the people there were women; the men had probably started work many hours before. An interior all white and gold with pale refined un-Spanish statuary, and three girls doing the Stations of the Cross, giggling and chattering from agony to agony. I remember what President Cárdenas had said in a public speech in Oaxaca, 'I am tired of closing churches and finding them full. Now I am going to open the churches and educate the people and in ten years I shall find them empty.' The girls giggled their way up Calvary and I wondered if Cárdenas had made a true prophecy. The very old priest at the altar knelt and rose and raised God in his hands; what did it matter in the long run, anyway? God didn't cease to exist when men lost their faith in Him; there were always catacombs where the secret rite could be kept alive till the bad times passed: during the Calles persecution God had lain in radio cabinets, behind book-shelves. He had been carried in a small boy's pocket into prisons; He had been consumed in drawing-rooms and in garages. He had Eternity on His side.

The old gentleman talked at breakfast about his bowels. He said, 'When I kept you waiting I thought I only had to do one, but I found I had to do both. It's eating cereals. They keep your bowels good.' He ran happily on; it might have been a dog speaking. And then he looked up from his dry wheat flakes, good and child-like and innocent, and said, 'I was scared you'd get lost last night. I hoped you'd knock on my door when you went by.'

Depression lifted with daylight. America after all stopped short at the hotel doors: in the Avenida Hidalgo a great bare pulled-about church hummed gently and continuously with the prayers of people doing the Stations of the Cross. There was no ignorance in this devotion – even old peasant women carried their books of devotion and knew how to contemplate the agony. Here, one felt, was a real religion – the continuous traffic of piety. They came and moved along the walls and went and others came. They were like relays of labourers making a road up Calvary.

On a hill behind the town stood the ruined Bishop's Palace coloured delicately with olive and green age. The ranges of the Sierra Madre, grass dying out against the stony-toothed ridges, lay all round, rank behind sharp rank. This palace, like a mosque in heavy broken stone, was built at the end of the eighteenth century, when religious architecture in England was dying and Baptist chapels were rising everywhere with their empty dignity enclosing the bare table and crossless hall and the tank for total immersion. Yet this ruined palace and chapel were as beautiful as anything out of the Middle Ages – I don't think it was the bullet marks which made it so, the holes knocked in the walls for Pancho Villa's machine-guns. Has the Church in Mexico, I thought, been maligned if it created works of art so late as this? I have no sympathy with those who complain of the wealth and beauty of a church in a poor land. For the sake of another peso a week, it is hardly worth depriving the poor of such rest and quiet as they can find in the cathedral here. I have never heard people complain of the super-cinemas – that the money should be spent in relief – and yet there's no democracy in a cinema: you pay more and you get more; but in a church the democracy is absolute. The rich man and the poor man kneel side by side for Communion; the rich man must wait his turn at the confessional.

I had forgotten it was Ash Wednesday till I reached

the cathedral again and found the long packed queue the whole length of the aisle lined up to receive the ashes. ('Remember, O man, that thou art dust, and shalt return to dust again.') There were as many boys and young men now as old people, for the work of the day was over. At least two hundred and fifty must have been waiting in the aisle; it took me a quarter of an hour to reach the priest, and by that time the queue had renewed itself completely and there was no sign of any slackening in the slow tide of penitence. Thousands must have received the ashes that evening. They came out again like witnesses to stream through the sunset town with the heavy grey cross on their foreheads – a few years ago and they would have suffered imprisonment for it: I began to think that after all Cárdenas had not been right. That is the danger of the quick tour, you miscalculate on the evidence of three giggling girls and a single Mass, and malign the devotion of thousands.

At dinner the old gentleman couldn't get over the joke of it: here I'd been walking miles about town and he'd gone all round in one hour by street car – for five cents American money. 'But I like walking,' I kept on telling him uselessly. 'I'm going to tell them that back home,' he said, 'about my English friend who walked all day and saved five cents American.'

At night I found a little square scented with flowers and leaves, a silent fountain, and demure courtships going on upon every bench – I thought of the couples sprawling in ugly passion on the Hyde Park grass or on chairs performing uglier acts under the shelter of overcoats. It was as if these people hadn't the need for lechery, their nerves were quieter, the marriage bed was the accepted end. They didn't feel the need of proving their manhood by pressing on the deed of darkness before its time. Fear was eliminated: they each knew where the other stood. One was not thinking, 'What does she expect me to do?' nor the other, 'How far can I let him go?' They were happy together in the dark bound by the rules of a game they both knew; no fear, no exasperated nerves; what was left, sentiment and the demurest sensuality – a hand on a hand, an arm along the back, the faintest of contacts. And again if only I'd known it, I was taking the tourist view – on the strength of one prosperous town on the highway, on the strength of a happy mood, I was ready to think of Mexico in terms of quiet and gentleness and devotion.

SAN LUIS POTOSÍ

The cacti stood in groups like people with feathered head-dresses leaning together and engaged in intimate whispered conversations – hermits who had come together in some dismal stony waste for an urgent purpose, and didn't look up to see the train pass. Roads were like the lines on a map; you saw them meandering thinly for an immense distance, dying out at the margin among the rocks and cacti. The cacti had no beauty – they were like some simple shorthand sign for such words as 'barrenness' and 'drought'; you felt they were less the product than the cause of this dryness, that they had absorbed all the water there was in the land and held it as camels do in their green, aged, tubular bellies. Sometimes they flowered at the tip like a glowing cigar-end, but they had no more beauty even then: an unhealthy pink, like the icing in a cheap pastry-cook's, the kind of sugar cake you leave upon the plate. Only sunset cast some kind of

gentle humanising spell over this rocky cactus desolation
– a faint gold, a subjective pity, as if one were looking at
the world for a moment through a god's anatomical and
pitying eye, 'He judges not as the judge judges, but as
the sun falling round a helpless thing.'

Somewhere among the cacti and the stones Nuevo
León gave drearily out and the state of San Luis Potosí
began. I am writing now when they are waging guerrilla
warfare in those hills – the day before yesterday the rebels
dynamited a train and the rebel leader, General Saturnino Cedillo, is being hunted from aerie to aerie, tiny
landing-ground to tiny landing-ground, and a censor-
ship imposes silence (what has happened to one's
friends?). It is only a few months since I was there and
everything is out of date already: it belongs to history.*

In those days (the first week of March 1938) San Luis
Potosí was a little capitalist pocket in Socialist Mexico,
ruled less by the governor than by the Indian General,
Cedillo, from his ranch among the hills at Las Palomas.
For a year now they had been talking rebellion in Mexico,
with Cedillo as the potential leader, one of Carranza's
old Indian fighters, the man who had put down the
Catholic rising in Jalisco eleven years before. Cedillo
himself was born a Catholic, but he didn't practise it; he
was rumoured to have a pious sister, yet the real reason
why in San Luis Potosí the anti-religious laws were not
enforced was the one he gave to an American reporter,
'Perhaps I do not believe in all this religion myself, but
the poor people want it, and I am going to see that they
get what they want.' For some reason, perhaps because

* Very much out of date, for soon after this was written General
Cedillo was shot by Government troops in the mountains of his
own state.

39

there are no good hotels, the tourists do not get off the train at San Luis, or if they do one night at a Mexican hotel is enough for them – the dingy room, the symbolic dead beetle, and the smell of urine. Like my old friend, they catch the early-morning train to Mexico City. The old voice speaking at dawn down the room phone stirred an exaggerated emotion – goodness and simplicity are rare things; he was speaking with a little concern and anxiety because I was staying behind and he was going on alone, and I tried to reassure him. I said, 'In Mexico City you're sure to find someone from Wisconsin,' and rang gloomily off.

I had plenty of days ahead, more than I needed, though San Luis is a lovely town – narrow balconied streets and rose-pink churches against a mountainous blue; an industrial city, but the industry is hidden away at the edge of town; an unhappy city, but you don't discover that at first. You notice only that your tap doesn't run when you go to bed at night. Later you learn that there's not enough water to go round – the whole administration of the place is rotten, dependent on the General at his farm in the hills; the city is literally drained dry for the sake of *his* fields. It is useless to put all this into the past tense: there are always other generals in Mexico. Everything is repeated there, even the blood sacrifices of the Aztecs; the age of Mexico falls on the spirit like a cloud.

And then you go into the cathedral for Mass – the peasants kneel in their blue dungarees and hold out their arms, minute after minute, in the attitude of crucifixion; an old woman struggles on her knees up the stone floor towards the altar; another lies full length with her forehead on the stones. A long day's work is behind, but the mortification goes on. This is the atmosphere of the stigmata, and you realise suddenly that perhaps *this* is the population of heaven – these aged, painful, and ignorant faces: they are human goodness. Five minutes have passed and the old man's arms, weary already from the fields, are still extended; a young girl is making her aching way up the nave upon her knees carrying a baby in her arms, and behind her in the same attitude her sister – a slow sad procession towards the foot of the cross. You would say that life itself for these was mortification enough, but like saints they seek the only happiness in their lives and squeeze out from it a further pain.

Outside lies the market – a grim place at sunset, far more squalid than anything I had ever seen in the West African bush. A few potatoes, a few beans; pottery and basket work in ugly arty shapes and colours (there were no tourists to attract: the genuine native craft takes the Chelsea-Cotswold form); hideous little toys and trinkets, and second-hand revolvers lying among the vegetables, death for a few dimes. The dust got in the throat; the cantinas were crowded and dirty – a drunken man leaned on a billiard cue. In a small cleared space a young clown performed, with painted face and long black Indian hair. He was dressed in a grey ragged night-shirt. Perhaps he was fifteen years old; he strutted before his strange surrealist laboratory – a couple of megaphones, a bottle of alcohol, a board stuck with nails, an iron, and a little brazier – the hard soles of his feet proof against steel and fire – mortification for money, the stigmata of the pleasure fair. He had a little band of grinning assistants; not one of them was more than fourteen.

A little farther on and there was the front of the

seventeenth-century Templo del Carmen crowded with figures and flowers carved by Indians. When you looked closely at individual faces they were merely the old European bearded prophets with smug expressions and a Bible pressed to the breast, but when you moved away from the terracotta façade the effect was Indian more than Christian – a kind of turbulent materialism, bubbling grossly up towards the sky.

On the balcony of the Government offices the politicians stood all day. After Mexico I shall always associate balconies and politicians – plump men with blue chins wearing soft hats and guns on their hips. They look down from the official balcony in every city all day long with nothing to do but stare, with the expression of men keeping an eye on a good thing.

SUNDAY LUNCH

A Scotswoman gave Sunday hospitality over the store she'd run for many years now, ever since she'd lost her farm in one of the revolutions. Independent, outspoken, Protestant, she was a pillar of common sense among wild, shifting fanaticisms. She put everybody in his place, including Cedillo – acid, courageous, with little frank grossnesses like an Edinburgh wynd. A smell of good coffee drifted up the stairs from the store, and a daughter came in from tennis at the American Club. But there was an empty chair; it wasn't filled till near the end of lunch.

The newcomer, C, was British by blood, but he had been born in Mexico and he had a Spanish-American accent. Thin, dark, and shiny, he was a little too polite, he had a look of suburban refinement: he was the sort of person you avoid at a party. He began to explain why he was late – he had had to make a long detour driving up from Mexico City. A friend had warned him that the roads round Querétaro were unsafe because of the revolutionaries (it was the polite Mexican word for bandits). His friend the other day had lost all his money and all his clothes. He picked his words pedantically, making conversation. This was Mexican small talk.

Over the coffee a little bitterness crept in. His father had been a rich man with estates in Morelos and he had sent his son to England to be educated; then the father's lands had been confiscated and he had sent for his son and died. The son was in a mining company now, and he looked back with a raw nostalgia to the days of Díaz. (You find them all over Mexico, hotel-keepers, old ladies, professional men remembering Díaz – whose only fault perhaps was that he forgot the poor, who have forgotten him.) He hated Mexico with a little refined adder-like hatred, but his mining experience was of no value anywhere else in the world; he was a prisoner here.

And then something opened behind the pedantry and the wormwood, a doorway into God knows what braveries and acceptances – 'making the best of things', he'd call it with his reptilian bitterness. In 1927 he had been kidnapped by rebels and held for ransom together with a young American from the same mine. He had been expecting something of the sort for days, but the American didn't believe in banditry – it was too like fiction or the films – it wasn't *true*. C used to try to scare the young man by calling out to him that the bandits were coming – the first time the American had believed it, but not again. And then the bandits *did* come. He had a few minutes' warning when they rode in and he tried to call the American out of bed. 'You lay off,' the young

43

man said, 'you can't scare me' – and then the room was full of them. They were looking for money and there was no money there. They pushed their prisoners against the wall. 'I thought they were going to shoot. You should have seen that American's face. I was laughing. There wasn't anything else to do . . .'

I believed him. He had lost too much in Mexico to mind – one came across others in Mexico like that, foreigners and Spaniards who had lost everything except despair, and despair has its own humour as well as its own courage. Perhaps his laughter saved them – it must be difficult to shoot a laughing man: you have to feel important to kill. That is why a brass band plays at a cock-fight and people put on big hats and charro trousers. The bandits carried them both into the mountains and demanded a ransom of twenty thousand American dollars. For four days they were without food or water, dragged from place to place at the tails of horses, beaten . . . Then fourteen thousand dollars were paid by their company and they were released, twenty-five miles away from home in the scrub.

'What rebels were those?'

'The Cristeros,' he said. That was the Catholic rising against Calles. It's typical of Mexico, of the whole human race perhaps – violence in favour of an ideal and then the ideal lost and the violence just going on.

COCK-FIGHT

On Sunday afternoon there was a rodeo in the bull-ring, but there wasn't enough money in the San Luis pockets for a really good company. The decorated seats of honour were empty. One had the feeling that all the activities in

San Luis were half-hearted – one eye was always fixed on the road to Las Palomas (and that eye reported many things – the Governor of Texas entertained at lunch, an American, hot and dusty carrying a lot of money with him, even poor old hunted Rodríguez's chief agent); everything went on under the shadow of future rebellion.

Two cocks were prepared for the ring. Men in big decorated cartwheel hats and tight charro trousers watched behind the fence; they had plump mild operatic faces; they might have come out of a Hollywood musical starring John Boles. They felt the cocks as if they were buying chickens in the market, plunging their fingers into the feathers; then a procession of horsemen entered, led by a band of fiddlers wearing bright-coloured serapes. They played softly and sang a melancholy chant about flowers, standing in a little group as if they were talking to each other and no one else was there. Two of the charros took little bright spurs out of beautiful red leather cases and bound them on the cocks' feet with scarlet twine, very slowly, very carefully. All this singing and procession were just a prelude to the scurry on the sand, pain in miniature, and death on a very small scale.

But death dictates certain rites. Men make rules and hope in that way to tame death – you shall not bomb open towns, the challenged has the choice of weapons . . . Three lines were drawn in the sand: death was like tennis. The cocks crowed and a brass band blared from the stone seats and sand blew up across the arena; it was cold in the wind, in the *sombrá*, among the hills. And suddenly one felt an impatience with all this mummery, all this fake emphasis on what is only a natural function; we die as we evacuate; why wear big hats and tight trousers and have a band play? That, I think, was the day I began to hate the Mexicans. The cocks' beaks were pressed against each other, and the brass blared, and the cocks were placed on the outside lines, and the band fell suddenly silent. But the cocks didn't fight, death didn't perform; they turned their backs on each other, the spurs giving them an odd stilt-like walk, and then they stood quiet and indifferent, taking a look around, while the crowd hooted and jeered as if they had been cowardly or unsuccessful bull-fighters.

Again their metallic beaks were touched, as if an electric spark could be engendered by contact, and this time it worked. They were released quarrelling in mid-air; it was all over in a minute; there was no doubt of the victor – a great green cock who sailed above the other and forced it down by weight of feathers on to the sand. The plumage blew out like a duster, the thin bird collapsed and flattened, and there was a wicked punch, punch, punch at the eyes. It was a matter of seconds and then the beaten bird was lifted up and held head downward, until blood came out of the beak, pouring in a thin black stream as if out of a funnel. Children stood up on the stone seats and watched it with glee. The afternoon was very cold and a little rain began to fall and the rodeo was incompetent, men trying to throw horses with lassoes and failing; with death over, it wasn't worth staying for all the rest: the blasts of music and the botched climax. Outside the bull-ring were the barracks – soldiers marching up and down, up and down – and the Church of the Virgin of Guadalupe, and the prison, and a tram going into town, and a drum beating.

I went into the Templo del Carmen, as the dark dropped, for Benediction. To a stranger like myself it was like going home – a language I could understand –

'*Ora pro nobis*.' The Virgin sat on an extraordinary silver cloud like a cabbage with the Infant in her arms above the altar; all along the walls horrifying statues with musty purple robes stood in glass coffins; and yet it was home. One knew what was going on. Old men came plodding in in dungarees on bare feet, tired out with work, and again I thought: how could one grudge them the gaudy splendour of the giltwork, the incense, the distant immaculate figure upon the cloud? The candles were lit, and suddenly little electric lights sprayed out all round the Virgin's head. Even if it were all untrue and there were no God, surely life was happier with the enormous supernatural promise than with the petty social fulfilment, the tiny pension and the machine-made furniture. When I came out, little groups of Indians sat on the sidewalk eating their evening meal; they carried their homes with them, like tents, to be set up anywhere.

TOUR OF THE CATACOMBS

I wanted to see General Saturnino Cedillo – the city owed to him so much of its happiness and unhappiness. You couldn't drink enough water, but you could have your children taught that Christ had risen. Catholic Action was strong in San Luis, but not even here could it be quite openly pursued: there was a Government agent in town, and for six months the priest who organised the schools had kept away from them. While I waited on in San Luis to see Cedillo – hours of waiting in the Government office for the private telephone to ring from Las Palomas, long interviews with an official, interminable assurances that I was not seeking money, that I would let no one in Mexico know that I had seen the General, and then the half-hearted consent for five days ahead – the priest showed me a few of his activities: revolution in the form of the Sermon on the Mount, treason as a class in domestic economy. Down a long narrow pink passage, past a birdcage and a few melons, a door; impossible to foresee from the street the huge space behind the door – the courtyard surrounded by small rooms where classes for girls were being held, classes in cooking, in sewing, and one for high school girls in apologetics – and the main door led to a great hall the size of a church supported by four old massive pillars. Here the weekly religious class was being held for poor girls, domestic servants and the like. The priest talked to them, gently, with many jokes – they were in the catacombs, learning the dangerous lessons of modesty and love. He was an intellectual, with a European doctorate in philosophy, but war made understanding easy between very different minds; he was like a beloved officer going the round of his company in the trenches. Outside in the town – somewhere – was the Government agent; they were violating the Constitution; the whole building could be confiscated. He spoke very quietly, never raising his voice – he gave the effect of great confidence and great love. One thought of the blue-chinned politicians on the balcony, the leaders of the state, with their eyes on the main chance, the pistols on their hips, with no sense of responsibility for anyone at all. The girls here would go back to the daily drudgery, but they had a leader they could trust, they were not alone. We went on to a working-class school – one big room with classes graded from small children up to grown men. Fathers sat in the same room with their sons, learning to read and write, learning elementary arithmetic and

48

sociology, the teaching of the encyclicals against capitalism and Communism. The teachers were women with Government licences – their Catholicism was secret.

Outside was complete irresponsibility – waves of it breaking over a countryside – lawless roads, the reversed signpost, the desert pressing in. It wasn't merely a question of General Cedillo at Las Palomas irrigating his own land and neglecting the state, protecting religion simply because his own people believed, believing nothing himself, with his eye for a crop and his eye for a woman, round which a dozen dark legends grew in San Luis – a protector no Catholic cared for, a capitalist no other capitalist would trust. It wasn't merely an Indian general in an obscure state of a backward country: it was a whole world. I remembered the game called 'Monopoly' they were playing at home with counters and dice, the girl of fifteen on the railway-line, a world where the politicians stand on the balcony, where the land is sold for building estates and the little villas go up on the wounded clay with garages like tombs.

THE PHILOSOPHER

The priest and I went up the stairs in a dingy building near the market to find the old German teacher of languages who would come out with me to Las Palomas in case I needed an interpreter; some years before he had lived with the General and tried to teach him English and German, but there were always too many people waiting with petitions, seldom fewer than sixty a day, never any chance of a quiet time with the irregular verbs. We beat on the door for a long while, until at last it was secretively opened by a young man in a raffish grubby dressing-gown, one-eyed and pockmarked. The flat was dusty and unaired; a few books lay about on the floor, and hideous boarding-house pictures hung askew; there were a blackboard and some broken teacups. It was like a place temporarily put together by gipsies. The old professor had thin white hair, a long white moustache, and blanched and bony hands. He had an air of melancholy breeding; he was very clean and very worn; he was like an old-fashioned vase standing among the junk at the end of an auction.

He was a philosopher, he managed to insist, while he haggled gently over the pesos he was to be paid.

'Motion is life,' he said, 'and life is motion.'

Somewhere the pockmarked boy moved restlessly like Polonius behind the tapestry.

'As for food,' the old man said, 'my wants are very simple; the General will know what I will like. A little vegetable, a glass of water.'

He had pale yellow eyeballs; he was like a German before the Empire; you could picture him master of music in some little principality, all plush and gilt and courtesy. I wondered what odd whim of Providence had landed him here – a teacher of languages in a Mexican mining town.

That night there was a thunderstorm, the lights went out all over town, one had to find one's way back slowly to the hotel by the lightning flashes; the streets were empty and the rain came down. Did one turn left or right? It was like being forgotten in a maze when the ticket man has gone home; I thought of the good old American with vacancy behind the smooth pink skin, of the turkey breeder back home with no one to talk to and the gun under his pillow; everyone existing alone in his little personal maze and the ticket man gone.

A DAY AT THE GENERAL'S

It was four hours' drive from San Luis into the brown and stony hills. The cacti pressed up along the road, leaning towards us, turning away, a whole people rank behind rank stretching up out of sight into the mountains, waiting for someone to pass. A car went lurching by full of puffy *pistoleros*, churning up the dust of the unsurfaced road, but presently they broke down and we passed *them*. They too were on the way to Las Palomas – the road, I think, led nowhere else at all, simply petered out four hours away in the General's yard.

The old German talked continuously, clasping an umbrella between his knees. His parents had died when he was very young and he had left Germany and come to Mexico. Why Mexico?

'If you are a philosopher,' he rebuked me, 'every place is the same. Why not Mexico?'

He had lived for decades in San Luis; he was there when Madero was jailed, he was there when Villa and Carranza fought Huerta. Men he taught became generals and later corpses; there were times when you didn't go outside your door for a few days (another month or two, if only we had known it, and the shooting was to begin again). Then a few years ago he began to go blind; it was awkward, for he lived alone.

'Awkward!' I exclaimed. 'Terrifying.'

Oh, no, no, he said, not to a philosopher. We bounced furiously on the back seat of the car, rising into cold mountain air. The doctors had given him up. Well, he had thought about it, he didn't believe in doctors anyway; he began to exercise his eyes and to poultice them every few hours with hot and cold towels. They began to clear, he found he could see a few yards, across a street; now his eyes were as good as they had ever been, and he gave me a long hawk-like look out of his yellow eyeballs to convince me. Bump, bump, bump, climbing into cloud.

'Never mind,' he said, 'it is good for you. Motion. That is my philosophy. Motion is life and life is motion.'

Suddenly there was a barrier across the road, a hut, a few men peering in. The driver said, 'Las Palomas' and the Mexican businessman who sat beside him and acted as my sponsor said, 'General Cedillo.' We were waved on. It was a private passport station set up by the General an hour and a half from his farm. The road at last stopped climbing; it came out on to the precipitous edge of the hills and curved down – so rough and narrow you felt it could be held by a few men against a regiment – towards a great flat bowl with a few signs of cultivation, tiny scratchings on the plain below, miniature trees, a roof or two. I had been told that Las Palomas itself was well hidden, and so it was – not until you were in the plain itself and the road had taken a loop round a rocky outcrop of the hills did it come into sight a few hundred yards away. But it was only the romantic notion of ignorance that the farm could be easily defended; it wasn't chosen and hidden for that purpose: a few hours after General Cedillo broke into rebellion Federal troops were in possession. It had been built with care as a place from which escape was easy – into the rough, friendly, complex hills.

We bumped slowly between a few cultivated fields

towards some scattered white buildings in a dusty yard. An armed man swung the gate open, and a young dark Indian in riding breeches with a khaki topee and a scarred handsome face came down from a veranda to meet us. The veranda was crowded with politicians waiting for the General to appear, with guns on their hips, the holsters and the cartridge belts beautifully worked, a decorative death (I believe there is a law confining the carrying of arms to Government employees, but it didn't operate in San Luis Potosí any more than in the south). We sat down in wicker chairs and the old philosopher began to talk. It was midday. He talked – for hours. The young Indian, who was the major-domo and a deputy in the state legislature, offered us beds, but we sat on. A little farther up the hillside was the General's new house, a bungalow like the one we sat in but shinier, glossier. In the yard a whirlwind, small and domestic, raised a pillar of dust; it was very hot, and the politicians stood there patiently waiting while the hours passed, waiting to get something: money, an appointment, a promise – one man had come from as far as Yucatán. A blind-from-birth boy called Tomás, with slit eyes and little unreflecting pupils, came up the stairs and felt his way jovially from face to face, laughing at his own blindness. 'Someone said, "The light's gone out." I said, "What's that to me?"' He was the telephonist.

Then everyone stood to attention as if a national anthem had been played, and up the stairs from the dusty yard came the General – the only man without a gun – looking except for the Indian face like any farmer, a good and well-worn suit and a coarse shirt and no tie, an old soft hat perched back from the damp bull's forehead, and one gold tooth like a flaw in character. He went from man to man, embracing them all ceremoniously – a longer embrace than usual for the old German teacher. I had thought out some formal questions to explain my visit – the sort of foolish questions newspapermen are supposed to ask – about Fascism and Communism and foreign trade and the elections two years hence. We trooped after him into another room and the questions were read out to him; he looked puzzled, at a loss, a little angry; he said he'd answer them properly in writing – later – after food: we would find food ready for us at his house.

The major-domo led us across to the new bungalow and we drank whisky in the hideous *sala* while maids, pretty and nubile and faintly insolent, laid food. There was New Art furniture which might have come from the Tottenham Court Road and alligator skins, bought for a few pesos in Tabasco, and little statuettes and occasional tables and a framed colour print of Napoleon lying on the floor. It was like the house of a bachelor without personal taste who has tried to make a formal gesture to represent home. There was the pathos of the betwixt and between – of the uneducated man maintaining himself among the literate. On the wall was a coloured picture of the young Cedillo – the innocent Indian face under a big hat – seated on a horse, rifle in hand, a trooper in some old revolution. He didn't look like a future general – far less like a future minister. The major-domo's revolver holster creaked on the ugly easy chair and the young maid stared at us with a kind of sexual impertinence across the occasional tables. Cedillo was supposed to be dangerous – that was pathetic too among the statuettes. A man would never bring his wife or daughter

54

here, and yet many people had a kind of affection for him – an affection for an animal whose cage you enter with caution. A year or two back he had been a very sick man; the politicians ceased to visit him – they began to prepare their change of allegiance; only a few professional men came, from a sense of pity. Then they returned to San Luis and spread their legends – how many of them true, it is hard to say – of this woman and that. A lady took me on one side in San Luis and said, 'If you go out to Las Palomas you must be very careful – you know what I mean – not to look at any women he has at his house, or comment. He is a very jealous man.' And all the time we sat there the five hundred troops were waiting at Las Tribas for orders to move, while the dangerous man padded on his great flat feet round the farm.

The major-domo didn't eat lunch; he sat and watched us and pushed across the plates – with his dark scarred courtesy. And the old German teacher ate as if he hadn't tasted so much food for a long time, with complete absorption. Afterwards I thought we would get the answers to my questions and be off, but interviewing the General wasn't so simple as all that. We went back to the old bungalow – the General had disappeared, and the same crowd waited on the balcony. The major-domo showed the three of us into a little stuffy bedroom and went away; there was nothing to do and nothing to read but one little pamphlet on Communism published in Mexico City: it looked as if the General was doing his best to understand politics.

It was nearly five o'clock before the General appeared again, out of a shed where the electric-light plant was kept. But he didn't want to answer questions – not yet, there was a time for everything; presently I should get his replies in writing; now we were to see the farm, and off we bumped in the late golden light along the ruts of the unhedged fields, and behind at a discreet distance came another car – with the major-domo and his gun. The sun slid behind the mountains and shot its paling rays like a torch into the sky, and a very little green showed its head above the dry fields. The General sat in the front seat; the great back and rounded shoulders reminded me of Tommy Brock in Beatrix Potter's book – 'he waddled about by moonlight, digging things up'. Every now and then we got out and looked at a field, a crop, an irrigation canal. The night came suddenly down and we bumped back towards the yard over the hard dark ruts. Somewhere the oil engine chugged and a few lights – not many – went on correctly, and a foundry rang and rang under the blackening hills. The peasants drifted into the cookhouse, maids passed carrying tin dishes, smoke went up, and the dust of the day settled. Every now and then a car arrived and more men got out with their guns and milled boisterously on the veranda. The blind boy wandered round, roaring with laughter, feeling a stubble chin and a holster, saying, 'Juan. It's Juan.' If the General hadn't time for them that day, they'd stay the night and eat his food (two oxen had been killed in five days) and see him in the morning. It was all rather movingly simple and, in spite of the guns, idyllic. The peasants sat silently against the cookhouse wall, with their rugs drawn up around their mouths. The General gave them no pay, but food and clothes and shelter and half of everything the farm produced, and ready cash too if they asked for it and he had it. They even took the fifty chairs he bought for his little private cinema. And they gave him labour and love. It was not a

56

progressive relationship, it was feudal; you may say it was one-sided and he had everything – the New Art furniture, the statuettes, the alligator skins, and the coloured picture of Napoleon, but they possessed at any rate more than did their fellow-peasants in other states, living at best on the minimum wage of thirty-five cents a day, with no one caring if they lived or died, with all the responsibility of independence.

The General said he couldn't answer my questions that night. I had better sleep at the farm and then by midday he would be able to see me and I could get back to San Luis the next night . . . I couldn't afford it: I had hired a car and a chauffeur. I said in that case I must be off; I wanted to be in Mexico City next day. The General blew himself out: his neck and cheeks extended like rubber. I could see from the faces of the German teacher and the businessman that I had committed an atrocity. Suddenly the General gave way, sent for his secretary, and led the way into a room away from the veranda where the politicians waited.

The door blew shut and we were in the dark: the electric light had apparently failed. The obscurity was hot with the General's resentment. He grunted breathlessly near my shoulder and the business man said, 'No, señor,' 'Sí, señor,' with immense obsequiousness. Something rattled metallically on the floor: it was the old philosopher's umbrella. Presently somebody thought of trying a switch and the light went obediently on, a bare globe beating on a cracked mirror, a few hard chairs, a miniature billiard table with a ragged cloth. The teacher began to read out my questions, and the General dictated his answers to the secretary. He hated the whole business; you could see he didn't think in our terms at all.

Yes, he said, he believed in religious toleration ('*Soy respetuoso de todas las creencias*'), and in San Luis he had given his people toleration. Yes, he approved, too, of the new Socialist schools Cárdenas was building all over Mexico, so long as they taught children the practical things of life – but there were some teachers who were making their schools sectarian and serving 'mean political interests'. He hedged all the time – I don't think he could forget the Federal troops waiting at Las Tribas, the watchers and the listeners. The President's agrarian policy – the break-up of the big estates, land for the Indians – he even agreed with that, heavily diplomatic in the middle of his dark acres – but . . .

When it came to the 'buts', he sweated and rolled his eyes. He felt himself 'on the spot'. Questions were being asked which people didn't care to ask in San Luis – his attitude to the great trade union organisation CROM, whether he meant to stand as President at the next election – and the obsequious capitalist was listening carefully to what he said. He swelled out indignantly like a bull-frog and sweated; hospitality held him uneasily curbed. True, I was a Catholic (I could never have got leave to visit him otherwise, for he didn't receive foreign newspapermen), but he knew that Catholics regarded him with insecure gratitude. Not one of them really wished to exchange even the harsh laws of Cárdenas for his corrupt administration.

So the 'buts' came rolling out. He approved of the Agrarian Laws in principle, but they were being applied by individuals disastrously – 'to serve mean political interests'. As for Fascism and Communism, he didn't believe in either – he stood for parliamentary government 'if possible'. (He used the word democracy, but you could tell he'd been taught that. You always slipped it in when people talked politics.)

Sitting there under the bare globe near the billiard table I couldn't really believe any longer in the twenty thousand disciplined troops he was said to have at his call. Of course one doesn't trust the word of a general or a politician, but there was something genuine in the bull-frog rage, the hopeless bewilderment of the man when I asked him about the German officers. He spluttered, he turned eyes of desperate inquiry on the old teacher . . . what would his enemies say next? He was caught in a maze of friends and enemies with similar faces. That is how I see him – the young Indian trooper with the round innocent face turned middle-aged, the bitterness of political years souring the innocence. People who were his friends milked him, and he had to milk the state, and then there was a drought and the water system was antiquated and the governor had no money to deal with it – and the trade unionists complained to the President, the President who wouldn't have been at Chapultepec now without his help, without the support of the troops which had enabled him to deport Calles. He had to get money from the state – for his friends, for his farm – and from capitalists. And capitalists wanted 'things' in return, things like the suppression of labour agitation, and so politics crept in. I think he was inclined to hate the man who came bothering him with questions about Fascism and Communism. He swelled and sweated and said, 'Democracy'. He had been happier at sunset, jolting over the stony fields in an old car, showing off his crops and his canal.

59

They were not to be his two months hence; I think he already felt the steady pressure to rebel. Mexico was coming to the boil. A week before, the Mexican Supreme Court had upheld the Federal Labour Board's award against the foreign oil companies. In ten days' time President Cárdenas was to sign the decree expropriating them; the machinery of propaganda was already at work which was to set the tide of patriotism flowing and to give the President the chance of settling accounts with Cedillo. Left to himself, Cedillo, I think, would have gone on hesitating. He may have enjoyed being the centre of intrigue; it was another matter altogether to sacrifice his farm and take to the mountains in middle age. But the screw was turning: that very night officers were on the way from San Luis to tell him that the military commandant of the city, who was his friend, had been removed and fresh uncontaminated troops were entering the state. A fortnight later he was to be appointed military commandant of Michoacán, Cárdenas's own state, where he would be safely shut away from his friends with all Guanajuato between him and San Luis. He pleaded illness and hung on at Las Palomas, but by that time the tide was flowing strongly, and Cárdenas made his sudden and dramatic appearance unguarded in San Luis, addressed the people in his enemy's stronghold, accused Cedillo of preparing rebellion, and demanded the disarming of his peasantry. The war was on – at the right moment for the Government; bombs were dropped, there were skirmishes in the hills, Las Palomas was occupied, and Cedillo was chased from small landing-ground to small landing-ground. Supporters of his as far south as Las Casas in Chiapas were jailed; a general was shot near Puebla; the rebellion was over and the banditry was on – the dynamiting of trains, the useless cruelty.

Even when the General had disposed of that last question, we were not free to go. The answers had to be typed and the typescript passed. So, more long hours dragged by on the balcony with the *pistoleros*, a seedy American manager with a stubbled chin and a little round belly, a young scented Mexican journalist who said he'd been warned not to come – the rebellion was starting that day – and blind Tomás feeling round. At ten o'clock we were led back to the new bungalow and fed. Little fires were burning in the yard and women with cooking-pots stirred the embers; tongues of flame wavered like tiny snakes and the night pressed down. Somewhere far away a thunderstorm shifted cumbrously in the hills (a week before two peons had been killed by lightning) like cargo unloaded in a railway-yard. Two painted flashy women with fine legs sat in the *sala* waiting for the General and bed, and again the major-domo watched us eat, the revolver creaking as he passed the salad, and again a maidservant passed by, faintly impertinent with her dim suggestive smile. It was like the scene in a play which attempts too much: the businessman and the bandit, the old philosopher (tucking the food away as if he had to supply himself for a long desert march without wells or rations), the world of the flesh slinking around, and heaven cracking up outside.

We got away about eleven – the teacher had a petition to present and that kept us another half-hour. Suddenly he emerged as a family man, with a son out of work and another son who had died a few weeks before in Veracruz of infection; he had been a doctor. The General dictated a few words which would ensure his boy a position in the Government departments of San Luis, until, I suppose, the rebellion came, bringing a few violent deaths and much fun and excitement for the professional *pistoleros* and overtoppling here and there some small, obscure, and private life, like that of the teacher's son.

Then we drove away towards the storm. The white farm gates swung open, a man waved a rifle cheerily in the headlights, we climbed into the hills. The storm lay like a threat across the future – on the other side of the private passport station which we passed at two in the morning. The businessman and the chauffeur sang side by side in the front seat and the old philosopher slept uneasily, clutching his umbrella, the fine aristocratic face with the silky white hair bobbing up and down on the torn upholstery, lit by the storm. The cacti leapt up like sentries on the mountain slopes against the green flapping light, and on either side of the pass the lightning stood for seconds at a time vibrating in the ground. It was impossible to see at all before that vivid illumination: we drove blindly from left to right, missing the cacti by inches, coming closer and closer to the spears of fire. It was like a barrage we had to pass through – the electric fire rocketed down on the road a mile ahead. And then suddenly we swerved – turned away – outwitted it. The storm faded noisily away on our flank, and somewhere in front of us between the hills a light blinked. The old teacher slept and the business man nodded and a premature cock began tentatively to crow and then slept again; and a dead town slipped like a lantern slide before the headlights. The storm had not frightened; it had exhilarated. Lightning and the gods have always been associated; terrible, majestic, deliberate, stabbing impartially, it was like a criticism of human violence, the little decorated pistol holsters, the absurd self-importance of killers. One thought of Oklahoma Jim and Dutch Kaplan – the dried skin and the bared ribs – who thought they had ruled their roost and were now exhibited in a booth. They all – even the General – had become figures of fun under the enormous storm.

TO MEXICO CITY

Only the big decorative poster-shapes of the maguey broke the monotonous landscape of mountain and parched plain. The scene, I suppose, was beautiful in a way, but I felt in sympathy with Cobbett, whose *Rural Rides* I had just been reading before I looked out of the window. He judged a landscape by its value to human beings – not as the Romantics did, in terms of the picturesque. The Romantics would have enjoyed the Mexican scene, describing it as 'sublime' and 'awe-inspiring'; they scented God in the most barren regions, as if He were a poet of escape whom it was necessary to watch tactfully through spy-glasses as He brooded beside a waterfall or on the summit of Helvellyn; as if God, disappointed in His final creation, had fallen back on one of His earlier works. They preferred the kind of Nature which rejects man.

But Nature appals me when unemployed or unemployable – I can give only lip service to the beauty of the African bush or the Cornish coast. 'The birches are out in leaf. I do not think that I ever saw the wheat look, take it all together, so well as it does at this time. I see, in the stiff land, no signs of worm or slug. The roots look well. The barley is very young; but I do not see

63

anything amiss with regard to it.' *That*, I can understand –
there is no subjective judgment there – Nature is
presented to us like a loaf of bread, and memory can
surround the concrete words, birches, wheat, barley,
with what haze of sentiment it pleases. I wondered in
what terms a Mexican Cobbett would have described
this barren picturesque strange land. 'As villainous a
tract as the world contains . . . the soil is a mixture of
stone and sand . . . I have observed all the way along
that the maguey is the only plant able to ripen.' And
then as the train drew into Huichapán, what exclama-
tions there would have been against 'the basest lick-
spittles of power', who under their pretence of freedom
have left so many chains. And yet, though this is the
tourist railroad from Laredo to Mexico City, I have seen
no references anywhere in the blithe optimistic American
books to the squalor of Huichapán station.

The whole long platform was given up to beggars, not
the friendly Indian women bearing tortillas and legs of
chicken, preserved fruits dried in the dusty sun, and
strange pieces of meat, who pass at every station down
the train, not even the kind of resigned beggars who
usually sit in church porches waiting dumbly and
patiently for alms, but get-rich-quick beggars, scrambling and whining and snarling with impatience,
children and old men and women, fighting their way
along the train, pushing each other to one side, lifting
the stump of a hand, a crutch, a rotting nose, or in the
children's case a mere bony undernourished hand. A
middle-aged paralytic worked himself down the platform
on his hands – three feet high, with bearded bandit face
and little pink baby feet twisted the wrong way. Someone
threw him a coin and a child of six or seven leapt on his

64

back and after an obscene and horrifying struggle got it from him. The man made no complaint, shovelling himself farther along; human beings here obeyed the jungle law, each for himself with tooth and nail. They came up around the train on both sides of the track like mangy animals in a neglected zoo. I remembered how once in a pleasure park on the outskirts of London I had come down a great sweep of beautiful treed turf, below a palace of arts where an organ was playing to thousands, and encountered tucked away in a tiny group of sheds – admission sixpence – a zoo, and no one about at all but a man with a rake and a pail. There wasn't much to be seen: a monkey scratched in a dark corner and a tiger turned and turned in a cage a foot or two larger than itself; it was half dark and stuffy, and far away you heard the organ playing. One will never exhaust these little store houses of human cruelty. They are tucked away like petrol from air-raids, in a street off the Tottenham Court Road, in a London park, at Huichapán – they are always there to be drawn on in case of need.

And then the capital. Troops were entraining – for San Luis Potosí. They made very little noise, small men moving in platoons, without good humour. Outside, the city was very dark, though it was not yet ten o'clock – the streets round the station were shabby, as in Paris, but the hotel was very new, too new. The room was all scarlet and black cellulose; there was a smell of paint, and the price tag hung on the chamber pot – 1 peso 25.

I went out and walked down the Cinco de Mayo, shining from a shower, and into the Avenida Juárez, which smelt of sweets – the white skyscraper of an insurance office, the Palace of Arts, white and domed and dignified, the great tame trees of the Alameda, a

65

park which is said to date back to Montezuma, expensive jewellers' and antique shops, libraries . . . it was difficult to realise that Huichapán was only a few hours away, and twelve hours off were the *pistoleros* waiting on Cedillo's veranda, as the lightning stabbed between the mountains. There was nothing to connect this European capital with the small wild farm and the Indians in the hills. They belonged to different continents – how could one ever help the other? This was like Luxemburg – a luxury town. The taxis drove up the great wide handsome avenue, the Paseo de la Reforma, and a green phosphorescent R shone out on the roof garden of the best hotel, above balconies and long glass halls glowing with tubular orange lighting; gold wings at the Statue of Independence: the last Aztec monarch in dark bronze glittered like laurel bushes with the late rain. There were few people about, and most of these were American, except that in the doors of shops in the Avenida Juárez, out of the wind, crouched small Indian boys, homeless, wrapped in blankets, singing low melancholy traditional songs – but you find that, I suppose, in every capital: the untouchables under the Paris fortifications, and old women rotting at night in Regent Street doorways.

3. Notes in Mexico City

How to describe a city? Even for an old inhabitant it is impossible; one can present only a simplified plan, taking a house here, a park there as symbols of the whole. If I were trying to describe London to a foreigner, I might take Trafalgar Square and Piccadilly Circus, the Strand and Fleet Street, the grim wastes of Queen Victoria Street and Tottenham Court Road, villages like Chelsea and Clapham and Highgate struggling for individual existence, Great Portland Street because of the secondhand cars and the faded genial men with old school ties, Paddington for the vicious hotels . . . and how much would remain left out, the Bloomsbury square with its inexpensive vice and its homesick Indians and its sense of rainy nostalgia, the docks . . . ?

The shape of most cities can be simplified as a cross; not so Mexico City, elongated and lopsided on its mountain plateau. It emerges like a railway track from a tunnel – the obscure narrow streets lying to the west of the Zócalo, the great square in which the cathedral sails like an old rambling Spanish galleon close to the National Palace. Behind, in the tunnel, the university quarter – high dark stony streets like those of the Left Bank in Paris – fades among the tramways and dingy shops into red-light districts and street markets. In the tunnel you become aware that Mexico City is older and less Central European than it appears at first – a baby alligator tied to a pail of water; a whole family of Indians eating their lunch on the sidewalk edge; railed off among the drug-stores and the tram-lines, near the cathedral, a portion of the Aztec temple Cortés destroyed. And always, everywhere, stuck between the shops, hidden behind the new American hotels, are the old baroque churches and convents, some of them still open, some converted to the oddest uses – the Cine Mundial, once the Convent of Jesús María; the Government Library, once the Betlemites' church; a warehouse which was a Catholic college; a shop, a garage, a newspaper office still bearing the old façades. Between November 11th 1931, and April 28th 1936, four hundred and eighty Catholic churches, schools, orphanages, hospitals were closed by the Government or converted to other uses. The National Preparatory School itself was formerly a Jesuit college, built in the eighteenth century.

Out of the Zócalo our imaginary train emerges into sunlight. The Cinco de Mayo and the Francisco Madero, fashionable shopping streets, run like twin tracks, containing smart Mayfair stations – the best antique shops, American teashops, Sanborn's, towards the Palace of Arts and the Alameda. Tucked behind them is the goods track – Tacuba – where you can buy your clothes cheap if you don't care much for appearances. After the Palace of Arts the parallel tracks are given different names as they run along beside the trees and fountains of Montezuma's park – the Avenida Juárez full of tourist shops and milk bars and little stalls of confectionery, and the Avenida Hidalgo, where hideous funeral wreaths are made, ten feet high and six across, of mauve and white flowers. Then Hidalgo wanders off where no one troubles to go and Juárez is closed by the great Arch of the Republic, which frames a sky-sign of Moctezuma Beer, and the Hotel Regis, where the American Rotarians go and the place where they draw the lottery. We turn south-west into the Paseo de la Reforma, the great avenue Maximilian made, running right out of the city to the gates of Chapultepec, past Columbus and Guatemoc and the glassy Colon Café, like the Crystal Palace, where President Huerta, the man who shot Madero and fled from Carranza, used to get drunk (when he became helpless, they turned out the lights and people passing said, 'The President's going to bed'; it wouldn't have been a good thing to *see* the President of Mexico carried to his car), on past the Hotel Reforma and the Statue of Independence, all vague aspiration and expensive golden wings, to the lions at the gates. And on either side branch off the new smart streets, pink and blue wash and trailing flowers, where the diplomats live, and the smell of sweets blows heavily along from Juárez.

PLANS

I began to plan the journey I had in mind. I decided it would be necessary to go down to Veracruz and find some cargo boat there which would take me to Frontera, in Tabasco. There are no railways in Tabasco and, as far as I could make out, no roads – one must travel by water to Villahermosa, the capital, and then somehow by water again to Montecristo on the other side of the state. From there apparently I could get horses to the ruins of Palenque in Chiapas – which were my excuse for wishing to visit the state – and then if I could (these things always look so simple on a map) I would make my way by horse to the railhead in southern Chiapas, by way of San Cristóbal de Las Casas.

One seemed to need some excuse of the Palenque kind – there was an uneasy conscience at work among Mexican officials on the subject of Tabasco and Chiapas. They are the only two states left where Catholics cannot receive the Sacraments of their faith except secretly, and if I had shown any particular interest in politics or religion, it would have been simple enough to thirty-three me. Plenty of foreigners have been thirty-threed in the past few years.*

No one seemed to know quite what the situation was in Tabasco and Chiapas – states more isolated than Yucatán, for Yucatán has the tourist traffic to Mérida and Chichen Itzá, while there is nothing to take the tourist to these two states, except Palenque. The few visitors to Palenque, perhaps from egotistic pride, have asserted that the ruins are the equal of Chichen Itzá, yet not many people but archaeologists – and visitors rich enough to charter a special aeroplane – care to face the minor hardships of the journey. There seemed to be no priests at all in Tabasco, and I was told in New York that they believed not a church was left standing – not even the cathedral.

* To thirty-three is to exercise the right under Clause 33 of the Constitution to expel any foreigner deemed undesirable, without giving cause, at twenty-four hours' notice. The process may be an expensive one for the victim, as he has to pay the cost of an escort to the frontier. I have heard of an American woman who found herself tied to a couple of guards for several weeks. They escorted her – first-class, of course – to either Juárez or Nuevo Laredo, and then found something wrong with her papers which enabled them to hang on in her company at a Mexican hotel, charging up every drink, until her money was exhausted, when she was allowed across the frontier.

I changed my hotel – it was too brand-new – for a dustier, noisier, more native brand, though it called itself by an Anglo-Saxon name. Here I got a room with a shower and three meals a day for 5.50 pesos, say, seven shillings. Lunch consisted of six courses with a cocktail and coffee. Music was supplied through the street door; a succession of marimba players took up a collection – the marimba, gentle, sentimental, with the pleasing tinkle of a music-box. Beggars came in all through the meal (why not? It is a good strategic time) and people selling sheet music, and even rosaries, and of course lottery tickets. You couldn't get away from lottery tickets, even in the courtyard of the cathedral. I shall always associate Mexico City with the sick smell of sweets and the lottery sellers. The lottery is the next best thing to hope of heaven – there is a draw every week, with first prizes of twenty-five thousand, fifty thousand, and sometimes one hundred thousand pesos.

CINEMA

I went my first night to Fritz Lang's *Liliom*, a naïve and rather moving film of heartlessness on earth and repentance in heaven. The audience was more interesting than the film; they accepted the sentiment just as any European audience would have done, but when the two messengers from God – dressed in sinister seedy clerical black – appeared beside the body and lifted Liliom's soul between them into the sky, legs trailing like stuffed dolls through the firmament, they hooted and cat-called. Many got up and went out: they were not going to have anything to do with heaven or hell; only later, when they found that heaven was to be treated with whimsicality and a touch of farce, did they settle down into their seats. When I came out the streets were dark, the cantinas empty, and the air at seven thousand feet felt cold and thin and lifeless. Only a few Indians sat on stone seats in a gawky and innocent embrace – fingers stuffed over the mouth or a great ham hand hanging over the shoulder – dungarees and shawls and no sense of passion at all.

ALL BOYS TOGETHER

As I was returning from the bank, I heard explosions in the Francisco Madero. Crowds blocked the end of the Gante. There was another explosion and the crowd bolted – I ran with them right into a haberdashery store. A group of young men rushed by throwing water out of pails over the sidewalk and into the shops. It was the opening of the university and this the traditional 'rag' – they put colouring matter into the water and if it gets on your clothes, they are ruined. Presently the police are called out, but they can never do anything: then the fire brigade, and that's the end of the 'rag'. Nobody minds, everybody thinks it a fine joke, they are all boys together. It is this boyishness, this immaturity, which gets most on the nerves in Mexico. Grown men cannot meet in the street without sparring like schoolboys. One must be as a little child, we are told, to enter the kingdom of heaven, but they have passed childhood and remain for ever in a cruel anarchic adolescence.

NUNS' BABIES

I was sitting in the lounge of my hotel waiting for lunch when an American planted himself firmly down beside me. He was middle-aged, with a firm weak face, as if he had taken a correspondence course in personality. 'You new here?' he said.

'Yes.'

'Then I'll tell you a thing or two.' He took a lot of papers out of his pocket – old envelopes scribbled with calculations. 'I'll tell you what you got to see. An' you don't want to let them cheat you, either. There's a lot of hooey at the agencies. You can do this place cheap if you know how.'

'I'm not staying long,' I said, with my eye on the restaurant.

'That's just it,' he said. 'I can be of use to you. What's experience for unless you share it? Now you started well. This is a cheap place.'

'Have you had your lunch?'

He laid a plump hand heavily on my knee and kept it there. 'Now you'll want to see Cuernavaca, Taxco, Puebla – they charge you a lot at the agencies, but I looked around an' you can go to all those places for a dollar, by bus. I'll give you the addresses.'

'I don't think I'll have time,' I said.

'There's something you mustn't miss,' he said, 'and that's the hidden convent at Puebla. But you won't find all they say's there. Nuns' babies.'

'Nuns' babies?'

'It's disgusting,' he said. 'Propaganda, propaganda all the time. I went to an agency in San Antonio, Texas. They said, "Are you a Freemason?" I said, "Yes." They said, "We've got just the thing for you. The hidden convent at Puebla. You'll be met by a Freemason. He'll give you the real goods – show you things. The bones of all these nuns' babies."' He paused and said with

73

suppressed fury, 'There weren't any bones of nuns' babies! It's all propaganda, propaganda, propaganda.'

FRESCOES

I went and saw Orozco's and Rivera's frescoes at the National Preparatory School and the Ministry of Education in the university quarter. The frescoes in the Preparatory School are mainly by Orozco. Rivera contributes only one mural with typical grandiloquence – all outstretched arms and noble faces, white robes and haloes. It is called 'Creation'; it is full of literary symbols – the Tree of Life, Dionysus, Man, Woman, Music, Comedy, Dance, Tragedy, Science, Temperance, Fortitude. It adapts Christian emblems to a vague political idea, and they become unbearably sentimental in the new setting, far more sentimental than repository art. That pale blue madonna with the seven swords does, however inadequately, represent an exact idea; but the Son in Rivera's 'Creation' – what is he but Progress, Human Dignity, great empty Victorian conceptions that life denies at every turn ? This is always Rivera's way – to try to get the best of both worlds. He is the Leighton or the Watts of the Revolution.

Orozco – however invalid one may believe his ideology to be – knows his own mind and his own world; it is very seldom that the great abstractions – 'Maternity' – billow their sentimental draperies across *his* walls. His subjects are 'The Trench', '*Soldaderas*', 'The Indian', 'The Missionary', 'St Francis', 'The Eternal Father' – guyed with white woolly beard and little birdlike beak, lightning, and grumpy eyes. The Franciscan monk clasping with huge arms the starving

74

Indian in a strangling embrace, the patient hopeless women trailing after their soldiers into the umber future, these represent emotions of pity and hate that one can respect.

In the Ministry of Education Rivera has it all his own way. Occasionally – very occasionally – his moral is where it should be, implicit, 'The Rural Teacher' – the little group of Indians sitting in a circle on the baked ground, while the woman speaks to them out of a book and the trooper sits his horse, his rifle ready, and the men plough a tiny field under the mountains; 'Inspection on Leaving the Mine' – the white-clothed worker standing on a plank across the abyss, head bowed and arms outstretched, while the officials search him for stolen silver. But even here we are aware of the stolen symbol – the cross, the agony.

Perhaps we have no right to criticise – Christianity itself adapted the feast days and the holy places of the older faiths. In Mexico City the cathedral is built on the site of the great Aztec temple, and perhaps we are only experiencing the uneasiness of the old Aztec priests when we turn impatiently away from these murals of rural teachers dressed in white with pious apostolic faces and fingers raised in blessing – 'Suffer little children to come unto me.' Perhaps they are only making things gentle for us, so that we shan't miss our faith in the new, drilled totalitarian day.

SUFFER LITTLE CHILDREN

It was a narrow by-street in the new part of town. When I asked for Father Q the door was slammed in my face. Perhaps I had come to the wrong house. A boy had just come out; he watched with cautious interest. I held out my letter of introduction printed with the address of a Catholic organisation in New York, and when he saw it he smiled encouragement and rang the bell for me. The door was opened, this time by a young man. He wore a stiff collar and a small bright tie – his suit looked somehow unlived in. He was Father Q.

Walking upstairs, he said it was unwise of me to have addressed a letter to him as the Reverend. Though there was a spell of quiet, at any time the Government might renew the searches and the confiscations.

The small house was active all around us – young women typewriting, men waiting for a conference: Catholic Action under way.

He was rushed: a conference was due; in an hour he had to take the train – somewhere. There was a sense of purpose and efficiency which had been absent in San Antonio. He could tell me, though, nothing about Tabasco or Chiapas. His main concern was education. It was in that field now that the battle was joined. He told me of the law that forbids religious education in the schools but does not forbid anti-religious teaching, of the provision that makes any house in which more than nine people have gathered for a religious purpose automatically Government property. At the moment in Mexico City the police were careless; none the less, the Church tried to hold all the schools it could in houses that were half ruined and might escape the cupidity of a politician.

Even foreign schools – English and American – had to obey the Government regulations on the subject of religious teaching and to accept the Government curriculum. No school could employ unlicensed teachers, and private schools therefore had to choose their professors from a list supplied by the Secretary of Education. Naturally – as far as possible – the Ministry saw to it that only one political complexion was represented on the list. The teachers when appointed usually formed a union, and controlled the school without reference to the owner. The sexual tradition operates in odd ways and in the case of one private school, where all the nine teachers were women, they elected the doorkeeper to their union and his sex made him its leader and automatically the head of the school. Of course schools still existed in the capital staffed by Catholics, but they were secret.

Mexican education is Fascist, or totalitarian, whichever you prefer to call it. It is not democratic.* Here is an extract from Article 3 of the Constitution:

'The education imparted by the State shall be a socialistic one and, in addition to excluding all religious doctrine, shall combat fanaticism and prejudices by organising its instruction and activities in a way that shall permit the creation in youth of an exact and rational conception of the Universe and of social life.'

It is a little pathetic, that muddled idealism which speaks of 'an exact and rational conception of the Universe': one thinks of men like Samuel Butler with hideous crippling childhoods; and in the dry Sonora or Michoacán plains, the homes of Calles and Cárdenas, childhood *was* no doubt crippled – in the Mexican way of the pistol shot and the crooked judge and the cockfight and nobody caring for another's life. Who can

* There is still an inclination to defend the Mexican Government on the part of labour organisations. But Mexico does not follow accepted ideological lines, as we may see in the oil deals with Italy and Germany.

77

blame these men if they tried to exercise responsibility? The State has certainly the right to decide what type of education the State shall pay for. It is in the second half of the same clause that totalitarianism leaks out – the revolt from irresponsibility carried too far. 'Only the State – Federation, States, Municipalities – shall impart primary, secondary, and normal education. Authorisation may be conceded to individuals who desire to impart education in any of the aforementioned three levels in conformity, in every case, with the following norms:

'1. The teachings and activities of private plants must adjust themselves without exception to that indicated in the initial paragraph ['exact and rational,' etc.] and shall be in charge of persons who, in the opinion of the State, shall have sufficient professional preparation and a morality and ideology that is suitable to and in keeping with this precept.' Then comes a rule that no minister or anyone connected with any religious society shall be allowed to teach or assist the schools financially.

'2. The formation of plans, programmes, and methods of teaching shall in every case rest in the State.'

The State . . . always the State. What idealisms have gone to the construction of that tyrant! One thinks of the Fabians and Mr Shaw in his Jaeger suit; and then suddenly the thing lives – and Pro receives the *coup de grâce* in the little dirty yard and no one any more is able to make the claim, 'The State is I.' The State is none of us; phrases like 'no taxation without representation' are meaningless, because we are all taxed and no one is represented. Perhaps the only body in the world today which consistently – and sometimes successfully – opposes the totalitarian State is the Catholic Church. In

Germany motor-cyclists distributed the Pope's encyclical secretly at night; in Italy the *Osservatore Romano* printed what no Italian paper dared to print – protests against the bombing of Guernica and attacks on open towns; and in Mexico, in a back street, the typewriter goes steadily on, and the young priest, ill at ease in his lay suit, laughs with genuine carefree mirth at his own arrest a few years back. He said, 'It was the happiest time of our lives.'

He was studying in a street seminary carried on right in the heart of the city, almost next door to the National Palace. Calles was still President. Suddenly one morning the house was surrounded – two hundred troops with rifles; it might have been a secret fort packed with munitions. Fifty plain-clothes detectives suddenly filled the corridors, herded the students into one room while they searched for religious emblems or treasonable pamphlets. They found nothing, except what Calles himself, in that moment of extraordinary infatuation, had distributed to the Press – the photographs of Father Pro's execution. These photographs had to be made the basis of a charge of treason. The pupils were packed off to jail and the seminary was confiscated. After a few days they were released – Calles had learned that making martyrs didn't pay. 'It was the happiest time,' Father Q said, chuckling, remembering the camaraderie of the cells, the hope and exultation, under the light of death.

And the work goes on. A training college for girls started at the time of the worst persecution to instruct leaders among the laity numbered six in 1926; now fifty-six thousand have been trained in theology and dogma. Catholic Action sends out instructed guides to work among those of the Government, who are licensed to take tourists round the 'show places' near Mexico City, propagandising all the time against the Church; now the Church's voice begins to be heard – among the Rotarians and the earnest social workers and the amateur painters and the business men out for a good time where the dollar buys so much; trailing round old monasteries and shattered churches, with Kodaks and little stools and sketch-books, here and there they encounter a Catholic voice. And that, I suppose, is treason too. For the State puts its own interpretation on the word treason – and never punishes anyone for his religion. It is the technique the totalitarian State has always employed: in the time of Elizabeth in England, just as much as in Mexico, Russia, or Germany today, and Campion's reply is still the valid one, 'In condemning us you condemn all your own ancestors – all the ancient priests, bishops, and kings . . . For what have we taught, however you may qualify it with the odious name of treason, that they did not uniformly teach? To be condemned with these lights – not of England only, but of the world – by their degenerate descendants is both gladness and glory to us.'

FUN AT NIGHT

El Retiro is the swagger cabaret of Socialist Mexico, all red and gold and little balloons filled with gas, and chicken *à la* king. A film star at one table and a famous singer, and rich men everywhere. American couples moved sedately across the tiny dance floor while the music wailed, the women with exquisite hair and gentle indifference, and the middle-aged American business-men like overgrown schoolboys a hundred years younger than their young women. Then the cabaret began – a

Mexican dancer with great bold thighs, and the American women lost a little of their remote superiority. They were being beaten at the sexual game – somebody who wasn't beautiful and remote was drawing the attention of their men. They got vivacious and talked a little shrilly and powdered their faces, and suddenly appeared very young and inexperienced and unconfident, as the great thighs moved. But their turn came when the famous tenor sang. The American men lit their pipes and talked all through the song and then clapped heartily to show that *they* didn't care, and the women closed their compacts and listened – avidly. It wasn't poetry they were listening to or music (the honeyed words about roses and love, the sweet dim nostalgic melody), but the great emotional orgasm in the throat. They called out for a favourite song, and the rich plump potent voice wailed on – interminably, a whole night of love. This was not popular art, or intellectual art – it was, I suppose, capitalist art. And this, too, was Socialist Mexico.

Then the Waikiki, on a lower level socially and morally. Armed policemen watched by the cloakroom (later that night the place was raided for Pérez, the drug trafficker). Lovely sexual instruments, wearing little gold crosses, lolled on the sofas; a man had passed out altogether beside a blue soda-water bottle. Small intimate parties struggled obscurely with shoulder-straps, and presently got up and made for the hotel a little way down the street. My friend thought I might be lonely and insisted on finding me an American girl – there was only one in the place, and she was called Sally. I said I didn't want her, but she obviously had for him (he was a Mexican) the glamour of foreignness. He said, 'She's nice. She's refined – and interesting. You'll like to talk

81

to her. You're a writer. She'll tell you all about her life.'

I said, 'I don't want to hear about her life.' You could see it all around without asking questions – in the red velvet sofas and the blue soda-water bottles and the passed-out Mexican. But my friend had got a girl and he wanted me to have an American – somebody I could talk to easily. He kept on asking everybody, 'Where is Sally ?' and presently they found her – so there she came, picking a refined way across the dance floor, pasty, genteel and a little scared, and very badly dressed. She said, 'Yes, sir,' 'No, sir,' 'Yes, sir,' to everything I said. The formality, the subservience, the terrible refinement were uncanny.

My Mexican friend said, 'She's pretty, eh ?' and I had to look at that infinitely plain pasty face with all the vacancy of drug-stores and cheap movies and say, 'Yes, fine.'

'And mine is good, too, eh ? Feel her here.' He pinched her thigh. 'If only she didn't have all those gold teeth' – he was a dentist. 'Open your mouth,' he said. 'Why do you have all those gold teeth ?'

'I like them,' she said.

'Feel her here,' he said. 'Go on. She is pretty good, eh ?' She was, indeed – a fine young instrument of pleasure. 'Go on and ask Sally about her life. You are a writer. You want to hear all about it.'

'Do you like it here ?' I said with embarrassment. It was like making conversation at a tea-party.

'Yes, sir.'

'Better than the States ?'

'No, sir.'

'She is interesting,' the Mexican said. 'Not like mine.

She is only good for one thing, eh?' and the other flashed her gold teeth at him and asked for another drink. Every time a drink came, five-centavo pieces were slipped under the girls' plates. The dentist began to talk about Huerta and Madero – he had been telling me about them at dinner.

He was the son of a rich southern landowner, but his family had lost everything in the revolution. He himself had been an army cadet at the time of Huerta's counter-revolution. He was in the National Palace when Huerta's men broke in – they had shot Madero there in front of his eyes in the palace, or so he said. The whole story that Madero had been taken in a car towards the prison and shot in the street was a lie – he had been there, he had seen. But so, of course, others had seen – the other shooting. The historian in Mexico is lost among eye-witnesses.

Half a dozen girls in yellow bathing suits did high kicks for a few moments and disappeared. I said to Sally, 'Is that all the cabaret there is?'

She said, 'Yes, sir,' sitting there with pasty rectitude, her hands folded in her Main Street lap.

'Got many friends among the girls here?'

'No, sir.'

'What brought you here?' I said. It appeared she had married a Mexican and come across the border – so she was a Mexican citizen.

'Then he dropped you?'

'Yes, sir.'

'She is very interesting,' the Mexican said. 'You ask her things.'

He bit his companion's ear and she nestled against him – brown hair and dark brown Jersey eyes, a figure

83

to pin on a wall. He began to tell jokes about Cárdenas. The President had visited Yucatán, where the henequen plantations had been divided up among the Indians. They had taken him to see Chichen Itzá. 'Mr President, nowhere else in the world are there such ruins.' But he turned impatiently away and said, 'They are nothing to the ones I shall leave behind me.' Always in totalitarian States you get these underground jokes, a bitter powerless humour.

'Do you like Spaniards?' I asked Sally. The dull face suddenly lit up with refined fury.

'No,' she said, 'they are vulgar. The Mexican is a gentleman, but the Spaniard's vulgar.'

'And the Indian?'

'Oh, the Indian's a fine man, sir.'

The bill for drinks was enormous for Mexico. About thirty shillings. I had only five pesos left, and the Mexican dentist wanted to have his girl. 'She will only cost twenty pesos,' he said, 'but then there is the hotel – that will be five. I have only twenty.'

'I can't lend you any.'

'It is very awkward.' All the same, he brought her with him – the man still sat collapsed beside the soda-water bottle. He thought he might be able to borrow five pesos somewhere. I took them as far as my hotel in a taxi; it was four o'clock in the morning. I saw them trailing off down the Cinco de Mayo, the girl a little behind, brown and docile, dragging her evening dress through the grey early light.

I dreamed that a woman and I had committed a murder and buried the body, but the smell seeped up to us through the ground until the whole world seemed to carry the scent of decay.

I went to Mass in the huge cornery cathedral – great twisted gold pillars and dark pictures of love and agony. Outside the cathedral they were selling cards consisting of small photographs of Father Pro – sitting with his superior in Belgium, his face a little sullen and immature, with heavy mouth and too serious eyes; in a police photograph, wearing a jumper and a cheap striped tie, unshaven, the mouth senstitive now and controlled and no less obstinate; kneeling in prayer in the dreadful little execution yard behind police headquarters; standing with arms outstretched and closed eyes between the two old dummy figures used for rifle practice; lying with legs doubled up and arms still crosswise, receiving the *coup de grâce;* in the mortuary, lids not quite closed and the obstinate mouth dropping open to show the big stony teeth, and the vacant face like a mask taken off and ready for any wearer. A prayer is printed with the photographs, a prayer which they say is often answered. People preserve his relics (the dentist's mother had a handkerchief dipped in his blood): he is beatified already by popular election.

The Alameda on a Sunday is like a scene from a René Clair film: the bourgeois families under the great trees, and the photographers, with odd Edwardian painted backgrounds, all pale blue and pink, roses and *châteaux* and lakes and swans and absurd flying machines, dating back to the Wright brothers, lumbering overhead. Everywhere churches lift up their bruised and antique heads above the walls and trees. A Holy Child stands in a Libera Religiosa with lottery tickets spread over his outstretched arms. On the ceiling of San Fernando potentates are tossed lightly up into the cerulean, jack-boots buoyed up by the enormous torrent of air, clouds thrown about like tennis balls by winged figures, an effect of freedom and jubilation (all crippling gravity cut off) as we mount to the Son of Man radiant on a blue globe.

All the world that doesn't go to the bull-fight goes to Chapultepec, and the streets of the city are empty. Chapultepec Park, as well as the Alameda, is said to date back to Montezuma: huge old trees – one of them is two hundred feet tall and forty-five feet round – draped with Spanish moss, lakes with little boats, sham caves and cold rocky tunnels out of the sun, and, on the precipitous rock above, the unoccupied castle guarded by small careless soldiers, who go wandering off into shrubberies after a girl, or sit on the parapet by the guardroom reading a cheap novel; the palace of Maximilian with a glass front like the Crystal Palace tacked on to the staid eighteenth-century stonework, and down below a monument to useless heroism – to the Cadets who fell, at the time of the American invasion, guarding the Castle. The last Cadet to survive wrapped the Mexican flag around his body and leapt from the rock – the same old flag people wear on shirts and paint on gourds for tourists, the eagle eating the snake. All the monuments in Mexico are to violent deaths.

In the paper there were two assassinations of senators. One was shot in Juárez on the American border, and the other last night three minutes' walk from my hotel, at the other end of the Cinco de Mayo, in the Opera Bar. He was plugged full of bullets after a discussion and the assassin walked away to his car and escaped from the city. These deaths are distinguished from all the other details that happen every day only by the senatorial rank.

'Riddled with bullets' is the stock phrase.

Perhaps it is the atmosphere of violence – perhaps only the altitude, seven thousand odd feet – but after a few days not many people can escape the depression of Mexico City.

A little party of peons came down the hill from Chapultepec Castle wearing big hats; they carried bread in the brims. Oh, it's comic too sometimes – in a way – like the cock-fight.

NO GOLD-DIGGER

I ran into the dentist and asked him how things had gone. 'I liked her,' he said. 'She was not a gold-digger. She accepted fifteen pesos.'

THE OLD FRIEND

And then I met my good old friend from Wisconsin, mooning not very happily down the Francisco Madero. He had bought a new walking-stick – a hideous scarlet Mexican affair with painted emblems. He wasn't very happy, except that he was off home next day and was glad of that. We went back to his hotel and he took a bottle of Canadian Club out of his little black bag and made me drink a dose out of his toothglass. Then I took him in a bus out to Chapultepec. He still buttonholed everybody he saw with embarrassing directness – when he wanted to ask about buses, he put out his stick and tapped a traffic cop's gaiters. Then we went to the Regis and had Bacardi cocktails and got a little lit and talked of the American debt and the Immaculate Conception, which he had thought was the same as a virgin birth – 'I was married to a Roman,' he said, 'and she never told me any different.' He was tipsily suspicious. He said the Romans in Wisconsin believed the two things were the same, anyway. Then he told me how the churches here were covered in gold, 'when people went hungry,' he said. And afterwards we went to Sanborn's and had waffles and sausages – 'The food here's safe' – and he said to the waitress, 'I want you to meet my English friend, Mr Greene of London. I told you about him. He looked after me on the way down. I've got a joke on my friend – he went walking all day in Monterrey when I had a ride around for five cents.' And he said to me, 'I want you to meet my friend here who looks after me an' sees my food's hot.' Then he introduced me to the black doorman – 'How's your foot, Joe?' – and I saw him back to the Regis and we said we'd remember each other. He began to say, 'You oughta meet——' and then he was swept up into a noisy gang of Rotarians from Houston, Texas, wearing little labels, and I could only catch 'looked after me'. I felt lonely when he'd gone, and I couldn't sleep.

COOK'S TOUR

One day I went on a Cook's tour to the Monastery of San Augustín Acolman and the pyramids of Teotihuacán. The monastery lies below the level of what was once all lake; it had to be abandoned more than a hundred years ago. It was founded by twelve survivors of twenty Augustinian friars who landed in Mexico at the beginning of the sixteenth century, before the city of Mexico had fallen to Cortés. The monastery was built first and the little balcony still remains where Mass was said in view of the Indians on the plain outside. Then after twenty years, in 1539, the great tall church was completed, and one wonders how it was that twelve friars, picked at random by Providence to survive, were able to plan a building of such beauty. They planned, I suppose, on the lines of what they knew, but what an exact – and loving – memory they must have had of the Spanish monasteries. We think of these churches now as Mexican, or Colonial; but in those first decades in a continent which had been discovered less than fifty years before, in the appalling strangeness of a land which should have been over the world's edge, they must have seemed not a style of architecture, but an acre of home. In the cloisters are the remains of the oldest wall painting in Mexico – the faint line still visible of some representation of Hell and Judgement whitewashed over when that lesson had been learned by the Indians, the crude and elementary idea of punishment in terms of flame and cauldron and pincers. What remains today is the last and most difficult lesson of all – the lesson of love and the mysterious death of the Creator on the cross, and the little quiet European countryside, copied by Indians, still going quietly and securely on as the Universe ends: with both a sun and moon in the sky.

In the great grey courtyard of Teotihuacán, surrounded by the platforms of small pyramidal temples, you do get the sense of a continent over the world's edge – a flatness, a vacancy, through which peer plumed serpents and faces like gas-masks over orifices that might be the mouths of Lewis guns or flame-throwers. Archaeologists maintain theories of what happened here from the number of steps in each pyramid – mathematical computations that lead to a human sacrifice or a struggle between rival cults, rather in the same way as the British Israelites foretell the future from the comparative measurements of the Egyptian pyramids. It is fantastic and credible. The mathematical sense seems to have run riot – everything is symmetrical; it is important that the Pyramid of the Sun should be sixty-six metres high and have five terraces and the Pyramid of the Moon be fifty-four metres high and have – I forget how many terraces. Heresy here was not an aberration of human feeling – like the Manichaean – but a mathematical error. Death was important only as solving an equation. In the museum you see the little black glassy knives with which the breast of the sacrifice was opened – they look as hygienic as surgeon's instruments. Only the Temple of Quetzalcoatl is decorated – with horrors, serpents, and gas-masks – and he was the white Toltec god of culture, the mildest god of the lot, and was defeated by this stony mathematical discipline. One expects to see Q E D written on the paving of the great court – the pyramids adding up correctly, the number of terraces multiplied by the number of steps, and divided by the square metres of the surface area, proving – something, something as inhuman as a problem in algebra.

A young American girl, attached to two elderly ladies who complained of the heat, scrambled up to the second terrace of the Temple of the Sun and stuck – small and pale and plump and scared – on the huge slope of stone. She stared across the pyramids with amazement to where the whirlwinds moved under the mountains. The old ladies far away below like beetles sat on the grass with their backs to the pyramid and talked. She said, 'All these folk have been all over the place – to Europe. This seems just wonderful to me.' She had a complete lack of subterfuge, she was so completely without sophistication that she didn't even pretend, her simplicity affected you like goodness. She said, 'I've never been away from my home before.' It was only accident that she was here – somebody had fallen sick and someone else wanted a companion and so she'd emerged into this ancient and bloody land from her home town, a little place of five thousand inhabitants five miles from Jackson, Tennessee; she worked in Jackson, but she never even got to a cinema because she had to go straight back home after work. And here, suddenly, she was – half-way up a pyramid in Mexico: she panted and stared and gave herself away, every time she opened her mouth, generously.

MEXICAN BISHOP

I went with Dr C to call on the Bishop of Chiapas. People had told me he was regarded by the Government as one of the most dangerous and astute of the Mexican bishops. A month or two before, he had tried to return to his diocese, but he was put into a motor-car and driven back across the state border. I don't quite know what I had expected to see – some plump blue-chinned ecclesiastic with a quick eye and a cautious mouth, certainly not this unsophisticated good old man living with the utmost simplicity in surroundings of pious ugliness.

He looked like a village priest and showed a kind of humble confused embarrassment at my genuflexion. The little dark curtained room was stuffy with images and big obscure brown paintings of the love of God. No priests, he said, were officially allowed in Chiapas, although some of the churches were open now for the people to use. It was hard travelling there except in the south near the Pacific where there was the railway to Guatemala and a few roads. But in the north it was all mountain and forest and Indians who could speak no Spanish and could not even understand the language of the next village. He doubted very much whether it was possible to find a guide from Palenque to Las Casas.

San Cristóbal de Las Casas – he spoke of it with gentle regret – the old capital, before the Government removed to Tuxtla and the plain, lying eight thousand feet and more up in the mountains. It was, he said, 'a very Catholic town'; there were many churches, and one in particular, Santo Domingo, was among the most beautiful in Mexico. But most of the churches of Chiapas were not like those one saw in other parts of Mexico. Chiapas had always been a poor wild state, and the churches were very simple . . . He spoke of it gently as a foreign land to which he would never now be able to return. It touched my imagination so that I began to regard the city of Las Casas hidden there in the mountains at the end of a mule track, with only one rough road running south, as the real object of my journey – and the beginning of going home.

1997

The booth was wedged between two shops not far from the National Preparatory School. I walked down a little dark winding passage which at every curve disclosed a brightly lighted cell – with a monk in a cowl flogging a naked woman or interrogating one by torchlight, whip in hand. The women's bodies had been constructed with tender sensuality – pink haunches and round breasts. A little Indian and his woman preceded me down the passage; they stared with blank interest – I don't think it meant a thing to them – just a woman being beaten, that was all. Why not? The evil in the little stuffy passage didn't touch them – or the propaganda. They were innocent.

Upstairs there was Trotsky (who lived in a suburb of Mexico City, in Rivera's villa, a revolver on his desk, reporters searched for arms, the villa floodlit at night and guarded by Federal soldiers – the papers were full of a Stalinist plot against his life). He wore plus fours and a little pink tie and a Norfolk jacket – a Shavian figure. Two waxwork hands in a glass case were compared, the worn worker's and the sleek priest's, but which would Trotsky's have resembled most? A waxwork Indian bent over a glass coffin where a waxwork bishop lay in state, all gold and scarlet, and one remembered the old thin Bishop of Chiapas in seedy black and the hair shirt of St Thomas of Canterbury. There was a little scene of an Indian hut – a dying woman and her husband and a baby or two on the floor and an empty food bowl. The priest was blessing them and the legend said, 'Their capital fifty cents and they must pay one and a half pesos for a Mass.'

Anti-Catholicism often goes with a curious uncritical superstition. People must have something outside the narrow world to live for – whether it is the idea of the inevitable progress of the proletarian revolution or just that a black cat will bring them luck if it crosses their path – and here, in the little rationalist anti-clerical wax-work show, was a famous gipsy woman and a baby in a cradle – and the baby was the foreigner who she had prophesied would rule Mexico in 1997, from London, the capital of the world.

Guadalupe – a quarter of an hour's tram ride from the cathedral, in a suburb which retains the shape and air of a village as some parts of London do – is the most important shrine in Mexico, the centre of a whole nation's devotion. There isn't a town of any size which doesn't contain a church of Guadalupe with a facsimile of the famous relic.

The plain formal eighteenth-century church stands in a little plaza where a market is held every day of the week – ices and fruit, little sweet corncakes cooked while you watch and wrapped up in coloured paper like crackers, the blue Guadalupe glass, the colour of poison bottles, small crude toys. Outside the Chapel of the Well, a spring which is said to have flowed from under the feet of the Virgin, are stacks of empty whisky bottles in which to carry away the brackish healing water. Within the church the miraculous serape hangs above the altar, the dark-skinned Indian Virgin bending her head with a grace and kindliness you will find nowhere in mortal Mexico.

She appeared first at Amecameca, fifty miles away, but no one paid her any attention; then on December 9th 1531, an Indian peasant, Juan Diego, was climbing Tepayac hill, at the foot of which the shrine now stands. The Virgin appeared to him among the rocks – there was music suddenly and light – she called him 'my son' and told him to carry a message to Bishop Zumárraga that he was to build a shrine on that spot where she might watch and love the Indians. (Zumárraga was the bishop who, to the permanent grief of archaeologists, burnt the Indian manuscripts in the market-place of Tlaltelolco, the town to which Diego was going to receive instruction.)

It is as well to remember how revolutionary this vision must have seemed. It was only ten years since Mexico City had fallen to Cortés, the country was not yet subdued, and it is doubtful what kind of greeting the average Spanish adventurer would have given an Indian who claimed to have been addressed as 'my son' by the Mother of God. The legend, one is told by Mexican politicians, was invented by the Church to enslave the Indian mind, but if indeed it had been invented at that period by the Church, it would have been with a very different purpose. This Virgin claimed a church where she might love her Indians and guard them from the Spanish conqueror. The legend gave the Indian self-respect; it gave him a hold over his conqueror; it was a liberating, not an enslaving, legend.

The Bishop, of course, disbelieved Diego. Priests and bishops are human – they share some of the prejudices of their nation and time. 'My son' may have stuck even in the Bishop's throat, however much in theory he believed in his kinship with the Indian (just as the Pope's encyclical *Rerum Novarum* stuck in the gullet of the Bishop of San Luis Potosí, so that he kept it stacked in his cellar where a priest found it after Carranza's revolution). On Sunday, December 10th (the legend is well documented with dates), the Virgin appeared again to Diego on Tepayac hill and he asked her to send some more important messenger – some Spaniard, he may have implored her – whom the Bishop would believe. She might have appeared to Cortés himself, who could have commanded anything.

But the wisdom of man is nothing to the wisdom of God, and one wonders what would have been the future of that vision if it had been sent to the conqueror instead of to the conquered. Undoubtedly there would have been a rich shrine built – but would the Indians have attended it? One may be sure it would have been closed eventually like every church in Mexico, just as the vision itself would have been overlaid in the conqueror's mind by affairs of state and politics and war. But this shrine of Guadalupe, even at the height of the persecution, remained open – no government dared to rob the Indian of his Virgin, and it helped to break the career of the only man who ever threatened it. When Garrido Canabal, the dictator of Tabasco, arrived in the capital, accompanied by his Red Shirts, to take his seat as Minister of Agriculture in Cárdenas's Cabinet, he gave private orders to his men that the shrine was to be destroyed as the Tabascan churches had already been. The image was guarded day and night and Garrido was eventually driven from Mexico to exile in Costa Rica. The Virgin of Guadalupe, like St Joan in France, had become identified not only with the faith but with the country; she was a patriotic symbol even to the faithless . . .

So the Virgin sent the Indian peasant back to Bishop Zumárraga, and the Bishop demanded – with not unnatural caution – a sign. For the third time Diego listened to the Virgin, who told him to return next day and she would give him the sign for which the Bishop asked, but next day Diego's uncle was very ill and he forgot – or more likely the immediate *fact* of the dying man semed more important, more true, than a vision he may himself have discounted when the Bishop talked, full of the wisdom and the slowness and the sane scepticism of the church authority. On Tuesday, the twelfth, he had to return to Tlaltelolco to fetch a priest for his dying uncle, but he was afraid of that particular stony path he associated with his vision, and took a different way – as if he could escape the immanent Godhead and its messenger on one path more than another. He showed the same materialism as the sceptical Catholics today who discount the vision because *this* Virgin was dark-skinned, apparently believing that race is an attribute of the spirit as well as of the flesh.

But Diego could not escape. The Virgin blocked his new path too, without reproach. No vision of the Mother of God has ever been associated with the idea of punishment. She told him his uncle was already well and directed him to go to the top of the hill to gather roses from the rocks and take them to the Bishop. He wrapped the roses in his serape and when he opened it to give the roses to the Bishop, the image of the Virgin was there stamped on the cloth, just as it hangs above the altar today.

An old Spanish lady, Señora B, was showing me Guadalupe – sceptically. She took me through the vestry into the small room where the votive paintings are hung – thanks to the Virgin expressed in little primitive daubs, like the paintings of talented children, explained in short ungrammatical sentences; a wife in bed watching her drunken husband; little men with awkward hands and pistols firing at each other: 'the tragic shooting of Señor So-and-so'. Afterwards we climbed the steep winding stairs which go up Tepayac hill behind the shrine to the chapel built on the spot where the Virgin first appeared. At every corner photographers stood with their old hooded cameras on stilts and their antique screens – an early steamship, a train, a balloon, improbable aeroplanes out of Jules Verne, and of course the swans and lakes, Blue Danubes and roses, of that nostalgic period. Little braziers burned, and there was a smell of corncake all the way up. Near the chapel is the rich man's cemetery, huge tombs with Spanish coats of arms of lichened stone, huddling for safety near the peasants' shrine. There is no earth on Tepayac hill; it has to be carried up by human labour; and every grave must be drilled out of the solid rock.

The old lady sought for her ancestors among lanes of mausoleums like those of a new building estate where every house is different. She had lost all her money, lived in a small bed-sitting room where she entertained her grandchildren every Wednesday, the tea kettle boiling beside the bed; she had immense courage and vivacity and the will to endure. She was a descendant of a general who had fought for Iturbide and independence, and then had been exiled by Iturbide when he took the crown. But General B could not be kept out of his country; he secretly returned and, moving from place to place, he left his features everywhere among the children of Mexico. At his death, according to his wishes, his heart went to Guadalajara, where he first met his wife, and his right arm to Lerma, where he won his victory, and the rest of his body to Guadalupe. And Señora B retained the panache and the pride, but the aristocratic attitude, balked of the power to act, had become bitter, defiant, useless. The enemy of Cárdenas, she was also the enemy of Cedillo, whose father had been an Indian peasant on *her* family's estates in San Luis Potosí. She was too proud to choose between two evils – she was typical of many Spaniards of birth who have simply withdrawn into bed-sitting rooms and small hotels.

She was a Catholic too, but with an aristocratic scepticism. She wouldn't believe in Diego's vision and the miraculous image – it was a popular fantasy. She withdrew again, as in politics, from the source of life. It was enough for her to know that there was a parallel to this vision in Spain. She, for one, would have been more ready to accept the vision if it had come to the conqueror and not to the peasant, to the grown mind and not to the child's.

Next day I was to leave for Orizaba and Veracruz, the first stage to Tabasco and Chiapas. After a journey the Mexican Catholic returns to thank the Virgin of Guadalupe for her care; I told myself, kneeling again at the bottom of the hill before Juan Diego's serape, that I would do the same. The old lady knelt, saying her 'Hail Mary'; she didn't believe – but among Catholics even the sceptical are courteous.

4. To the Coast

JOURNEY DOWNHILL

I felt glad to be leaving Mexico City – the shops full of tourist junk, silver filigree and gourds and rugs and dead fleas dressed as little people inside walnuts, all the fake smartness and gaiety, El Retiro and the Cucaracha Bar and the Palace of Art, the Avenida Juárez smelling of sweets, and all the hidden hate. How right Lawrence was when he wrote, 'This city doesn't feel *right* – feels like a criminal plotting his next rather mean crime,' and again, 'I *really* feel cynical about these "patriots" and "Socialists" down here. It's a mess,' underlining his words like Queen Victoria. 'You know Socialism is a dud. It makes just a mush of people, and especially of savages. And seventy per cent of these people are real savages, quite as much as they were three hundred years ago. The Spanish-Mexican population just rots on top of the black savage mass. And Socialism here is a farce of farces, except very dangerous.'

Dangerous it certainly was – like an electric tram gone wild, sparking and jabbing down the Embankment. In my paper, as I sat in the train waiting for it to go off (a beggar came down the aisle – you couldn't escape them even inside a train), I read that the President had signed a decree expropriating the foreign oil companies. One had been aware, of course, at the back of the mind that trouble was boiling up; but it had been boiling for nearly a year now – nobody had been expecting this sudden crazy action. Or crazy it appeared to be during those first days, when the country was stupefied and scared for its savings, and the exchange began to rocket down.

It was in the middle of December that the Federal Labour Board had published its award, after the petroleum strike of the previous summer. No need to go into all the details now – two provisions alone make it unarguably clear that no company could have accepted the award and continued operations. The working days were to be reduced to two hundred and twenty-three during the year, and workers were to be given the right to be absent from their duties for three days on an unlimited number of occasions, for any personal or family reason, and were to be paid in full for time lost. It does not need any knowledge of book-keeping – only of human nature – to know that such an award was unworkable. On March 1, the day I got to Monterrey, the Supreme Court upheld the Labour Board's decision, but that seemed to be only the beginning of the usual interminable litigation designed to put money into the pockets of judges, counsel, and solicitors. Temporary stays, injunctions, these the companies had been able to win – no Mexican to whom I had spoken had expected this sudden climax; it must have been a rude shock to the legal profession. I was to see the immediate result in Chiapas – social services shut down, roads and reservoirs stopped, and everywhere talk of revolution.

The train pulled out by the shrine of Guadalupe. It was early in the morning, but the little tortilla stalls were already up, and the crowd was eddying round the sanctuary. It pulled away from the dingy Parisian skirts of the city, out on to the long wide plateau – white and pink haciendas with their frilly façades and their broken chapels. At every station the food-sellers came by, bearing the best food in Mexico – legs of hot fried chicken to be eaten in the fingers and tortillas wrapped round dark rich anonymous scraps of meat; and different stations had their different tourist traps – at Apizaco hideous little painted clubs and walking-sticks, at Rinconada little grey stone mortars for pounding corn made hideous with blue and scarlet birds' beaks. The volcanoes, Popocatepetl and Ixtacihuatl, were hidden in cloud, as they had been all the time I was in Mexico City, and the Peak of Orizaba, the highest mountain in Mexico, was hidden too. Two small boys boarded the train at San Marco with guitars and played in the middle of the coach for centavos – sweet melancholy bogus voices and large brown actors' eyes. Then they went reeling over the plates, towards the Pullman. Dozens of whirlwinds fumed up across the brown plain like the chimneys of a factory city.

And suddenly after Esperanza, more than eight thousand feet up, the line comes dramatically to the edge of the plateau; it is cold there even in the mid-day sun, the air even more thin and depressing than in Mexico City. But during the next sixty-four miles the train goes down six thousand four hundred feet; it moves in great loops into summer, the seasons change as you watch, the air thickens, and exhilaration stirs in the flaccid lungs – until you begin to believe after all that this is a country to be happy in. Far away, below the huge straight wooded gorge, lies Maltrata, like a town seen from an aeroplane, a little German toy, washed clean by distance and the long rush of air; but it takes nearly an hour to get there, the train edging round and round the same mountain towards the plain. From Boca del Monte at the cliff edge to Alta Luz there are only nine miles of track, and the altitude changes by more than a thousand feet; ears buzz with the descent and it is a shock at the little station to find yourself still looking *down* at the soaring birds. Summer is advancing: strawberries and lemons are for sale; and then you are in the bottom of the valley at Maltrata only to discover it is the beginning of another descent – to Santa Rosa, where the great scarlet tulipans are out, roses and magnolia in March, and bright yellow lemons on the trees, and, after Santa Rosa, Orizaba and the papers from Veracruz announcing that the Bank of Mexico has suspended dealings in foreign exchange and that the country remains quiet – sinister phrase.

ORIZABA

Orizaba, you would say at first sight, is a town in elegant decay – within the hotel patio the doves whispered and a fountain splashed. There was a gentle moaning from an automatic organ, and an American wandered sentimentally round the bird-cages hung above the patio on the first floor, chirping gently himself. It was like an escapist's paradise – nothing new or dangerous, nothing bitter: little bridges over sharp torrential streams and the mountains pressing in and the clouds falling; hidden squares with fountains and cupids and broken bows, like a de la Mare poem, and the grass pushing up; flowers in private patios, and not many people about, a sense of desertion – '"Is there anybody there?" said the Traveller.'

It was the Feast of St Joseph, but even the churches were empty – except two, full of young children whose thin responses couldn't carry far. In the market flowers and flies and ordure and sleep. The long white stringy hair of a tired woman fell across a table; a young man leaned asleep against a wooden partition – black hair, consumptive face, and tipped-back chair. In the cathedral a woman wailed in what seemed to be an inexpressible physical agony of grief and then fell silent, brushed her skirts, and rose – it had been a formal expression of a formal contrition; a peon Christ sat beaten and bleeding in his scarlet robe with no one by. A whole street of dentists' shops (it's the most thriving trade in Mexico: gold teeth everywhere) with little white-washed empty waiting-rooms and the tops of drills above the windows. The politicians sat on the balcony rail of the CROM headquarters, doing nothing. Could anything ever happen in this place? Or would the cupid's bow just moss a little more as the flowers dropped and the clouds came lower down and somebody wailed formally in an unused church for what nobody really cares about in the warm, sweet, empty air?

The answer, of course, was that something had already happened – only six months before. Until then there had been no churches open in the state of Veracruz; Masses were said secretly, as in Chiapas, in private houses. Then one Sunday in Orizaba police agents followed a child who had been at Mass; she ran from them and they fired and killed her – one of those sudden inexplicable outbursts of brutality common in Mexico. Mexicans are fond of children, but some emanation from the evil Aztec soil seems suddenly to seize the brain like drunkenness, then the pistol comes out. The result of that death was an outburst of religious zeal all over Veracruz state; the peasants got into the churches in Veracruz itself and locked the doors and rang the bells; the police could do nothing, and the governor gave way – the churches were opened. The indignation was spent like an orgasm – sleep returned to Orizaba.

I wanted to go to confession – it would probably be my last chance before I returned to Mexico City – but it wasn't easy to find a priest who could understand English, and my small amount of Spanish could cope more easily with the simple ideas of politics than with those of human sin. Darkness began to fall; the children had left the churches to emptiness; the CROM politicians still lazily gobbled and watched on their balcony – it was their great day, I suppose, the day of the expropriation. There would be pickings for everyone except the workers. Already it had been announced in the President's message to the people that belts had to be drawn in; though wages if possible were to be maintained, holidays and social services – everything for which the worker had been persuaded to fight – would be cut; and a great loan was to be raised to pay an indemnity to the companies. What possible hope had the worker that conditions would ever reach the old capitalist level in *his* lifetime? Oh, how weary one gets of this fight to help future generations! I wandered from church to church seeking help for myself, not for an unborn soul.

Last I came to the church dedicated to St Joseph. Loud-speakers were braying sentimental music from the radio shops and the bells of the church clanged back. A little row of booths had been set up along the gutter where you could buy rosaries and candles and corncakes; acetylene flares flickered on the thin paper streamers blowing in the cold wind off the peak; inside the church a few women prayed before a carpet of flowers. It was a small celebration: not much money to spend, and an enormous inanition eating away the faith. They had risen here to their great moment – the death of the child who had the thin taste of the Host still on her palate. But the great moment was over – here in Orizaba it was like Galilee between the Crucifixion and the Resurrection – all the enthusiasm had been spent.

SAINT'S NIGHT

Then suddenly it became one of those evenings that conspire for happiness, when everything for a while goes right, and during a few hours you experience peace.

Mauriac in his *Vie de Jésus* speaks of the Catholic who has the habit of frequently changing his confessor, how suddenly he will receive from a strange priest an unexpected consolation. So in Orizaba – from a thin, unshaved, impoverished man with a few words of English – one gained a sense of peace and patience and goodness, which includes, like the Roman virtue, courage and endurance. He had lived through so much; what right had an English Catholic to bitterness or horror at human nature when this Mexican priest had none? He asked me where I was going. I said Tabasco.

'Oh, an evil land,' he said mildly, as he would reprove a common vice.

That night a crowd collected outside the church in the warm fresh air; little braziers burned along the pavement, and the bell clanged in the tower, shaking out sparks with every heavy oscillation. A Catherine wheel whirled in the road, and the rockets hissed up into the sky and burst in flippant and trivial stars. The church door was open; between the dark shoulders of the crowd you could see a bearded Joseph surrounded with light; the noise of the bell and the rockets and the crowd faded out at the church door and inside was quiet and the smell of flowers. This, I felt, was how a saint's day should be celebrated – joyfully, with fireworks and tortillas, domestically.

THE MORNING AFTER

Happiness never lasts long and the next morning was not so good. At early Mass one missed the mortifications of the Mexican plateau – it was more like an English Mass, sedate and unenthusiastic and familiar until one turned the head and saw a black-haired baby face working out from under a shawl – thick hair and tiny skull like a shrivelled head from Ecuador, with large brown lustrous heartless eyes. What had it to hope for in thirty years? Even Cárdenas could not procure it the certainty of thirty-five cents a day, unless perhaps it joined the army and became – one saw what it would become in the Hidalgo barracks.

The bugles played desultorily in the little pink ruined square, and the small Indian soldiers lounged in grubby uniforms outside their quarters. A woman in a white nightdress trailed a bucket across a dingy yard, and on the other side of the square was a little decaying chapel of pink stone which the soldiers couldn't enter (no soldier is allowed to attend Mass). If they *had* gone in they would have seen only a grim Christ stretched out in a glass coffin under a white lacy cloth with a horrible open sore under the eye – a man who had been beaten up by men of their own profession. At times in these

Mexican churches the separation of God and Man seems too complete: God, you may say, is on the altar – but in these churches the sanctuary light is out. He is not there, for fear of desecration. What had, I suppose, been the presbytery was now the offices of the Third Military Sector; they hemmed the little church in like something dangerous.

Beside the river a rubbish dump lay stinking under the sanitary notice forbidding it; the politicians lounged on the balcony of CROM and everywhere leaflets lay about urging the workers and peasants of Orizaba to stand behind the President at this critical moment of the expropriation.

TO VERACRUZ

Again, from Orizaba, the line drops, and for a while the spirit rises; man is not made to live on mountains, and when he does settle himself there for centuries, more than seven thousand feet above the sea, what can you expect but some derangement? First the Aztec and then the Spaniard, their lungs expanding to fit thin air; human kindness withering out like a flower in a vacuum flask. We were going down, dropping towards the too tropical plain. Only half-way between the two could you catch a glimpse of life as it should be.

A football game went on beside the line; half the teams just lazed on the grass; little stalls sold sweets and fruit juice and a horseman watched like a statue between the goal-posts . . . At Fortín the flower-sellers came crying down the train, 'Gardenias, gardenias.' For twenty centavos or less (say, for two pence) you could buy a hollow cane ten inches long filled with blooms.

The compartment became scented like a hothouse: flowers dangled from the luggage racks. Blooms on short stalks would be stuck in a cane, like the spokes of a star, around one scarlet hibiscus. Here you could count your blessings: the lovely baroque churches, the belief in God, the fountains and the flowers . . . it was like life before the road went irremediably wrong, before it plunged into the hot and fevered plain.

The moment passed almost as quickly as a dream, which tradition tells us lasts a few seconds only: at Córdoba politicians came on board. Like the cracked bell ringing down the stone school stairs they marked another day. They tied a streamer to the outside of the coach, leaning from the windows shouting and tugging on ropes as the train plunged down the huge ravines towards the plain. They were drunk; they carried with them, as a kind of clown to entertain them, a drunken youth with a thin wild face who flapped his hands and crowed like a cock. Awful orgasms mounted in his throat; he flapped his hands and pointed to his tongue and swilled warm beer and burst into high explanatory screams, pointing to the roof, buzzing like an aeroplane. Outside, all the vegetation died out into a black and hopeless soil; somewhere far across the flat land a lighthouse winked as the sun went down.

At Veracruz a fat homosexual porter tried to take my bag, archly. I sat in the little square in front of the Hotel Diligencias and the fans played and the girls went round and round in the thick heat under the deep sky. Commercial men in white drill suits sat limply in the romantic night. Little bright tramcars with open sides pulled up and pulled away like cars on a scenic railway, and somewhere music played and a Pennsylvanian with pouchy insomniac eyes warned me against Havana, staring gloomily out over the bright square. 'It's awful,' he said, 'the things they do. I've been in Paris an' I can stand a lot, but these Cubans . . . the things they show you.' It was as if the world were being found out at last by even its most innocent inhabitants.

5. Voyage in the Dark

'AS GOOD A SPORT . . .'

I hadn't expected to leave quite so soon. I thought I'd
stay awhile in Veracruz and get accustomed to the heat
and read more Trollope and rest. It is a gay and pretty
town with its little balconied houses, and shell-boxes
and shell picture-frames and rosaries of shells, and the
cantinas open to the street to catch whatever breezes
there may be. And the shabby Villa del Mar joined by
tramway to the town with its big wooden dance hall
raised on piles and its little dingy houses smearing out
on to the silver sandhills. A little blonde girl of two lay
wearily asleep in her nurse's arms, washed out and
fragile as a shell, with her tiny ears already drilled for
rings and a gold bangle round the little bony wrist –
handcuffed to sophistication at birth – like goodness
dying out in the hot seaport.

But I went back to town, past the bank where there
was a run on the silver, people queueing up and standing
on windowsills and pushing their way towards the
counter to exchange their notes for silver – all because
of the expropriation of the oilfields. I pushed open the
swing cantina doors of the vice-consulate, and there was
the consul going through his weekly lottery tickets,
seriously, as if it were a game of skill. With a sense of
uneasiness I learned there was a boat for Tabasco
leaving that night. The consul was American; he regarded me as a fool; he had never known a foreigner to

use one of these boats before. 'You don't know what you are in for,' he said.

'Are they very small?'

'Small?' Words failed him. He said, 'I wouldn't go in one of those boats for a thousand dollars.'

'Aren't they safe?'

'They don't often sink,' he said, 'unless you hit a norther.'

'But the norther season's over.'

'You can't tell. Anyway,' he said grimly, 'they insure you for five thousand pesos when you buy your ticket.'

And buying the ticket in the shipping office I again had the uneasy feeling that I was regarded as a fool – or ignorant; they seemed to be talking about me among themselves with pity and amusement, but chiefly amusement.

That afternoon I took a guide, a bright dapper young man like a hairdresser's assistant, round town shopping and seeing the meagre sights – the little squat church Cortés built, the oldest in America, barred and bolted and scorched by flame. A mob had tried to burn it down about two months before – their motive was not really anti-clerical (they had left the presbytery alone): it was simply to embarrass the new mayor, who was not a Veracruzian. As we got on to a tramcar, the guide met a friend, a big burly man in overalls, who laughed all the time. We left the tramcar at the first stop and sat in a cantina and drank beer. 'He is always like that,' the guide said, 'always laughing.' Nothing one could say failed to feed that enormous flame of mirth: it roared like a draught in a chimney, sucking up words like scraps of paper. 'I think . . .' 'Do you know . . .' – no time for a complete phrase. He was employed in the customs office, the guide said, and, 'I am a customs officer for my sweetheart, too,' the man bellowed mysteriously in my ear with a leer and a belch. It was like trying to read Rabelais in the original. His boisterous company melted the constraint between me and the guide – we were all friends together. The time of the guide's employment wore out; he said it was too late in the afternoon to find another customer, so he might as well stay on with me as a friend. He had come from Tabasco years ago in the same boat that I was to travel in, the *Ruiz Cano*. He said, 'Nothing – nothing will ever make me go on that boat again. You don't know – it's terrible.'

Perhaps, I said nervously, I wouldn't go after all. I might change my ticket for another boat.

The customs man roared with laughter.

'The other boats,' the guide said, 'are smaller. The *Ruiz Cano* has a flat bottom. That is good. It will not sink easily. And they pay five thousand pesos if something happens.'

'Who to?'

'Your family.'

'But my family,' I said, 'are in England.'

'Of course,' he said, 'they would have to prove who they were. It would not be easy. A lot of the money would be spent in lawyers' fees. It might not be worth while.'

'And they wouldn't even know it was due to them.'

'I tell you what,' he said, 'tomorrow morning I will go and see the consul and tell him you have sailed, and if anything happens he must get the money for your family.' I didn't like the serious way he took this matter of the insurance; this was graveyard talk. The boat couldn't be as bad as all that.

It was. It was worse.

We came to it in a taxi with my single suitcase, bumping over the Veracruz quay. An English liner of about ten thousand tons was docked, and there were a few coasting steamers and out in the gulf a grey gunboat.

'There's the *Ruiz Cano*,' the taxi-driver said.

I couldn't see it anywhere; we had passed the colliers; I looked right over the top of the ship where it lay against the quay – a flat barge with a few feet of broken rail, an old funnel you could almost touch with your hand from the shore, a bell hanging on a worn piece of string, an oil-lamp and a bundle of turkeys. One little rotting boat dangled inadequately from the davits.

I had pictured something the size of the colliers you see in the Thames off Wapping – but this: I wouldn't have gone down the Thames in her. Forty-two hours or so in the Atlantic, in the Gulf of Mexico – I had never in my life been more frightened.

We climbed over the rail with the suitcase, and a sailor led the way down a few stairs into the engine-room, where one old greasy engine sat like an elephant neglected in its tiny house. There were two cabins close beside the engine, dark padlocked cells with six wooden shelves in each. I laid my bag on one and went gloomily up into the fading tropical afternoon. I had the feeling that my journey had only just begun; Laredo wasn't the frontier, and I thought with nostalgia of that first Mexican hotel and Mr Arabin and the thunder cracking over the skyscraper across in the United States.

I said, 'Let's go and have a drink.'

The boat didn't sail till eight.

We went back to the Diligencias and ordered food and a couple of tequilas each and beer. A little girl came round selling lottery tickets and I bought one, the first I'd ever bought – a gesture to fate. After the tequilas I began to feel better, to think grandiloquently in terms of adventure. And my friend blossomed too – he wished he could accompany me. He would like to show, he said, that a Mexican was 'as good a sport' as an Englishman. He would come as a friend, not as a guide. He would charge nothing. We would ride together across Chiapas and have interesting conversations.

'Why not?' I said.

'I have no clothes.'

'We could take a taxi to your house.'

'No time.'

'Then we could buy them in Tabasco.'

The second tequila worked – wildly – in his eyes.

'All right,' he said, 'it is done. I will prove that a Mexican is as good a sport . . . Just as I am, I will come with you.'

We pledged ourselves in beer and shook hands drunkenly.

A little boy carrying a dog stopped on the sidewalk and stared at us. My friend called him over; he was a nephew whom he was looking after while his mother was away in Mexico City. He said, 'I am going with this Englishman tonight to Tabasco. Just as I am. To prove . . . Can you look after yourself while I am away? Three, four weeks. Have you any money?'

The little boy clapped his hands with excitement. One saw in the ten-year-old eyes hero-worship. He flung his arms around his uncle's neck and embraced that little dapper man furiously. A couple of English people from the pleasure liner at a nearby table watched with intense disapproval, suspecting I don't know what Latin iniquities. We bought some ham and got into a taxi all three. The driver wouldn't take the dog, so it ran behind, gate-crashing past the sentry at the entrance to the docks. It was quite dark now; music was playing on the pleasure liner, and not a light showed on the barge, except an oil-lamp in the bows. Little knots of people stood on the quay, somebody wept, and the turkeys rustled. My friend began to explain to everyone; they gathered round admiringly.

'I am going tonight to Tabasco. Just as I am. No clothes. Because this Englishman and I are friends. I am going to prove to him that a Mexican is as good a sport as an Englishman.'

I felt myself moved by an immense self-esteem: to have evoked such a friendship, in a few hours. The little boy stood holding his dog. My friend besought him to say *now* if he could not look after himself. An old night watchman appeared at the edge of the group and offered to take last messages. Then we climbed on board, and the little boy went home with his dog, ecstatically, his uncle's great adventure in his heart.

Suddenly we were alone in the dark, and it was cold. I said I had a jumper down below which he could have. We sat on a bench and shivered. The water lapped like doubt and the turkeys moved. Then the captain came on board, a stout youngish man in shirt-sleeves who only grunted when my friend whipped out his saga – 'no clothes . . . just as I am . . . as good a sport . . .'

The captain went into his tiny deckhouse and changed his trousers in the dark. The crew came on board and the other passengers: two young girls travelling with their brother, an old woman, a family which wrapped itself in rugs and lay down among the turkeys blocking

116

the deck (you couldn't tell how many they were – they broke up later in daylight into three or four children, one at the breast, and a man and wife). The girls sang softly in the stern, and the engine began to shake; everything knocked and rattled, and we moved a couple of feet out from the quay.

I looked at my friend; a sudden wild doubt came up into his eyes like a face at a window. I said, 'Do you really want to come?'

He muttered something about his nephew – couldn't leave him alone – and scrambled on to the lifeboat. The old davits cracked under the strain – we were three feet from the quay. He gathered himself together and jumped, landing on his knees. He called out, 'If I had any clothes,' one reason too many, and we waved shame-facedly to each other. But he was soon cheerful again and began to tell everyone on the quay about his nephew . . . We moved, shakily, out of earshot.

There was no light at all on the little deck and none below, only the oil-lamp in the bows. The searchlights of the English liner moved right over our heads, missing us altogether, and the captain began to write up his log by the light of an electric torch a sailor held for him. After an hour one bare globe went on outside the sleeping cells below, above a tin wash-basin, and the wind rose. We sailed in almost complete darkness into the Gulf.

THE GULF

There were no sex divisions in the dark cabin: in the bunk below me a woman lay for the whole forty-two hours, never stirring, never eating. A young school teacher was on my left hand; his shelf, when he went on deck, was littered with pamphlets – about the petroleum dispute, about the Church. He lent them to the sailors – you came on a sailor bunched by the lifeboat absorbed in the President's message to the people. All the time the companies were appealing to the Supreme Court and the Labour Board was arguing its case the presses must have been busy with that message; long before the Supreme Court decided in favour of the workers and the companies refused to implement the award, long before expropriation was announced, the President had his message in type. It followed me everywhere: it was read out in remote Chiapas inns.

The boat rolled horribly all night. I wondered if the wind was from the north, but I no longer cared. It is before you cross a frontier that you experience fear. Now I lay there in my clothes, on my wooden shelf, with dim curiosity and wonder. It was too bizarre and inexplicable – rolling on a Mexican barge across the Gulf. Why ? On my right hand the younger girl lay on her face, her legs exposed up to the thighs by the dusty light of the globe outside. The school teacher began a gentle flirtation in a protective way: he lent her a copy of the President's message and she lent him a cheap song-book: they hummed to each other softly in the oily night. My riding-boots, for which there was no room in my suitcase, rolled in a composite mass with the packet of ham, the sun helmet, and my electric torch.

In the morning I got on deck. The Atlantic rollers rode in under a grey cold sky. The girls' brother lay with sick abandon on a straw mat. A folding table was opened, and breakfast was handed up through a hatch in the deck from the engine-room – a loaf of bread and a plate of anonymous fish scraps from which the eyeballs stood mournfully out. I couldn't face it, and rashly made my way down to the only privy: a horrible cupboard in the engine-room with no ventilation, no flushing, and the ordure of I don't know how many days and voyages. That finished me for the rest of the day; I lay on my shelf through the morning and the afternoon and struggled up only once more before night.

And next morning everything was worse – not better. The sun was out and sucked out all the smells there were on the little ancient barge. Twice I dashed for the privy and the second time the whole door came off in my hands and fell on to the engine-room floor. Then in the late morning we came into smoother water and I got up on to the deck again – twenty feet of it on either side the smokestack, with two benches long enough to hold perhaps a dozen people. The captain stood in the bows with a toothpick in his hair, and everywhere you moved you found sailors doing up their trousers. The coast was in sight – a long low line of trees and sand like West Africa. I ate a ship's biscuit – there seemed to be cause for celebration. Thirst, though, was greater than hunger, but there was no beer nor mineral water on board; at meal times they made a shocking kind of coffee, but otherwise there was only the dubious water in a tin filter above the wash-basin, and that ran out completely after twelve hours.

FRONTERA

We arrived at Frontera at two-fifteen, forty-one hours from Veracruz, in an appalling heat. Only, I think, in Monrovia had I experienced its equal, but Frontera like Monrovia is freshened a little by the sea. To know how hot the world can be I had to wait for Villahermosa. Shark fins glided like periscopes at the entrance to the Grijalva River, the scene of the Conquistadores' first landing in Mexico, before they sailed on to Veracruz. Frontera itself was out of sight round a river bend; three or four aerials stuck up into the blazing sky from among the banana groves and the palm-leaf huts: it was like Africa seeing itself in a mirror across the Atlantic. Little islands of lily plants came floating down from the interior, and the carcasses of old stranded steamers held up the banks.

And then round a bend in the river Frontera, the frontier. So it will remain to me, though the Tabascan authorities have renamed it Puerto Obregón: the Presidencia and a big warehouse and a white blanched street running off between wooden shacks – hairdressers and the inevitable dentists, but no cantinas anywhere, for there is prohibition in Tabasco. No intoxicant is allowed but beer, and that costs a peso a bottle – a ruinous price in Mexico. The lily plants floated by; the river divided round a green island half a mile from shore, and the vultures came flocking out, with little idiot heads and dusty serrated wings, to rustle round the shrouds. There was an election on: the name Bartlett occurred everywhere, and a red star. The soldiers stood in the shade of the Presidencia and watched us edge in against the river bank.

This was Tabasco – Garrido Canabal's isolated swampy puritanical state. Garrido – so it was said – had destroyed every church; he had organised a militia of Red Shirts, even leading them across the border into Chiapas in his hunt for a church or a priest. Private houses were searched for religious emblems, and prison was the penalty for possessing them. A young man I met in Mexico City – a family friend of Garrido's – was imprisoned three days for wearing a cross under his shirt; the dictator was incorruptible. A journalist on his way to photograph Tabasco was shot dead in Mexico City airport before he took his seat. Every priest was hunted down or shot, except one who existed for ten years in the forests and the swamps, venturing out only at night; his few letters, I was told, recorded an awful sense of impotence – to live in constant danger and yet be able to do so little, it hardly seemed worth the horror. Now Garrido is in Costa Rica, but his policy goes on . . . The customs officers came on board, their revolver holsters creaking as they climbed the rotting rail. I remembered a bottle of brandy in my suitcase.

Their search was not a formality. They not only went through the cargo but the captain's cabin: you could see them peering under his bunk. They felt in the lifeboat and insisted on having unlocked the little cupboard where the plates and knives were kept. Presently the passengers were summoned below to open their boxes; I allowed myself to forget all my Spanish. People came and explained things with their fingers. I could hold out no longer and went down. But the customs men had come to the end of their tether; the heat in the cabin was terrific; everybody was wedged together – I slipped quietly away again and nobody minded. On the quay they were unloading beer – it was our main cargo: a hundred and fifty dozen bottles, to be sold only by Government agents. Puritanism pays.

I went for a walk on shore; nothing to be seen but one little dusty plaza with fruit-drink stalls and a bust of Obregón on a pillar, two dentists' and a hairdresser's.

The vultures squatted on the roofs. It was like a place besieged by scavengers -- sharks in the river and vultures in the streets.

One introduction I had here, to the merchant who owned the warehouse on the quay, an old man with a little pointed beard who spoke no English. I told him I wanted to go to Palenque from Villahermosa. He tried to dissuade me – it was only a hundred miles, but it might take a week. First, as there were no roads for more than a few miles outside the capital I should have to return to Frontera, then I'd have to wait till I could get a barge up another river to Montecristo – or Zapata, as it was now called. There I could get horses. But the river journey would take two or three days and conditions would be – horrible. After all, I said, I had endured the *Ruiz Cano*. The *Ruiz Cano*, the old man said, was a fine boat . . . I went back to the ship discouraged. They were still unloading beer; they wouldn't be moving that night, for it was still ten hours to Villahermosa and they needed daylight for the passage.

At sunset the mosquitoes began – a terrifying steady hum like that of a sewing-machine. There were only two choices: to be eaten on deck (and probably catch malaria) or to go below to the cabin and the appalling heat. The only porthole was closed for fear of marauders; mosquito-nets seemed to shut out all the air that was left. It was only eight o'clock. I lay naked under the net and sweated; every ten minutes I tried to dry myself with a towel. I fell asleep and woke again and fell asleep. Then somewhere I heard a voice talking English – hollow over-civilised English, not American. I thought I heard the word 'interpreter'. It must have been a dream, and yet I can still remember that steady cultured voice going on, and the feel of my own wet skin, the hum of mosquitoes, and my watch saying 10.32.

I went for a walk with one of the sailors and we drank sweet unpleasant fruit drinks at a stall in the market and he tried – rather hopelessly – to sell me his secondhand crocodile-skin notecase for three pesos, about the price you pay for a whole crocodile. Then at nine-thirty we we got under way up the monotonous, not unbeautiful river, shaking and rattling into the interior. There is always something exhilarating about moving inward from the sea into an unknown country. All the way along, the low banks were lined with bananas or coconut palms; sometimes a tributary stream ambled muddily off to God knows where.

A sailor came and told me there was a second gringo on board: he was sitting on the bench the other side of the smokestack. The boat was crowded now with passengers from Frontera, where he had come on board sick, unshaven, in an old black greasy hat. He wasn't very good to look at, sitting there with his mestizo wife and two blond washed-out little boys with transparent eyelids and heavy brown Mexican eyes. I couldn't foresee that I was to spend, oh, days in his company.

He was a dentist, an American, Doc Winter, and he hadn't been out of Frontera to Villahermosa for five years. But yesterday a long sickness had reached its climax; he said, 'If I don't get away, I guess I'll die.' He had tried to walk the two hundred yards to the ship to take his passage, but he couldn't make it. He had to send his wife, and this morning, well, he'd just struggled down and reached the bench, and he guessed he wouldn't move from there for an hour or two. In Villahermosa there was an English doctor – he didn't talk much English and he'd never been out of Mexico, but he was English all right – Dr Roberto Fitzpatrick, and he would fix him up. It was the stomach, but what he most wanted was just a change of air, and the big stubbly western face sniffed for a breeze on the hot listless river.

I couldn't help wondering what had landed him in Frontera, the only foreigner there, and how he made a living in that dreary little river port. The answer to the second problem was, of course, gold fillings; I might have guessed that: they flashed at you from every face, like false *bonhomie*. He had the best practice, he said, in Frontera, for apparently that tiny town supported at least three. The people preferred to come to him rather than go to their own countrymen, who treated them like dogs. So his colleagues hated him. They wouldn't have hesitated, he said, at murder – if they had had the guts. Once a gunman did play for him – came to his consulting-room and instead of sitting down in the chair pulled a gun. Doc Winter was younger in those days: he'd kicked the man in the stomach and sent his gun flying and landed him on the point of the jaw. He groaned slightly as the engines rattled, and sniffed greedily for air. He was like the tough case of something labelled fragile.

What a country! he kept on exclaiming. God, what a country! He had to get Japanese drills from Mexico City because they were cheap, and they never lasted – sometimes they broke down after a single use. How he longed to get out, but what a chance! Every time you made money there was a revolution. And now this oil business and the exchange falling – he heard you could get five pesos for a dollar in Mexico City. Oh, things had been all right once in Tabasco – in the days when people still used mahogany furniture. There were a lot of American traders then, in timber. That was why you had names like Bartlett among the Mexicans. They came down after the Civil War from the South and intermarried and forgot their own tongue and took Mexican citizenship. But now there was no money left in Tabasco: everything was just rotting into the rivers.

'Well,' I said, 'I suppose things are better than in Garrido's time.'

Not on your life, he said. There was discipline in those days . . . Garrido was right, only his friends went too far. 'Why,' he said, 'that woman there, my wife, she's his niece. I was Garrido's dentist in Villahermosa. He never went to anyone else.'

'Did he pay you?'

'I never sent a bill,' he said. 'I wasn't that crazy. But I got protection.' All that was wrong with Garrido was – he went against the Church. It never pays, he said. He'd be here now if he hadn't gone against the Church.

'But he seems to have won,' I said, 'no priests, no churches . . .'

'Oh,' he said illogically, 'they don't care about religion round here. It's too hot.'

That was incontestable – the heat increased not only as the day advanced, but as the boat screwed farther in to Tabasco. 'Frontera's nice and fresh,' the dentist said, 'not like Villahermosa.' At about two o'clock in the afternoon we went aground – backed furiously, swung this way and that, driving right up against the bank, slid off and landed – hopelessly – on sand. Our luck was in:

we had chosen the only place in the whole river where there was another ship to help us. We hadn't been there twenty minutes when she came chugging round a bend, dragging a chain of barges laden with bananas. It had been intolerably hot, motionless there on the shoal, and we cried out to them to let us have some bananas; and casually, as you might throw feed to chickens, they threw great bunches on board – a hundred or more fruit to a bunch – as if they were weeds. Then they attached a chain and dragged us off. 'Comrades,' the captain called, raising his fist.

With the dark, the early hasty tropic dark, the fireflies came out – great globes of moving light, like the lamps of a town, flickering over the banana trees. Sometimes a canoe went by paddled by Indians – white and silent and transparent like a marine insect, and the oil-lamps in the bow and stern gave a sharp theatrical appearance to the sabre leaves on the bank. The roar of the mosquitoes nearly extinguished the sound of the engines; they swarmed across from the banks and shrivelled against the oil-lamps. I wondered nervously what would happen if we went aground now, with no hope of release till daylight and nearly fifty passengers on board and the mosquitoes drumming in. And then, of course, we did begin to go aground. Somebody shone an electric torch on a man in the bows taking soundings; the ship moved backwards and forwards, swung this way and that – inches at a time. Cries came up to the little dark bridge – naming the soundings – '*seis, siete*,' and then quickly down to '*tres*'. Then the electric light would wane and die and a new bulb be fitted in. '*Seis, siete, cuatro*.' For nearly half an hour we sat there in the river, swinging gently, before we got through.

And then suddenly, about eleven hours from Frontera, Villahermosa burst out at us round a bend. For twelve hours there had been nothing but trees on either side; one had moved forward only into darkness; and here with an effect of melodrama was a city – lights burning down into the river, a great crown outlined in electricity like a casino. All felt the shock – it was like coming to Venice through an uninhabited jungle – they called, triumphantly, '*El puerto, el puerto!*' and in the excitement we nearly ran aground for a third time – the bow swung round and dipped into the bank.

6. The Godless State

That effect of something sophisticated and gay in the heart of a swamp did not outlast the night – it was the swamp that lasted. I never, till the day I left, discovered what building had shone like a crown through the night – there certainly wasn't a casino, and the lights I had seen were not visible when once one was an inhabitant.

We tied up to a steep mud bank crowned by a high dark wall; under the shadow of Villahermosa – 'the beautiful city' – the lights had all gone out. In the obscurity we could make out faces as the fireflies went by. A plank fifteen feet long bridged the mud river to the mud bank, and somebody switched on an electric torch to guide us. I began to slide on down the bank until a man took my arm and propelled me upwards. By the light of an electric torch I saw a policeman – or a soldier. He took my suitcase and shook it, listening for the clank of contraband liquor. It was like landing at the foot of a medieval castle: the ramp of mud and the old tall threatening walls and a sense of suspicion.

One came, as it were, through a crack in the walls to the only possible hotel, which stood in a small plaza on the main landing quay. An electric dynamo filled the hallway and the hotel itself began on the first floor at the head of a wide staircase, where an unshaved malarial creature sat rocking up and down in a wicker chair talking to himself. My room was a huge bare apartment with a high ceiling and a tiled floor and a bed set down somewhere in the middle. There was a private shower which put the price up by a peso a day, and it was only later that I found it didn't work; now, after the boat's dark cell, this room was luxury.

Somewhere music was being played: it came faintly down the hill to the riverside through the sticky night. I followed it to the plaza. I was excited and momentarily happy: the place seemed beautiful. Under the trees of the little plaza the young men and women promenaded, the women on the inner circle, the men on the outer, moving in opposite directions, slowly. A blind man dressed carefully in white drill with a straw hat was led by a friend. It was like a religious ceremony going on and on, with ritualistic repetition – indeed it was the nearest to a religious ceremony you were allowed to get in Tabasco. If I had moved a camera all round the edge of the little plaza in a panning shot it would have recorded all the life there was in the capital city – a dentist's, with a floodlit chair of torture; the public jail, an old white-pillared one-storey house which must have dated back to the Conquistadores, where a soldier sat with a rifle at the door and a few dark faces pressed against the bars; a Commercial Academy, the size of a village store; the Secretariat; the Treasury, a florid official building with long steps leading down to the plaza; the Syndicate of Workers and Peasants; the Casa de Agraristas; a few private houses with tall unshuttered windows guarded with iron bars, through which one saw old ladies on Victorian rocking-chairs swinging back and forth among the little statues and the family photographs. A public dance was going on with faded provincial elegance – you could see the couples revolving at a slant in the great brewery mirrors marked 'Cerveza Moctezuma'. At nine-thirty promptly all the main lights – the groups of four globes like balloons which stood at each corner of the plaza joined by ugly trailing overhead wires – went out. And I suppose the dance came to an end. For this was the puritan as well as the Godless state.

I went back to the hotel to bed and began to read *Dr Thorne*, 'There is a county in the west of England not so full of life indeed, nor so widely spoken of as some of its manufacturing leviathan brethren in the north, but which is, nevertheless, very dear to those who know it well. Its green pasture, its waving wheat, its deep and shady and – let us add – dirty lanes, its paths and stiles, its tawny-coloured, well-built churches, its avenues of beeches . . .' Trollope is a good author to read in a foreign land – especially in a land so different from any-thing one has ever known as this. It enables you to keep touch with the familiar. A cockchafer came buzzing and beating through the room and I turned out the light – the light went out all over Barsetshire, the hedges and the rectories and paddocks dropped into darkness, and as the cockchafers buzzed and beat one felt the excite-ment of this state where the hunted priest had worked for so many years, hidden in the swamps and forests, with no leave train or billet behind the lines. I remem-bered the confessor saying to me in Orizaba, 'A very evil land.' One felt one was drawing near to the centre of something – if it was only of darkness and abandonment.

A DAY IN THE BEAUTIFUL CITY

Something went wrong with my watch in the night, so that I presented my only letter of introduction at seven-thirty in the morning when I thought it was ten-thirty. The man was away by plane, visiting a hacienda, but his wife received me with perfect courtesy as if she was used to foreigners arriving at that hour. We spoke of the Church in Tabasco (she was a Catholic), sitting in a little dark room out of the heat with her mother. There was no priest, she said, left in Tabasco, no church standing, except one eight leagues away, now used as a school. There had been one priest over the border in Chiapas, but the people had told him to go – they couldn't protect him any longer.

'And when you die?' I said.

'Oh,' she said, 'we die like dogs.' No religious ceremony was allowed at the grave. The old people, of course, felt it most – a few weeks before they had smuggled the Bishop of Campeche in by plane to see her grandmother who was dying. They had money still . . . but what could the poor do?

I went back to the hotel: heat and flies, heat and flies I found the dentist there, but not his family. 'That woman – my wife, you know, she's staying with relations. A man's gotta be alone sometimes.' He had shaved and was looking better. 'Maybe tomorrow,' he said, 'we'll go for a walk – up to the plaza.' There was a continual sour smell from the river like decaying fruit and a continuous thirst – every time I passed through the plaza I had a drink, of warm, sweet, gaseous chemicals. By the end of the day I had got through two bottles of beer, four and a half bottles of various mineral waters, and one bottle of so-called cider, as well as coffee, three large cups of it. As for the food, it was unspeakable, worse than anything I had eaten or was to eat in Mexico. The hotel served no food, and there was only one restaurant in town – flies and dirty tablecloths and meat on the point of turning in this wet oven of a place, and a proprietor in a kind of yachting cap. And it was expensive, too, by Mexican standards – eighteen pence a meal.

I went and saw the chief of police, a big, blond, cheery creature with curly hair, dressed too tightly in white drill, with a holster at his fat hip. He laughed aloud when he saw my passport, putting an arm round my shoulder with that false Mexican camaraderie. 'That's fine,' he said, 'fine. You've come home. Why, everybody in Villahermosa is called Greene – or Graham.'

'Are there English people in the town, then?'

'No, no,' he said. 'The Greenes are Mexicans.'

'I'd like to meet one.'

'Come back this afternoon at four and I'll introduce you.'

On the way down from the plaza I met the dentist again – he had struggled out a hundred yards or so and stood at a street corner spitting. 'Revisiting old haunts,' he said. 'Well, well, that's the Southern Banana Company now; it used to be . . . and that clock, that clock's been there ten . . . twenty years.'

'Seen the doctor yet?'

'All in good time,' he said. 'I don't want to hurry. I know what's wrong. Why, I drank iced milk in New Orleans thirty years ago. That acted just the same. The trouble is I took a purge this morning. I oughtn't to have done that. It's locked me. Seen my family?'

'No.'

'They're out looking for me,' he said. 'They've been at the hotel. Don't you tell them I'm around.'

Heat and flies, heat and flies. I felt a dreadful inanition at the thought of the journey I had to make and all the things I must buy for it: hammock, serape, kettle, snake-bite remedy. I got the last in a bottle, Dr Somebody-or-Other's snakebite cure – take a dessertspoonful right away, and then another spoonful every half-hour till the bottle is empty. Everybody said it was a good thing, but what happens if you get bitten twice? That's your bad luck, I suppose.

Then I went and saw the aviation company. I couldn't face the idea of that long double river journey to Monte-cristo.

I think there were only two classes of men I really liked in Mexico – the priests and the flyers. They were something new in Mexico, with their pride in history, their dash, their asceticism; non-drinkers and non-smokers living a mess life together in the only clean well-built house in Villahermosa, brilliant flyers, if a little less than efficient as mechanics. I hadn't been in the office ten minutes before I was being lectured on Cortés. I said I wanted to get a guide if I could from Palenque to Las Casas, which was the old capital of Chiapas before the politicians moved down into the plain, to Tuxtla. It will be a fine journey, the man said, if you can make it – you'll know what Cortés had to face in heavy armour on his march to Guatemala. And when the manager came in – an American airman, once Garrido's pilot, but forbidden now by Mexican law to fly a passenger plane – he, too, talked of Cortés: the problem of where he landed in Tabasco and what was the old course of the Grijalva – he had flown over it time and again with that in mind. Once again my plans had to be altered. I could fly to Montecristo instead of making the long river journey, but there wasn't a reliable guide, they said, to be obtained there or at Palenque.

The best thing was to fly to Salto de Agua, where there was a storekeeper who would help me first to a guide to Palenque and then to a guide to Yajalon, a village in the mountains. In Yajalon there was another storekeeper they could recommend who would find me a guide to Las Casas; and, what was better still, a Norwegian lady who spoke English lived there. From Las Casas everything was easy – a kind of road going south to Tuxtla, and from Tuxtla there was a regular air service to Oaxaca or Mexico City. But I'd just missed a plane to Salto; now I should have to wait – nearly a week.

A whole century separated these men – trained in the States, with their quick bird's-eye view of Mexico, their self-discipline – from the other inhabitants of Villahermosa, from the chief of police whom I tried to see again that afternoon. The appointment was for four; I sat on a bench in the courtyard of the police station for an hour. The dirty whitewashed walls, the greasy hammocks, and the animal faces of the men – it wasn't like law and order so much as banditry. The police were the lowest of the population: you had to look for honesty on the faces of the men and women waiting to be fined or blackguarded. You gained an overwhelming sense of brutality and irresponsibility as they took down their rifles from the rack and sloped away on patrol or ambled drearily across the yard in the great heat with their trousers open. These were the men who a few weeks later were to fire into a mob of unarmed peasants attempting to pray in the ruins of a church. I got tired of waiting in the end, and one of the policemen was assigned to hunt out the chief of police with me. We walked from one end of town to the other through the hot afternoon, looking in all the billiard parlours, but we couldn't find the chief.

I had dinner with the dentist; he was feeling better, but a little hunted: his family had been into the hotel again looking for him. A lottery seller came round and suddenly I remembered the ticket I had bought in Veracruz – it seemed a month ago. There it was in the long list of the smaller prizes – I had won twenty pesos with my first ticket. That sold the lottery to me: I bought at least a small share in a ticket in every town I came to, but I never won again. The dentist and I took a walk up to the plaza and sat down. You couldn't call it the cool of the evening: there was no cool. The old ladies sat swinging, swinging, and the parade went by. A young Mexican dentist called Graham joined us – he had known my dentist when he worked in Villahermosa – and presently in the parade the Señoritas Greene went by – raven hair, gold teeth, and the dumb brown eyes of Mexicans. It was astonishing that some young women in this place – of open drains and no water but the river – did manage to present themselves with a cleanness, a freshness, an *esprit* . . . The dentist sang softly to himself, 'I don't like the food I don't like the food,' and something about 'Your eyes of blue,' fanning himself with his straw hat. Then he'd chew a while and spit and murmur, 'No sugar in my urine' (he had apparently got to the doctor after all), and, 'Your stomach's the whole thing.'

In the night beetles woke me, thumping against the wall. I killed two – one in the very centre of the great tiled floor, but when I woke there wasn't a sign of it. It was uncanny. Had I dreamed? Then I looked for the other and found it surrounded by ants, which swarmed up in relays between the tiles. They must have eaten the first one altogether. It had been a bad night. I had thought feverishly over and over again of the opening of a short story – all through the night stuck in an opening paragraph, like a needle in a cracked record – and I woke with a thick throat, so that it was difficult to swallow: the effect of the green sour river outside. I tried to write my story, but the indelible pencil melted on my hand.

A VICTORIAN ADVENTURER

It is curious how the most dismal place after twenty-four hours begins to seem like home. Even the *Ruiz Cano*. And now this town. It is, of course, fear of the next step. 'Envy me, envy me,' a character remarks in one of Stevenson's stories, 'I am a coward.' And it is something to have some emotion to cherish in a place like Villahermosa, even if it's only fear. I began to cling to what I knew – the big tiled room, the fly-plagued restaurant, the walk uphill to the plaza, and to the people – the dentist and Dr Roberto Fitzpatrick.

Dr Fitzpatrick was an elderly Scotsman who had never been out of Mexico – not even to the States. He talked his native language slowly and brokenly, telling me of the fly in Chiapas which sends you blind, showing me horrible medical photographs and a scorpion in a little glass bottle. No one looking at this small man with the stubbly grizzled beard, the quick Latin movements, and the steel spectacles would take him for British. He had been absorbed nearly as completely as the Greenes and Grahams, and there was something rather horrifying and foreboding in this – for an unabsorbed Greene. Time goes so slowly: a few days were like months at home. Señorita Greene went swinging round the plaza on the evening promenade; and one found oneself haunted by fancies, as if fate intended to take in its octopus coils yet another Greene . . . The chief of police had – forcibly – kept his promise and summoned a rather scared Greene to see me in the police station. His name was De Witt Greene; he had Dutch, American, English, and pure Indian blood in him, for his grandfather, who had come from Pennsylvania after the Civil War, had married a cacique's daughter. His great-grandfather had come from England.* As we walked across the plaza together he had pointed – 'There's another Greene' – at a seedy Mexican, with a drooping hat and a gun on his hip, descending the Treasury steps.

But Dr Fitzpatrick was saved from complete absorption by an immense family pride. Sitting in the Victorian *sala* of his home, among the shiny mahogany furniture, the occasional tables, and the little china ornaments and picture-frames, I looked at old faded photographs, testimonials of his dead brothers who had been educated in the States; Tom, with a great spade beard, and brilliant Cornelius, who had died young – somewhere far back in the nineties. There was a gold medal from Seton Hall, New Jersey, and school reports (he was top in every class) and a letter from the warden to his father and yellowed clippings from a local paper about the degree celebrations in Orange and Cornelius Fitzpatrick's name underlined in old tarnished ink . . . But

* The other day, reading in d'Urfey's anthology *Pills to Purge Melancholy* (1720), I came across a Mr Witt Greene, the author and composer of a formal Restoration song – 'Never Sigh but Think of Kissing'. Certainly family migration may be a daunting thing.

137

most remarkable of all was the father. There are heroic adventurers the world knows nothing of: papers recording incredible achievements rot in old drawers, houses in the Midlands still surrender astonishing secrets; but one had not expected to find in Villahermosa the record of such an adventure. Dr Fitzpatrick took down from a shelf a little calf-bound notebook with loose torn leaves, the diary his father had kept when he came to Mexico in 1863 seeking a practice to support his wife Anna and his two-year-old baby Tom. (He had left England in 1857 at the age of twenty-seven, married a girl from a New Orleans convent, and never, I believe, saw England again unless for a brief period before he tried his fortunes unsuccessfully in Africa.)

He had left the two of them in New Orleans, and his first attempt to make a living petered miserably out in Tampico, now the great hot ugly oil port. Then came his first stupendous adventure of which the record, alas, has been lost! There remains in the existing diary only the brief statement, 'A year ago today I left Tampico with forty-seven cents, to walk to New Orleans' – three hundred odd miles to the present Mexican border, and more than twice that distance more through Texas and Louisiana. He stayed in New Orleans a few months only; stubborn and Scotch, he set out again, this time to Panama, where, for some unknown reason, he imagined there were good prospects for a doctor. From this time on we have the day-to-day entries of his disillusionment and laconic despair.

As a Scottish Catholic he was shocked by the condition of the Church in Panama; as a lonely young man of thirty-one, who had very little Spanish, he found himself consorting more and more with the disreputable and kindly Padre Rey. His brief entries build up a pathetic picture of his disapproval and his grudging friendship for this bizarre priest who lived with his wife and daughter (he said in excuse that he had married her before he became a priest) and kept live mice in a glass lamp. Stories about the Bishop of Panama reached Dr Fitzpatrick's ears. A girl was about to have a child, and Dr Fitzpatrick asked whether the rumours were true – that the Bishop was the father. 'Not this time, I think,' said Padre Rey . . . It wasn't the sort of Catholicism Fitzpatrick had been used to in Scotland.

And all the time his money was draining away and no patients came. On Christmas Day he was reduced to eight dollars, and he felt an intolerable loneliness, thinking of 'my beloved Anna and dear little Tom'. He posted letters which she would probably never receive, and got none himself. Then at last, with the help of Padre Rey, he found a patient and earned enough money to take his passage on a boat for El Salvador – it was at least a little nearer to the States.

Then began the second great adventure. El Salvador was at war with Guatemala, but in spite of that, without money and without arms and without Spanish, he took a horse and rode nine hundred and ninety-seven miles (he was always exact in his calculations) to the Atlantic, seeking in vain for a home and a practice – across Salvador (arrested as a spy and released), across Guatemala (meeting the Indian dictator with his soldiers in the field) and into Mexico, right across Chiapas, climbing the eight thousand feet to cold Las Casas, then down again into Tabasco and the tropical heat, and so to the sea. There is nothing in the diary to show he was conscious of the magnitude of his adventure; Indian superstitions, native medicines described with medical frankness, so many miles covered – most of the entries are Scotch in brevity and matter-of-factness. Only at moments when he thinks of Anna and Tom (he doesn't even know if they are still alive: he left them in the midst of the American Civil War) does the individuality of the young homesick man break through into the diary. Once he sang 'God Save the Queen' to keep his spirits up, climbing a mountain in Chiapas.

It is pleasant to know that he found his way safely back to New Orleans, that his wife and baby were well, and that eventually they all found prosperity – in Villa-hermosa of all places. His reputation as a doctor extended to Mexico City and across the Gulf to Mérida: he was called in by Porfirio Díaz to treat his wife, and died in 1905, in Campeche – a town he had always hated – on his way to see the Governor of Yucatán. There are photographs in the Mexican *sala* where the unpublished record lies on a shelf – Anna, a middle-aged woman in a crinoline, with one of those calm Victorian faces that hide years of the wildest anxieties; 'dear little Tom', looking like a Dean with that fierce black spade beard; and Dr Fitzpatrick himself, old and stern, with a beard as fierce as Tom's, wearing a long frock coat. The young Scotsman who had tramped from Tampico with forty-seven cents, who had ridden those thousand miles to the Atlantic, sleeping in Indian huts and depending for his life on the charity of a plate of beans and a cup of native coffee, turned into this rather awe-inspiring figure, a man who never wore a shirt more than twice and who rode about the streets of the tropical town, among the vultures and the mosquitoes, in the long dark broadcloth he would have worn in Edinburgh.

Of the old Dr Fitzpatrick's Villahermosa – of San Juan Bautista, as it was called then – very little remains: a few houses like the Hotel Tabasqueño, which must once have been lovely; a little classical plaza in pink stone with broken columns; the back wall of a church (what was the nave is a heap of rubble used – but rarely – for road mending). Of the cathedral not even that much remains – Garrido saw to that – only an ugly cement playground marks the site, with a few grim iron swings too scorching hot to use.

I said to Dr Fitzpatrick, small bitter exiled widower, caged in his Victorian *sala*, with the vultures rotting on his roof, 'But I suppose *some* good came out of the persecution. Schools . . .'

He said the church schools were far better than those that existed now . . . there were even more of them, and the priests in Tabasco were good men. There was no excuse for the persecution in this state – except some obscure personal neurosis, for Garrido himself had been brought up as a Catholic: his parents were pious people. I asked about the priest in Chiapas who had fled. 'Oh,' he said, 'he was just what we call a whisky priest.' He had taken one of his sons to be baptised, but the priest was drunk and would insist on naming him Brigitta. He was little loss, poor man, a kind of Padre Rey; but who can judge what terror and hardship and isolation may have excused him in the eyes of God?

TABASCAN SUNDAY

The anonymity of Sunday seems peculiarly unnatural in Mexico; a man going hunting in the marshes with his dog and his gun, a young people's fiesta, shops closing after noon – nothing else to divide this day from all the other days, no bells to ring. I sat at the head of the stairs and had my shoes cleaned by a little blond bootblack – a thin tired child in tattered trousers like someone out of Dickens. Only his brown eyes were Mexican – not his transparent skin and his fine gold hair. I was afraid to ask his name, for it might have been Greene. I gave him twice what I usually gave (twenty centavos – say, three pennies) and he returned me ten centavos change, going wearily down the stairs with his heavy box into the great heat of Sunday.

Garrido has fled to Costa Rica and yet nothing is done. 'We die like dogs.' There were no secret Masses in private houses such as are found in the neighbouring state, only a dreadful lethargy as the Catholics died slowly out – without Confession, without the Sacraments, the child unbaptised, and the dying man unshriven. I thought of Rilke's phrase, 'An empty, horrible alley, an alley in a foreign town, in a town where nothing is forgiven.'

There are, I suppose, geographical and racial excuses for the lethargy. Tabasco is a state of river and swamp and extreme heat; in northern Chiapas there is no choice between a mule and the rare plane for a traveller, and in Tabasco no choice between plane and boat. But a mule is a sociable form of transport – nights spent with strangers huddling together in the cold mountain air, talk over the beans and the embers; while in a boat you are isolated with the mosquitoes between the banana plantations.

And then there are no Indians in Tabasco, with their wild beliefs and their enormous if perverted veneration, to shame the Catholic into *some* action. Too much foreign blood came into Tabasco when it was a prosperous country; the faith with the Grahams and Greenes goes back only a few generations. They haven't the stability of the old Spanish families in Chiapas.

Nothing in a tropical town can fill the place of a church for the most mundane use; a church is the one spot of coolness out of the vertical sun, a place to sit, a place where the senses can rest a little while from ugliness; it offers to the poor man what a rich man may get in a theatre – though not in Tabasco. Now in Villahermosa, in the blinding heat and the mosquito-noisy air, there is no escape at all for anyone. Garrido did his job well: he knew that the stones cry out, and he didn't leave any stones. There is a kind of cattle-tick you catch in Chiapas, which fastens its head in the flesh; you have to burn it out, otherwise the head remains embedded and festers. In northern Chiapas the churches still stand, shuttered and ruined and empty, but they fester – the whole village festers away from the door, the plaza is the first to go.

So in Villahermosa there is nothing to do all the long Sundays that go on and on but sit in Victorian rocking-chairs, swinging back and forth waiting for the sunset and the mosquitoes. The vultures group themselves on the roofs like pigeons: tiny moron heads, long necks, faces like Carnival masks, and dusty plumages, peering this way and that attentively for a death. I counted twenty on one roof. They looked domesticated, as if they were going to lay an egg. And I suppose even a bird of prey does sometimes lay an egg.

Nothing to do but drink gassy fruit drinks (no miracle in the Godless state will turn this aerated water into wine) and watch the horrifying abundance of just life.

143

You can't open a book without some tiny scrap of life scuttling across the page; the stalls are laden with great pulpy tasteless fruits, and when the lights come out, so do the beetles: the pavement by the green sour riverside is black with them. You kill them on your bedroom floor, and by morning, as I have said, they have been drained away by more life – the hordes of ants which come up between the tiles at the scent of death or sweetness. I bought some sugar one morning to take with me to Chiapas, and when I lay down in the afternoon an army of ants was trooping along three sides of my room.

The only place, if you are a Christian, where you can find some symbol of your faith is in the cemetery up on a hill above the town – a great white classical portico and the legend 'SILENCIO' in big black letters, the blind wall round the corner where Garrido shot his prisoners, and inside the enormous tombs of above-ground burial, glasshouses for flowers and portraits and images, crosses and weeping angels, the sense of a far better and cleaner city than that of the living at the bottom of the hill.

A DENTIST'S LIFE

I visited it with the dentist. He was feeling much better, though his family had at last caught him. 'That woman – my wife' had arrived after dark with both children and moved in on him for the night. I don't know what they did about beds. He was accosted just outside the hotel as we started out by a man who offered to sell him any drink he needed, not a bootlegger but a friend of a friend or a relation of a relation in the Government. All the Government offices are honeycombed with unreality: there is a picture of Cárdenas on every wall, but the man supposed to be administering his policy may be a Catholic . . . a conservative . . . We had a cup of chocolate in the market, a great foaming cup beaten up from a little hard pastille – the only good drink obtainable in Tabasco – and went on up the hill towards the cemetery. At the street corners the dentist stopped to spit – his throat was always full of phlegm. Something – perhaps the heat – had destroyed memory. Every few minutes he would bring out the one fact he had caught hold of, 'You going off by aeroplane, eh ?'

'That's right.'

'Where to ? Frontera ?'

'No. I told you. Salto – for Palenque.'

'You don't want to go to Salto. You want to go to Zapata.'

'But I told you. I can't get reliable guides there to Las Casas.'

'Las Casas ? What you want to go there for ?'

He would pause for what seemed hours at street corners, unable to remember, I really believe, where he was going, standing like a cow chewing. 'So you're going off by plane, eh ?'

'Yes.'

'To Frontera.'

And the whole explanation would begin again. It was inexpressibly tiring.

I learned slowly a little of his life and of how he'd ended up here in Tabasco. He stood at a street corner chewing and spitting and mooning, hitching his belt, 'Why, that house was a dentist's ten years ago.'

He had been partner in a dentist's firm in the States when he was a young man and caught smallpox. Everyone avoided him after that because for months his face

145

was peeling. People walked round him on pavements. He tried to enter his office, but his partner stood at the top of the stairs and waved him away. '"You'll ruin the practice." I thought, aw hell – and went straight back home and packed a grip.' Then he went to Atlanta, Georgia – no luck at all. Then New Orleans . . . Houston, Texas . . . San Antonio. His face had stopped peeling by that time. In San Antonio he met a Mexican who told him there was good business to be done across the border – with gold fillings. He went to Monterrey, Tampico, Mexico City – at last Tabasco. That was in the time of Porfirio Díaz. Then the revolution came – the peso lost value – and he could never get out.

'All the same,' he said, 'I'm going. There's going to be trouble, you see.' Over the radio last night they had been told that the American people wanted to boycott Mexican goods. People were apt to get things into their heads about foreigners. We walked into the cemetery and out again. 'Well,' he said, 'so you're going off by aero-plane ?'

'Yes.'

'To Frontera.'

'No, no, to Salto – for Palenque.'

'You don't want to go to Salto. You want to go to Zapata.'

And then the whole explanation again while he chewed and looked around and the heat fell hopelessly across even the desire to remember. 'Las Casas ? What you want to go there for ? There's going to be trouble. I wouldn't be out of reach of an aeroplane now – not for a hundred dollars.'

I tried to distract him, pointing at some stone memorial in the street. 'What's that ?'

He mooned at it, chewing. 'I guess it's to someone they shot.' His mind for a while did succeed in running on a track, for at the restaurant door he said thoughtfully, 'I believe in revolution. Gives people ambition. Puts money in circulation.'

And he proved himself on occasions a man of resource. He would drink the olive oil at lunch out of a spoon – 'Your stomach's the whole thing' – and once when he swallowed a fish-bone he vomited without a second's hesitation on to the floor. It was, in its way, an extraordinary feat. Skulking abstractedly round the corner of the hotel with his eyes open for his family, spitting at the street corners, suddenly lost to all the world with his chewing gum, humming in the plaza, 'I don't like the food. I don't like the food,' without a memory and without a hope in the immense heat, he loomed during those days as big as a symbol – I am not sure of what, unless the aboriginal calamity, 'having no hope, and without God in the world'.

TROLLOPE IN MEXICO

No hope anywhere: I have never been in a country where you are more aware all the time of hate. Friendship there is skin deep – a protective gesture. That motion of greeting you see everywhere upon the street, the hands outstretched to press the other's arms, the semi-embrace – what is it but the motion of pinioning to keep the other man from his gun? There has always been hate, I suppose, in Mexico, but now it is the official teaching: it has superseded love in the school curriculum. Cynicism, a distrust of men's motives, is the accepted ideology. Look through the windows of the Workers' Syndicate in

Villahermosa and there on the wall of the little lecture-room are pictures – of hate and cynicism: a crucified woman with a lecherous friar kissing her feet, a priest tippling with the wine of the Eucharist, another receiving money at the altar from a starving couple. They are admirably designed in great bold poster colours, and one's mind goes back to the picture teaching of the Augustinian friars. With them at any rate the lesson of punishment was followed by the lesson of love. But this hate – one cannot believe it will be succeeded by anything at all: it poisons the human wells; like rats we shrivel internally, suck water with a frantic thirst and swell and die. One saw the symbol of it everywhere, even in the little ragged military band marching around the town while some proclamation was read from the governor – they carried rifles as well as bugles and drums.

It was my last night in Villahermosa, the plane left for Salto in the morning; I sat on a rocking-chair at the head of the stairs with the old proprietor, and we swung backward and forward, trying to stir a breeze. He was an old man with a pointed beard and an aristocratic Spanish face; he sat in his shirt-sleeves, wearing an old pair of braces and a belt, and swung and swung. He, too, like the dentist in Mexico City, looked back with nostalgia to the days of Porfirio Díaz. There had been a governor of Tabasco in those days who had ruled for thirty years and then died poor. Now they ruled for three or four years and retired to Mexico City rich. The election campaign was on – between Bartlett and a man whose name I have forgotten – but no one really cared; a few people had been shot in Zapata; but it would make no difference at all to Tabasco who won.

It was an awful night. The pavement outside the hotel

was black with beetles. They lay on every stair up from the electric dynamo to the hotel; they detonated against the lamp and walls and fell with little plops like hailstones. Somewhere there was a storm, but the air in Villahermosa never cleared. I went to my bedroom and killed seven beetles; the corpses moved as rapidly as in life across the floor pushed by the swarms of ants. I lay in bed and read Trollope, with nostalgia. Every now and then I got out and killed another beetle (twelve altogether). I had with me only *Dr Thorne* and the first volume of Cobbett's *Rural Rides* (my other books were in Mexico City). Cobbett I had finished already and *Dr Thorne* I had to ration – not more than twenty pages a day, to include my siesta in the afternoon. Even at that it hadn't lasted me in Villahermosa, and it was a cruel blow to discover that the binders had left out four pages – a whole fifth of a ration – at the climax. Somewhere in those four pages Mary Thorne's life changed from misery to happiness – I wasn't to know exactly how.

What books to take on a journey? It is an interesting – and important – problem. In West Africa once I had made the mistake of taking the *Anatomy of Melancholy*, with the idea that it would, as it were, match the mood. It matched all right, but what one really needs is contrast, and so I surrendered perhaps my only hope of ever reading *War and Peace* in favour of something overwhelmingly national. And one did want, I found, an *English* book in this hating and hateful country. I am not sure how the sentiment of *Dr Thorne* – of Frank Gresham divided from Mary by his birth and by the necessity of marrying money if Greshambury were to be maintained, and of Mary's rich inheritance from her scoundrelly uncle after he had drunk himself to death –

I am not sure how it would have gone down at home. I think there would have been mental reservations before one surrendered to the charm, but here – in this hot forgotten tropic town, among the ants and the beetles – the simplicity of the sentiment did literally fill the eyes with tears. It is a love story and there are few love stories in literature; love in fiction is so often now – as Hemingway expresses it – what hangs up behind the bathroom door. *Dr Thorne*, too, is the perfect 'popular' novel – and when one is lonely one wants to claim kinship with all the simple friendly people turning the pages of their *Home Notes*. With what superb skill Trollope maintains a kind of fictitious suspense. We know exactly from an early page that Frank will be faithful to Mary, that Sir Roger Scatcherd will die and leave her a fortune, that Lady Arabella will be humbled and old Dr Thorne be able to resume his friendship with the squire, that Frank and Mary will live happy ever after; but we co-operate with the author in his management of the plot, we pretend to feel suspense, and that frank co-operation is a mark of the popular novel, for the great sentimental popular heart doesn't care for *real* suspense, to be in genuine doubt of the lovers' destiny. In *Barchester Towers* Trollope says in so many words that he will have no mysteries in his story – the widow, he tells you, will not marry Mr Slope: the reader need have no fears. In this more 'popular' story, he doesn't deny his creed; the suspense is patently unreal, but he allows us to *pretend* we fear, and sometimes it was a real strain – to stop after twenty pages and lie and sweat upon the iron bed and not to *know*.

But it was worse to have finished the book altogether, to have finished with proud delightful Mary Thorne and have nothing to fall back on but the hopeless dentist and the hotel proprietor swinging in his chair dreaming of Díaz. I had badly miscalculated in Mexico City – I thought I should be back in three weeks, and the three weeks were half gone already. How slowly while the beetles flocked in I spun out the last paragraph! 'And now we have but one word left for the doctor. "If you don't come and dine with me," said the squire to him, when they found themselves both deserted, "mind, I shall come and dine with you." And on this principle they seem to act. Dr Thorne continues to extend his practice, to the great disgust of Dr Fillgrave; and when Mary suggested to him that he should retire he almost boxed her ears. He knows the way, however, to Boxall Hill as well as ever he did, and is willing to acknowledge that the tea there is almost as good as it ever was at Greshambury.'

So England faded out and Mexico remained. I had never in my life been so homesick, and the fault was Trollope's. His England was not the England I knew, and yet . . . I lay on my back and tried to project myself into home. Jules Romain once wrote a novel about just such a possibility; I built up the familiar in my mind carefully, chair by chair, book by book – the windows just there, and the buses going by, and the squeals of children on the Common. But it wasn't real: *this* was real – the high empty room and the tiled and swarming floor and the heat and the sour river smell.

7. Into Chiapas

When I got up, I threw away everything inessential –
like used socks – and put on riding-boots and breeches;
I wasn't to take them off very often in the next ten days.
I was still uncertain whether I was bound for Palenque
or not. I had set myself two jobs – to get to Villahermosa
and to cross Chiapas; Palenque was only a side issue, a
blind for officials, and now suddenly I found it taking
possession of my route – I was being driven there like a
sheep through a gate. The manager of the aviation
company had given me a letter of introduction to the
storekeeper at Salto, asking him to supply me with a
reliable guide – to Palenque. I was not an archaeologist.
I felt only the faintest curiosity about these ruins which
the few people who had visited them claimed to be finer
than Chichen Itzá. I was on my way home now by way
of Las Casas – I didn't want to delay any longer, and
my flying friends, with whom I had dined in mess the
night before, had told me Palenque was two full days'
ride from Salto. That meant five days in all. Well, one
could only leave it to fate.

The airport was up on top of the hill beyond the
cemetery. The great gateway, the black letters
'SILENCIO', and the wall where the prisoners had been
shot rolled by, and a few vultures lifted heavily.

A friend of mine, José Ortega, was flying the plane,
a little cramped red six-seater. I sat up in front beside

him and we took off ten minutes early. Far below Tabasco spread out, the Godless state, the landscape of a hunted man's terror and captivity – wood and water, without roads, and on the horizon the mountains of Chiapas like a prison wall. After a quarter of an hour we came down – no sign of a village – to a tiny clearing in a forest. A man sat on a horse and watched us taxi in, then trotted away down a narrow path and disappeared. Three people left the plane, a peasant woman with a basket and two men carrying leather satchels and umbrellas; they walked off – like season-ticketholders – into deep forest. We rose again and the same landscape unrolled like a Chinese picture: an endless decorative repetition. This was the dry season: you could see the hollows – like thumb-marks – waiting for the rains. The mountains came nearer – heavy black bars one behind the other – and a silver horizontal gleam upon the ground was a waterfall. 'You thought Villahermosa was hot,' Ortega said. 'You wait. And the mosquitoes . . .' Words failed him.

Salto lay right under the mountains on a bluff above a rapid green river which one must cross by dug-out canoe from the little rough landing field. The wooded mountains rose steeply at the back, shutting out ventilation. It was nine-thirty in the morning, and Chiapas, and no one spoke a word of English. A man carried my suitcase and my hammock ahead of me along the river bank, past the tin-roofed shacks where men lay in hammocks drearily swinging in the great heat, trying to construct a private current of air. Ortega's little red plane moved back across the merciless sky, like an insect on a mirror, towards Villahermosa. I had a sense of being marooned . . . even the dentist would have been welcome. The man carried my suitcase into a dark store with its back to a tiny dry plaza and laid it down; he said something I couldn't catch and disappeared. There were casks of – something, and Indians with curious pointed straw hats looked in and out again. I was overcome by an immense unreality: I couldn't even recognise my own legs in riding-boots. Why the hell was I here?

For the first time I was hopelessly at a loss because of my poverty of Spanish; always before there had been *someone* who spoke English – except on the *Ruiz Cano*, and my needs there had been few and my destination self-evident. Now I felt a mistake might land me anywhere. And, of course, that letter of introduction seemed doomed to land me in Palenque. It took a long time in my bad Spanish to make the storekeeper understand that I didn't really care a damn about Palenque: I was much more eager to get to Las Casas – that 'very Catholic' city – by the beginning of Holy Week. Could he find me a guide to Yajalon instead of to Palenque? He said he'd try, and every few hours during the day I visited him – to learn that he hadn't yet found a guide for anywhere at all. He *had* found me a lodging – a bed made out of packing-cases with a straw mat laid on the top in a room partitioned off with plywood from the rest of a one-room house. I was to pay two pesos fifty for room and food, and the food at lunch-time proved unexpectedly good. I don't really mean good: one's standard in Mexico falls with brutal rapidity.

There was nothing to do all day but drink warm expensive beer in the only cantina. The beer was expensive because it had to come on muleback across the mountains. In the plaza there was no life at all: two wooden seats, a mineral-water stall, some dogs and flies –

no church, of course. A horse tethered outside the schoolroom stamped and stamped, sometimes a mule team rattled across a little wooden bridge going towards the mountains, but long before midday the Indians had all cleared off and life went dead. There wasn't so much as a lottery seller here. At sunset I called desperately in at the store; no, he hadn't been able to find a guide for Yajalon; maybe in two or three days . . . but I hadn't even *Dr Thorne* to occupy me now. With a sense of doom I fell back on Palenque . . . Well, yes, he could find me a guide *there*, and by the time I got back again he would without doubt have found the Yajalon guide. And at Palenque, he said to encourage me, there was a German-American with a fine *finca* and a beautiful daughter – *muy simpática*.

This German with his beautiful daughter had been a legend, a mirage which had been flashing on and off ever since Mexico City. I had heard rumours of them first in the lounge of the bright chromium Reforma, but in Villahermosa the flyers had told me that the girl didn't exist – nor her father. And as the storekeeper had never been to Palenque, I took the information with reserve. Perhaps once – years ago – there had been a German with a beautiful daughter . . . Anyway, the mules and the guide were to call for me at five in the morning. How many days' journey? Only one day to the village, the storekeeper said, perhaps ten hours' riding, and rashly I left it at that – I was so eager to get on – although the flyers had told me it was a good two days' journey.

The dark came down punctually at six, and I sat outside my room on a hard chair, smoking to keep the flies away. My landlord sat on another chair, dumb with misery – he had toothache – and again inevitably with night the place took on the lineaments of home. This was what I knew well – a few hours were enough in so tiny and barren a place: the row of huts by the river, two parallel tracks running into the little plaza, the palms and the cantina at the corner, and the wooden bridge over a small ravine and a track running off into the hills. One might have been here for years without knowing the appearance of the place any better. The fireflies moved like brilliant pocket torches, and a small boy stood by the track with a flaming brand making mysterious animal noises into the dark.

At eight o'clock I climbed under my mosquito-net and put my mackintosh cape under my head as a pillow. Oddly enough, sleep came at once – luxuriously. A hard bed has its compensations: I remember once in a third-class compartment between Toulouse and Paris dreaming, with a rich sentiment and gentle sensuality, of Miss Merle Oberon and waking on the hard narrow vibrating seat to find the grey sky over the grey stone, the Paris suburbs already going by. So now, on the packing-cases, I dreamed of a Mr Wang, also known as Mr Moon, who was to guide me – somewhere. He was dressed in the most extravagant robes – all silk and gold embroidery and dragons – and when I said I much preferred walking to riding, he immediately assumed that I was offering him my horse. He was complacent and difficult – another more seedy guide complained that Mr Wang had 'put one over him' – but nevertheless Mr Wang left across the hard night an impression of enormous luxury, well-being, and romance. 'It is long since I saw the Prince of Chang in my dreams.'

Then somebody rattled on my door, and something animal muttered and stamped and blew windily in the

dark street. Mr Wang evaporated with his silken robe
into Chiapas air. I looked at my watch: it was only four
o'clock and I cried out a protest and turned over and
sought Mr Wang again in sleep. Somebody on the other
side of the wooden partition groaned and muttered, and
the animal stamped.

THE LONG RIDE

I left my suitcase behind, and because it seemed absurd
to think of rain I foolishly abandoned my cape and took
only the net, a hammock, and a rucksack.

At a quarter past four I got up and dressed by the
light of my electric torch, folded up the huge tent-like
mosquito-net. Everybody in Salto was asleep but my
guide – a dark, dapper young man of some education
who had come from Las Casas by way of Yajalon – and
his father, who had prepared us coffee and biscuits in
his home. It was the cool and quiet beginning of one of
the worst days I have ever spent. Only the first few
hours of that ride were to provide any pleasure – riding
out of Salto in the dark with one sleepy mongrel raising
its muzzle at the clip-clop of the mules, the ferry across
the river in the earliest light, the two mules swimming
beside the canoe, with just their muzzles and their eyes
above the water like a pair of alligator heads, and then
the long banana plantations on the other bank, the fruit,
plucked as we rode, tasting tart and delicious in the open
air at dawn.

The trouble was, the way to Palenque lay across a
bare exposed plateau, broken only occasionally by
patches of forest and shade, and by nine in the morning
the sun was blindingly up. By ten my cheap helmet

bought in Veracruz for a few pesos was just the damp hot cardboard it had pretended not to be. I had not ridden a horse for ten years; I had never ridden a mule before. Its trot, I imagine, is something like a camel's: its whole back heaves and strains. There is no rhythm you can catch by rising in the stirrups; you must just surrender yourself to the merciless uneven bump. The strain on the spine to the novice is appalling: the neck stiffens with it, the head aches as if it had been struck by sun. And all the time the nerves are worn by the stubbornness of the brute; the trot degenerates into a walk, the walk into an amble, unless you beat the mule continually. '*Mula. Mula. Mula. Echa, mula,*' the dreary lament goes on.

And all the time Palenque shifted like a mirage; my guide had never been there himself: all he could do on the wide plain was to keep a rough direction. Ten hours away the storekeeper had said, and after four hours I thought I could manage that quite easily, but when we stopped at an Indian's hut about eleven in the morning (six hours from Salto) and heard them talk as if it were now not quite half-way, my heart sank. A couple of wattle huts like those of West African natives, chickens and turkeys tumbling across the dusty floor, a pack of mongrels and a few cows listless in the heat under some thorny trees – it was better than nothing on that baked plateau, and I wished later we had stayed the night. They swung a string hammock up and I dismounted with immense difficulty. Six hours had stiffened me. They gave us tortillas – the fat, dry pancake with which you eat all food in the Mexican country – and an egg each in a tin mug, and coffee, delicious coffee. We rested half an hour and then went on. Six hours more, I said, with what I hoped was cheerfulness to my guide, but he scouted the notion. Six hours – oh, no, perhaps eight. Those people didn't know a thing.

I can remember practically nothing of that ride now until its close; I remember being afraid of sunstroke my head ached so – I would raise my hat for coolness, and then lower it from fear; I remember talking to my guide of the cantinas there would be in Palenque and how much beer and tequila we would drink. I remember the guide getting smaller and smaller in the distance and flogging at my mule ('*Mula. Mula. Echa, mula*') until I overtook him at a trot that wrenched the backbone. I remember that we passed a man with the mails travelling on a pony at a smart canter and he said he'd left Palenque in the night. And then somewhere on that immense rolling plain, in a spot where the grass grew long, the mule suddenly lay down under me. The guide was a long way off; I felt I could never get up on that mule again; I sat on the grass and tried to be sick and wanted to cry. The guide rode back and waited patiently for me to re-mount, but I didn't think it was possible – my body was too stiff. There was a small coppice of trees, some monkeys moved inquisitively, and the mule got on its feet again and began to eat.

Can't we stay the night somewhere, I said, in some hut, and go on tomorrow? But the guide said there wasn't a single hut between here and Palenque. It was two o'clock in the afternoon; we had been riding for nine hours, with half an hour's break; Palenque was, he said, about five hours away. Couldn't we string our hammocks up to the trees and sleep here? But he had no hammock and besides, there was no food, no drink, and lots of mosquitoes, perhaps a leopard. I think he meant a leopard – they call them tigers in Chiapas – and I remember how Victorian Dr Fitzpatrick had met one on his ride across these mountains, standing across his path. It is rather terrifying to believe you cannot go on, and yet to have no choice . . .

I got back into the saddle, thanking God for the big Mexican pommel which you can cling to with both hands when all else fails, and again the ride faded into obscurity – I didn't talk so much now about the cantina, I grumbled to myself in undertones that I *couldn't* make it, and I began to hate the dapperness of my guide, his rather caddish white riding-breeches – it was nothing to him, the ride; he rode just as he would sit in a chair. And then the mule lay down again; it lay down in the end four times before we saw, somewhere about five o'clock when the sun was low, a little smoke drifting over the ridge of the down. 'Palenque,' my guide said. I didn't believe him, and that was lucky, because it wasn't Palenque: only a prairie fire we had to ride around, the mules uneasy in the smoke. And then we came into a patch of forest and the ways divided; one way, the guide said – on I don't know whose authority, for he had never been here before – led to the German *finca*, the other to Palenque. Which were we to take? I chose Palenque: it was nearer and the lodging more certain, above all the drink. I didn't really believe in the German and his lovely daughter, and when after we'd been going a quarter of an hour we just came out on the same path, I believed less than ever in them. As the sun sank, the flies emerged more numerous than ever; they didn't bother to attack me; great fat droning creatures, they sailed by and sank like dirigibles on to the mule's neck, grappled fast, and sucked until a little stream of blood flowed down. I tried to dislodge them with my stick, but they simply shifted their ground. The smell of blood and mule was sickening. One became at last a kind of automaton, a bundle of flesh and bone without a brain.

And then a little party of riders came out of a belt of forest in the last light and bore news – Palenque was only half an hour distant. The rest of the way was in darkness, the darkness of the forest and then the darkness of night as well. That was how we began and ended. The stars were up when we came out of the forest, and there at the head of a long park-like slope of grass was a poor abandoned cemetery, crosses rotting at an angle and lying in the long grass behind a broken wall, and at the foot of the slope lights moved obscurely up towards a collection of round mud huts thatched with banana leaves as poor as anything I ever saw in West Africa. We rode through the huts and came into a long wide street of bigger huts – square ones these, raised a foot from the ground to avoid ants, some of them roofed with tin – and at the head of the street on a little hill a big plain ruined church.

My guide apparently had learned where we could get food, if not lodging – a woman's hut where the school teacher lived, and while food was prepared we staggered out on legs as stiff as stilts to find the drink we had promised ourselves all the hot day. But Palenque wasn't Salto; the Salto cantina loomed in memory with the luxury of an American bar. In the store near the church they had three bottles of beer only – warm, gassy, unsatisfying stuff. And afterwards we drank a glass each of very new and raw tequila; it hardly touched our thirst. At the other end of the village was the only other store.

We made our way there by the light of electric torches, to find they sold no beer at all: all we could get was mineral water coloured pink and flavoured with some sweet chemical. We had a bottle each and I took a bottle away with me to wash down my quinine. Otherwise we had to try and satisfy our thirst with coffee – endlessly; a good drink, but bad for the nerves. The school teacher was a plump complacent young half-caste with a patronising and clerical manner and a soft boneless hand: that was what the village had gained in place of a priest. His assistant was of a different type: alert, interested in his job for its own sake and not for the prestige it gave him, good with children, I feel sure. After we had eaten, he led us up the street to his own room, where we were to sleep. It was a small room in a tin-roofed hut beside the ruined church, which they used now as a school. He insisted that I should take his bed, my guide took my hammock, and our host tied up another for himself from the heavy beams.

I think the hut had once been a stable; now it seemed to be divided by thin partitions into three. In one division we slept, in another small children cried all night, and behind my head, in the third, I could hear the slow movements and the regular coughing of cows. I slept very badly in my clothes – I had cramp in my feet and a little fever from the sun. Somewhere around midnight there was the sound of a horse outside and a fist beat on the big bolted barn door. Nobody moved until a voice called, '*Con amistad*' (with friendship), and then the stranger was let in. I put on my electric torch and he moved heavily round the little room tying up a hammock; then he took off his revolver holster and lay down, and again I tried to sleep. It seemed to me that a woman's voice was constantly urging me to turn my face to the wall because that way I lay closer to Tabasco, the Atlantic, and home. I felt sick, but I was too tired to go outside and vomit. The hammocks creaked and something fluttered in the roof and a child wailed. There was no ventilation at all.

VISITING THE RUINS

Fate had got me somehow to Palenque, and so I thought I had better see the ruins, but it was stupid, after the long ride and the feverish night, to go next morning. And it was stupid, too, to start as late as seven, for it was nearly half-past nine before we reached them and the tropical sun was already high. It wasn't so much stiffness that bothered me now: it was the feel of fever, an overpowering nausea without the energy to vomit, a desire to lie down and never get up again, a continuous thirst. I had tried to get some mineral water to take with me, but our purchases had cleared the store right out, and all the time, if only I had known it, I was in one of the few places in Mexico where it was safe to drink the water. Springs rose everywhere; as we climbed through the thick hot forest they sparkled between the trees, fell in tiny torrents, spread out, like a Devonshire stream, over the pebbles in a little clearing. But I didn't drink, merely watched with sick envy the mules take their fill, afraid that the streams might be polluted farther up by cattle, as if any cattle could live in this deep forest: we passed the bleached skeleton of something by the path. So one always starts a journey in a strange land – taking too many precautions, until one tires of the exertion and abandons care in the worst spot of all. How I hated my mule, drinking where I wanted to drink myself and, like the American dentist, chewing all the time, pausing every few feet up the mountainside to snatch grasses.

Nobody had properly opened up the way to Palenque; sometimes the guide had to cut the way with his machete, and at the end the path rose at a crazy angle – it couldn't have been less than sixty degrees. I hung on to the pommel and left it all to the mule and anyway didn't care. And then at last, two hours and a half from the village, the ruins appeared.

I haven't been to Chichen Itzá, but judging from photographs of the Yucatán remains they are immeasurably more impressive than those of Palenque, though, I suppose, if you like wild nature, the setting of Palenque is a finer one – on a great circular plateau half-way up the mountainside, with the jungle falling precipitously below into the plain and rising straight up behind; in the clearing itself there is nothing but a few Indian huts, scrub and stone and great mounds of rubble crowned with low one-storey ruins of grey rock, so age-worn they have a lichenous shape and look more vegetable than mineral. And no shade anywhere until you've climbed the steep loose slopes and bent inside the dark cool little rooms like lavatories where a few stalactites have formed and on some of the stones are a few faint scratches which they call hieroglyphics. At first you notice only one of these temples or palaces where it stands in mid-clearing on its mound with no more importance than a ruined stone farm in the Oxford countryside, but then all round you, as you gaze, they open up, emerging obscurely from the jungle – three, four, five, six, I don't know how many gnarled relics. No work is in progress, and you can see them on the point of being swallowed again by the forest; they have looked out for a minute, old wrinkled faces, and will soon withdraw.

Well, I had told people I was here in Chiapas to visit the ruins and I had visited them; but there was no compulsion to see them, and I hadn't the strength to climb more than two of those slopes and peer into more than two of the cold snaky chambers. I thought I was going to faint; I sat down on a stone and looked down – at trees, and nothing but trees, going on and on out of sight. It seemed to me that this wasn't a country to live in at all with the heat and the desolation; it was a country to die in and leave only ruins behind. Last year Mexico City was shaken more than two hundred times by earthquake . . . One was looking at the future as well as at the past.

I slid somehow down on to the ground and saw my guide set off with the Indian who guards the site towards another palace; I couldn't follow. With what seemed awful labour I moved my legs back towards the Indian huts; a kind of stubbornness surged up through the fever – I wouldn't see the ruins, I wouldn't go back to Palenque, I'd simply lie down here and wait – for a miracle. The Indian hut had no walls; it was simply a twig shelter with a chicken or two scratching in the dust, and a hammock and a packing-case. I lay down in the hammock and stared at the roof; outside, according to authorities, were the Templo de las Leyes, the Templo del Sol, the Templo de la Cruz de Palenque. I knew what they could do with their temples . . . And farther off still England. It had no reality. You get accustomed in a few weeks to the idea of living or dying in the most bizarre surroundings. Man has a dreadful adaptability.

I suppose I dozed, for there were the Indian and the guide looking down at me. I could see the guide was troubled. He had a feeling of responsibility, and no Mexican cares for that. It's like a disused limb they have learned to do without. They said if I'd move into the other hut they would get me coffee. I felt that it was a trap: if they could make me move, they could make me get on that mule again and then would begin the two-and-a-half hour ride back to Palenque. An hour had lost meaning; it was like a cipher for some number too big to comprehend. Very unwillingly, very slowly, I shifted a dozen feet to another open hut and another hammock. A young Indian girl with big silver ear-rings and a happy sensual face began to make corn coffee – thin grey stuff like a temperance drink which does no harm. I said to the guide, without much hope, 'Why shouldn't we sleep here?' I knew his answer – mosquitoes; he was a man who liked his comforts. He brought up again that dream of a German with a beautiful daughter; I lay on my back, disbelieving. The *finca*, he said, was only a little way from Palenque. We'd go there tonight in the cool. I went on drinking corn coffee, bowl after bowl of it. I suppose it had some tonic effect, for I have a dim memory of suddenly thinking, 'Oh, hell, if I'm going to collapse, I may as well collapse in the village where the damned guide won't worry me . . .' I got on the mule and when once I was up it was as easy – almost – to sit there as in a hammock; I just held on to the pommel and let the mule do the rest. We slid down slowly over the tree-roots towards the plain. I was too exhausted to be frightened.

And when time did somehow come to an end, I fell off the mule and made straight for the schoolmaster's hammock and lay down. I wanted nothing except just not to move. The plump complacent schoolmaster sat on the steps and had a philosophical talk with a passing peasant – 'The sun is the origin of life,' a finger pointed upwards. I was too sick to think then of Rivera's school teachers in snowy white blessing with raised episcopal fingers the little children with knowledge, knowledge like this. 'That is true. Without the sun we should cease to exist.' I lay and drank cup after cup of coffee; the school teachers had lunch, but I couldn't eat, just went on drinking coffee, and sweating it out again. Liquid had no time to be digested; it came through the pores long before it reached the stomach. I lay wet through with sweat for four hours – it was very nearly like happiness. In the street outside nobody passed: it was too hot for life to go on. Only a vulture or two flopping by, and the whinny of a horse in a field.

SIGHT OF PARADISE

The *finca* did exist. When the sun was low I allowed myself to be persuaded back on to the mule, and there beyond a belt of trees it lay, only a quarter of an hour out of Palenque – over a rolling down and a stream with a broken bridge, among grazing cows, and as we waded through the river we could see the orange trees at the gate, a tulipan in blossom, and a man and woman sitting side by side in rocking-chairs on the veranda – as it might be the States, the woman knitting and the man reading his paper. It was like heaven.

There was no beautiful daughter, though I think there must once have been one, from a photograph I saw in the *sala* (she had married, I imagine, and gone away), but there was this middle-aged brother and sister with an unhurried and unsurprised kindliness, a big earthenware jar of fresh water with a dipper beside it, a soft bed with sheets, and, most astonishing luxury of all, a little sandy stream to wash in with tiny fish like sardines pulling at the nipples. And there were six-weeks-old copies of the New York papers and of *Time*, and after supper we sat on the veranda in the dark and the tulipan dropped its blossoms and prepared to bloom again with the day. Only the bullet-hole in the porch showed the flaw in Paradise – that this was Mexico. That and the cattle-ticks I found wedged firmly into my arms and thighs when I went to bed.

Next day I lay up at Herr R's – a bathe at six in the stream and another in the afternoon at five, and I should have felt fine if it hadn't been for the heat. My shirt was being washed and I had only a leather jacket lined with chamois to wear; the sweat poured down all day and made the leather smell, and the chamois came off on my skin. Like most Mexican things it was a bit fake. At the evening meal the lamp on the table made the heat almost unbearable; the sweat dripped into the food. And afterwards the beetles came scrambling up on to the porch. No, it wasn't after all quite Paradise, but it contained this invaluable lesson for a novice – not to take things too seriously, not to attend too carefully to other people's warnings. You couldn't *live* in a country in a state of preparedness for the worst – you drank the water and you went down to bathe in the little stream barefooted across the grass in spite of snakes. Happy the people who can learn the lesson: I could follow it for a couple of days and then it went, and caution returned – the expecting the worst of human nature as well as of snakes, the dreary hopeless failure of love.

Herr R had left Germany as a boy. His father wanted to send him to a military college, and he had told his father, 'If you do, I will run away.' He had run away and with the help of a friendly burgomaster had got papers and reached America. After that he'd never gone back. He had come down to Mexico as agent for various firms, and now he was settled on his own *finca*. There had been revolutions of course – he had lost crops and cattle to the soldiers and he had been fired on as he stood on his porch. But he took things with a dry cynical Lutheran humour; he had a standard of morality which nobody here paid even lip service to, and he fought them with their own weapons. When the *agraristas* demanded land he gave them it – a barren fifty acres he had not had the means to develop – and saved himself taxes. There had been, I suppose, that beautiful daughter (his wife was dead) and there were two sons at school now in Las Casas. He said of Las Casas, 'It's a very moral town.' I promised to take them out when I arrived: I should be in time for the great spring fair.

Walking in to the village to send his mail, we talked of the Church and Garrido. Though R was a Lutheran, he had no ill to say of any priest he had known here in the old days. Palenque had not been able to support a permanent priest, and the priests who came to serve Mass on feast days stayed usually with R at the *finca*. He had an honest Lutheran distaste for their dogmas which took him to queer lengths. There was one priest who was so sick and underfed that R insisted he should not go to Mass before he had breakfasted. To ensure this, when his guest was asleep, he locked him in, but when he went to call him he found the priest had escaped to church through the window. One felt that the Mexican priesthood in that politely unobtrusive act had shown up rather well. Another priest, one who sometimes came to Palenque, was an old friend of Garrido. He had great skill in brickwork, and Garrido invited him under safe conduct to come into Tabasco and undertake a building job. But friendship and safe conduct didn't save him – when the work was finished he was murdered, though possibly Garrido's followers had gone too far and the dictator may have had no hand in his friend's death.

Garrido's activities did not stop at the border. He sent his men over into Chiapas, and though in this state the churches still stand, great white shells like the skulls you find bleached beside the forest paths, he has left his mark in sacked interiors and ruined roofs. He organised an *auto-da-fé* in Palenque village, and R was there to see. The evil work was not done by the villagers themselves. Garrido ordered every man with a horse in Tabascan Montecristo to ride over the thirty-two miles and superintend – on pain of a fine of twenty-five pesos. And a relative of Garrido came with his wife by private plane to see that people were doing as they were told. The statues were carried out of the church while the inhabitants watched, sheepishly, and saw their own children encouraged to chop up the images in return for little presents of candy.

NIGHT ON THE PLAIN

It was six-thirty next day before we got properly started; the stiffness had been washed away in the shallow stream and my fever was gone, so we made far better time than

170

when we rode from Salto. In less than five hours we reached the Indian huts where we had eaten on our way. After stopping for coffee, we pushed on three leagues more – distances in Chiapas are measured always in leagues, a league being about three miles. This time we intended to make the journey in two stages. Just short of our destination a sudden blast of wind caught my helmet and the noise of crackling cardboard as I saved it scared the mule. It took fright and in the short furious gallop which followed I lost my only glasses. I mention this because strained eyes may have been one cause of my growing depression, the almost pathological hatred I began to feel for Mexico. Indeed, when I try to think back to those days, they lie under the entrancing light of chance encounters, small endurances, unfamiliarity, and I cannot remember why at the time they seemed so grim and hopeless.

The old Indian woman (you cannot measure the age of the poor in years; she may not have passed forty) had a burnt pinched face and dry hair like the shrivelled human head in the booth at San Antonio. She gave us bad corn coffee to drink and a plate of stringy chicken to eat with our fingers. I lay all afternoon and evening in my hammock slung under the palm-fibre veranda, swinging up and down to get a draught of air, staring at a yellow blossoming tree and the edge of the forest and the dull dry plain towards Salto, striking with a stick at the pigs and turkeys which came rooting in the dust under my legs. I dreaded the night. For one thing, I feared the mosquitoes here in the open, and though I had my net with me, I hadn't the moral courage to go against the opinion of the inhabitants, who said there were no mosquitoes at all. And for another, I feared, unreasonably, with a deep superstitious dread, the movements of the animals in the dark: the lean pigs with pointed tapir snouts, like the primeval ancestors of the English pig, the chickens, above all the turkeys – those hideous Dali heads, with the mauve surrealist flaps of skin they had to toss aside to uncover the beak or eyes. Suppose when night fell they chose to perch on the hammock? Where birds are concerned I lose my reason, I feel panic. The turkey cock blew out its tail, a dingy Victorian fan with the whalebone broken, and hissed with balked pride and hate, like an evil impotent old pasha. One wondered what parasites swarmed under the dusty layers of black feathers. Domestic animals seem to reflect the prosperity of their owners – only the gentleman farmer possesses the plump complacent good-to-live-with fowls and pigs; these burrowing ravenous tapirs and down-at-heel turkey cocks belonged to people living on the edge of subsistence.

And then a storm came cracking along the horizon through the heavy afternoon. It wandered in a circle, making the animals restless. They came in darts and rushes round the corner of the hut; the turkeys couldn't keep still; they scurried and hissed and raised their hideous and uneasy voices. I lay in the hammock and thought with longing of New York – Rockefeller Plaza rose in icicles of steel towards a cold sky; the ice-skaters moved in the small square under the stars; I thought of tea at the Waldorf, the little saucers of cinnamon sticks and cherries. This didn't seem to be the same world. I hit furiously at a pointed snout.

Punctually just before sunset the hens went to roost in the branches of a mimosa. The turkeys remained up later till dusk fell and then scrambled with difficulty into the overcrowded tree. Two children lit a fire at the end of a path going off towards the forest and then beat the path with brands from the fire. Why? Perhaps to ward off the spirits of the dead, perhaps to close the way out of the jungle to prowling animals. The sparks illuminated the mimosa tree with its strange dark feathered fruit. Somewhere on the plain too a great fire was burning, clearing the land for crops, and the lightning came edging up across the sky – the night was all flame and darkness. A few big drops began to fall.

At two o'clock everyone was asleep but the pigs and me; they still moved restlessly round the hut. Then the sound of horses came beating up across the plain – this is the romantic attraction of the Mexican countryside, the armed stranger travelling at night who may be a friend or an enemy. The door of the hut was barred shut. A horse whistled, stirrup irons jangled; when the lightning flared I could see four horses, and a man dismounting. He felt his way across the veranda and knocked at the door – '*Con amistad.*' His belt drooped with the weight of his gun. He seemed to be the leader; the three others dismounted and unsaddled, and for a moment time reversed and on the lawn under the forbidding wall I dreamed of Stevensonian adventure.

The night became alive again; the turkeys lumbered down from the tree and hissed and squawked; candles were lit and coffee served. There was political and incomprehensible talk around the table – hammocks were slung. The owner of the hut seemed to have some objection to the stranger's gun. He rolled up a trouser to show bullet scars in his leg. The stranger laughed, took off his belt, and tossed it into his hammock; the bearded arrogant faces shone in the candlelight. My guide slept on, and presently they too went to sleep. The leader had the table made up as a bed and – more sensible than I – draped a mosquito-net; the others wrapped themselves in serapes on the ground.

And then the storm broke overhead terrifyingly. The lightning struck the ground within a hundred yards; one tethered calf was thrown up by the light every thirty seconds or so, till I wearied of the sight of it. The night was bitterly cold and the rain poured in under the veranda, wetting my hammock. I put on my leather jacket, but I had no mackintosh; I retreated farther under the veranda, trying to avoid the men on the ground; the hens slept on in the mimosa. I was wet and frightened. I said 'Hail Marys' to myself and shivered with the cold. Why was I scared of this storm and not of the one in San Luis? I suppose the love of life which periodically deserts most men was returning: like sexual desire, it moves in cycles. At last the rain stopped and the lightning moved a little farther away. I got back into the wet hammock and dozed till four. I dreamed that I had returned from Mexico to Brighton for one day, and then had to sail again immediately for Veracruz. It was as if Mexico was something I couldn't shake off, like a state of mind.

8. A Village in Chiapas

At four-thirty I roused my guide and he saddled the mules by the light of an electric torch. Our stirring woke the strangers and they too began to saddle. We started at five-ten; I felt tired and stiff, and soon we were overtaken by the others and rode awhile in company, but I couldn't keep the pace (a mule against a horse) and we dropped behind. It was a cold dreary day of thin rain and cloud. It seemed an age before we reached the banana plantations and then the river again, the unsaddling, the canoe across – the spool, a little frayed, unwound the other way. Just before nine we rode into Salto and I jolted into a trot for the sake of appearance. In this drab lifeless village one had the sense of returning home. I swore – in vain – that I would never ride a mule again, if I could possibly travel any other way.

Things change all the time, everywhere; people move and go away; even in remote familiar villages you are disappointed by change. Here, too: I might have been away a year, not four days. There had been a daughter's wedding at my lodging the night before; all the partitions had been pulled down, and the room I'd slept in no longer existed at all; there were stacks of empty 'gaseosa' bottles instead. I changed and went to the cantina; I was determined to have there the orgy I had dreamed about in Palenque. I drank two bottles of orangeade and felt very sick indeed. So I listened to the storekeeper's excuses with satisfaction. He had been unable to find a guide to take me to Yajalon, that village in the foothills which was the first stage to Las Casas: it was, apparently, the wrong time of year – all the coffee had come down from the hills and the mules returned. But by great good fortune an aeroplane was leaving that afternoon – it should have left yesterday; it had come from Villahermosa, but it had been unable to go farther because of the low clouds; it was doubtful too whether it would be able to leave today. When was it due to start? One o'clock. I looked at the ridge of mountain above Salto: the clouds were half-way down the slope, and the thin rain fell continuously. There seemed no hope.

I had an early lunch with my landlord, his daughter, and the bridegroom – a middle-aged unshaven man with bad teeth. My landlord wore an air of quiet dignity like a suit he had slipped on in my absence; lunch went decorously on with subdued gaiety. It was only eleven o'clock, and while the bride was searching for her groom's revolver I walked out to try to pass the time, down the street to the river bank. On the little landing-ground there was a tiny scarlet plane, and with anxiety I watched the pilot give the propeller a twist. I ran for a canoe, sent for my luggage, and hurriedly crossed the stream, and who should come to greet me on the other side but my friend Ortega? But there was change even here: his nose was stuck over with plaster, and his face bore fresh scars. He had been trying out a plane in Villahermosa and the engine had failed. 'It was a British plane,' he said with gentle mockery.

There was one other passenger for Yajalon, Señor Gómez, the chief storekeeper there, to whom I had a letter of introduction from the aviation company. As the plane was due to leave at one o'clock, he, poor man, had not yet appeared. 'We'll give him five minutes,' Ortega said, 'and then we'll start.' You couldn't see the top of the mountain ridge for cloud; he said, 'I don't know if we can get through, but we'll go up and take a look round.' My suitcase arrived and we climbed into the little cramping plane – just room for four passengers. 'If we can't get through,' he said, 'we'll have to come back here.' The river dropped like a knife and was obscured immediately by thin cloud; a magnificent landscape opened up of rock and forest and sharp precipitous ridges; the low clouds broke at just the right points and let us through; an inky storm-cloud lay like a threat down a mountainside on our right. We climbed to about three thousand four hundred feet, and more mountains appeared above the propeller blade; we didn't fly over the mountains, we went between; long rocky slopes lifted to our level on either side; the world slanted up all round as if we were diving. 'We're through,' he shouted in my ear. We bumped downwards towards a white church on a little plateau completely surrounded by mountains; we were like a billiard ball dropping into a pocket. We landed very roughly, Ortega tugging at the joystick; when we came to a standstill, he said it had not been working properly – he thought he would have to take the plane back to Villahermosa. I was glad he hadn't told me that before we started.

And now for the Norwegian lady . . . A boy took my bag and led the way: a great square unused shuttered church, weeds growing out of the bell towers where the vultures perched; coffee laid out to dry all along the stone walks of the little plaza like yellow gravel; a little cobbled street between white bungalow houses, and the mountains terminating everything. The air after Salto even at noon seemed beautifully fresh: the village was two thousand feet up; I hadn't been so high since Orizaba. Through an open door in one of the little houses I came suddenly on a tall tragic woman with hollow handsome features and a strange twisted mouth – like an expression of agony – talking rapidly in Spanish. She broke off and stared at me. I asked rather stupidly if she could recommend a hotel.

Of course there was no hotel in Yajalon, but lodging could – sometimes – be got, she said, with a Señor López. She sent her daughters with me – two thin little blonde girls of fourteen and eleven, startlingly beautiful in a land where you grow weary of black and oily hair and brown sentimental eyes. The elder one disliked me on sight – I was the stranger breaking their narrow familiar life with demands – for lodging, conversation, company. They could both speak Spanish and an Indian dialect – the Camacho, I think – and a few words of English. I got a room – a wooden plank bed in a storeroom, behind the counter a few packets of candles, some empty tins, a few straw sombreros. I was to pay two pesos a day, and that included food.

At tea-time I went up and called on Fru R. She had coffee ready and cake and we drank on and on under the porch of the patio where her coffee was drying. A separator hummed in a shed like a harvest engine in an English autumn. That was to become a daily routine for a week – I was to look forward to it from the moment I got up in the morning. Somehow I had to pass the days till five o'clock, and then all went well for two hours. It was a kindness impossible adequately to repay.

Poor lady, her position was tragic enough. Both she and her husband were Norwegian by birth, and they had both gone to the States to work. Her husband had bought a coffee farm in the mountains above Yajalon and they had prospered in a modest way – they had been happy, until first her eldest daughter had died and then her husband, and she had been robbed of all their savings by her *compadre* while her husband was dying. (A *compadre* meant a fellow god-parent, a spiritual relationship regarded in Mexico as a close one.) She was left with practically no money, two daughters, and two sons. She had sent the boys to the States to her mother, to be educated, and she hadn't seen them for four years and was unlikely to see them for many years more. She scraped enough money out of separating and drying coffee to keep them at high school, and one of them had gone on to an agricultural college and would soon have a job. Her dream was that one day he would have a good enough post to return and fetch them away from Mexico. Her daughters she taught herself – the small one was learning *The Charge of the Light Brigade*; she got the lessons by post from America, and held periodic examinations in the little darkened parlour. And all the time the elder one was growing up; in a year, by Mexican standards, she would be marriageable; it is difficult to conceive the pain and anxiety of this mother.

She was a Lutheran like my host at Palenque, but she too had watched without sympathy the sacking of the church. Men had ridden in from outside just as at Palenque; the whole *auto-da-fé* had been arranged by the Government people at Tuxtla. They had burned the saints and statues. There had been one great golden angel . . . the villagers stood weeping while it burned.

They were all Catholic here . . . except the school-master, whom I would meet at my lodging. Like all the school teachers now, he was a politician. There had been a fiesta the night before at the school and he had made an impassioned speech on the oil expropriations (public affairs, which hadn't crossed the burning plateau to Palenque, had overtaken me now: I was not to hear the last of them). He had appealed to the people, 'Get rid of the gringos,' and, of course, sitting there in a back seat, she knew she was the only gringo in the village – except for a German who kept a little store and did photography.

I asked if here in Chiapas there was any hope of a change (I had found such a sense of hopelessness in Tabasco) and I learned from her for the first time of the rather wild dream that buoys up many people in Chiapas: the hope of a rising which will separate Chiapas, Tabasco, Yucatán, and Quintana Roo from the rest of Mexico and of an alliance with Catholic Guatemala. All plots against the Mexican Government get somehow confused with this dream, so that she spoke as if Cedillo were behind it, and mentioned a Catholic general, Pineda, of whom I was to hear more in Las Casas. German arms, she said, were being brought in by night from Guatemala and deposited in the mountains by a German airman.

I went back in the dark to the hotel: there is no street lighting in a Mexican village, and the dark falls early and makes the nights very long. I saw my fellow-lodgers for the first time at supper, which we ate at a table under the veranda by the light of an oil-lamp – a stout, white-toothed mestizo school teacher with an air of monotonous cheeriness (and one obscene English word which he repeated, with huge amusement, day after day), his pregnant wife, and his small son of a year and a half who ran up and down the floor of the *sala* every morning, admonishing in his father's manner the child nurse who with them occupied one room off the *sala*. And there were others who dropped in for meals only – a few grizzled, friendly men, a young married couple with their baby, and a clerk I grew to loathe, a mestizo with curly sideburns and two yellow fangs at either end of his mouth. He had an awful hilarity and a neighing laugh which showed the empty gums. He wore a white tennis shirt open at the front and he scratched himself underneath it. I didn't know that first evening that I was to be stuck in the village for a week – an aeroplane for Las Casas was due in three days; I couldn't foresee how familiar these faces round the table were to become, so that I could go nowhere in the village without seeing one or other of them – the mestizo looking up from his typewriter in the Presidencia and showing his fangs as I went by, a grizzled man waving a hand from a doorway, the schoolmaster's rich, powerful voice sounding all across the little plaza from his schoolroom, and the young married man pulling up his horse outside the cantina. It gave one the sensation of being under observation all the time.

There was nothing to do after supper, after the ceremonial gargle from the tin mug and the spit on the dirt floor, but watch the men playing rummy or sit on a rocking-chair in the *sala* admiring their wives and their children. A little Indian boy from the mountains belonging to nobody at all squatted on the threshold, staring in with wide wonder at civilisation – the square stone-paved room with all the chairs arranged round the edge, and the walls hung with big family photographs and monstrous wedding favours and embroidered carnations in scarlet silk. Round the walls in order stood a packing-case, a sewing-machine, a wooden sofa, three hard chairs, two rocking-chairs, a table with a radio which didn't work, a gramophone, and two oil-lamps. Here and there hung velvet streamers of mauve, orange and white; and at the door the little Indian face peered in with astonishment at the grandeur.

I went to bed and tried to pull out cattle-ticks, caught a flea, and lay by the light of a candle listening to rats rushing about overhead. I was overcome by a sense of disgust – Las Casas, that 'moral' city, that 'very Catholic' town, seemed like a promise of cleanness. Well, I told myself, only two days more of this and then the plane and a few hours' flight and I am there – in time for Holy Week and the Spring Fair.

ALAS, FOR TROY!

But in the morning, of course, the plane proved far less certain. Señor Gómez was not at the store – for hadn't we left him behind at Salto? – and his son, a dapper Chinese-looking youth, would promise nothing. The plane would 'probably' come on Wednesday, but he wouldn't take money for the ticket: with Serrabia's company at Tuxtla you could never tell. Sometimes he was a week, a fortnight, late.

Nothing to do all day till evening came but drink pale ginger beer at the cantina – real beer was still as expensive as in Tabasco – and eat chocolate, Wong's chocolate, almost the only kind obtainable in Mexico, the home of chocolate, a pale insipid imitation of English and Swiss makes. Nothing to do but stare out at the low white-washed houses under their mottled tiles and the clouds passing almost imperceptibly above the mountains. Canes were tied crosswise over closed doors (a religious symbol?), and over others black bags hung upside down (superstition?). The Indians with wispy hair on lip and chin and sad withdrawn faces came down from the mountains, across the little bridges, into Yajalon – naked to the waist, with pointed oriental hats of straw, bowed double under enormous crates supported by a leather belt across the forehead, plodding in with long pastoral staffs to squat by the side of roads, named absurdly even in this village Cinco de Mayo and Madero, and eat bananas out of a satchel. The schoolmaster would sit down beside me in the *sala*, very large and cheery and Socialist and optimistic, and tell me how the Spaniards had oppressed the Indians, making them into 'mere beasts of burden', and as he spoke the sad patient procession would plod by – men and women – just as it had for centuries. And afterwards, relieved of their loads, they would come peering inside the *sala* like dogs – cut off from intercourse, speaking no Spanish. The priests, who had learned the Indian dialects and acted as necessary interpreters between one village and another, who had shown interest in them as human beings, had been driven away. As for the school teacher, his large brown eyes were compassionate, he spoke with pity of their past, and knew no Indian dialect at all. In bad years they say hundreds starve to death, but no one knows – they retire like wounded animals into the mountains and forests, eating berries, lasting as long as they can, seeking no pity. And in the mountains, as I saw later, they have what the people of Yajalon do not possess – their crosses, their places of worship; Christianity existing like themselves wild and cut off and incomprehensible. After lunch the school teacher played the guitar, singing lustrous sentimental songs – 'Have I a Rose in My Field?' while the hot sun beat down on the outcasts. In the lavatory at the bottom of the patio some German had written up in careful loving script the lines about '*Wein, Weib und Gesang*'.

And then at last evening would come and cup after cup of coffee at Fru R's, and sad conversation as the dusk fell. Somehow the conversation turned to worms – perhaps I had remarked on the swollen bellies of the Mexican children. Her own daughter, she said, once got so stout that her dress would hardly meet, and she purged her of twenty worms, some of them a foot and a half long. Her children, she went on, speaking casually of the inevitable sickness, were always stubborn: they seldom evacuated more than half a dozen worms at a time. It was like the grave, the earth taking over before its day. Then the school teacher and a friend of his dropped in and the conversation became cautious and unilluminating. Flames flapped on the mountainside when the darkness dropped – fields being burned for a corn crop. The school teacher began oddly to complain that parents no longer felt a proper responsibility for their children, staring out across the God-banished village.

That night it was very cold and the rats were quieter; in bed I wore a vest, wool pants and tropical trousers, and my leather jacket, yet I was still cold. I dreamed I visited an art exhibition to buy a present for my wife. I had marked in the catalogue 'The Trojan Women', but it turned out to be, not a picture, but a surrealist object of black rubber, rather like a vacuum cleaner, which moved across the floor on wheels and said, 'Alas, for Troy!'

MISS BOWEN AND THE RAT

Next day there was still no news of the plane. It was expected. There was hope. Drinking ginger beer, buying chocolate, walking up and down the two parallel streets, lying on my bed reading Cobbett, somehow I got through the day – Cobbett on Tenterden, most English of market towns, 'It consists of one street which is, in some places, more perhaps than two hundred feet wide. On one side of the street the houses have gardens before them, from twenty to seventy feet deep. The town is upon a hill; the afternoon was very fine, and just as I rose the hill and entered the street, the people had come out of church and were moving along towards their houses. It was a very fine sight. Shabbily dressed people do not go to church. I saw, in short, drawn out before me the dress and beauty of the town; and a great many very, very pretty girls I saw; and saw them, too, in their best attire.' Out through the open door in the heavy sun I could see the Indians pass. I seemed to know everything. I might have been here a year. There was nothing in this country so beautiful as an English village, but then beauty is only an emotion in the observer, and perhaps to someone these forests and crags, these withdrawn and gentle Indians, abandoned churches, the mule teams ringing down the hillside might have given an effect of beauty. I felt something wrong in myself – tiredness and anxiety and homesickness can turn the heart to stone as easily as cruelty, sin, the violent act, the rejection of God.

That evening the Norwegian lady seemed more than

ever haggard, wide-eyed, distrait, given to bursts of hysterical laughter. She had once, I learned, been in an American beauty parlour – the awful undreamable changes life makes in our destiny – and the queer shape of her mouth was due to food poisoning which had paralysed her here in Yajalon for eight months. Looking in her shelves of books half ruined by the tropics, I found to my joy a copy of Elizabeth Bowen's *The Hotel* – the only novel by Miss Bowen I had never read. Apparently Mr R had belonged to the American Book-of-the-Month Club. (I never thought I should bless the existence of such clubs.) So I took the book off with me and nearly trod on a rat in the dark street; it slipped from under my feet like a rabbit.

Sitting in the *sala* after supper, I saw another rat, small, black, and elongated, run up the wall like a lizard and in through the open door of my bedroom. There was nothing to be done about it. I went into my room and shut the door: better to have one certain rat than a whole family, for at night I could hear them chasing one another in the *sala*. I am scared of rats, and it was an awful and absurd night that I spent with a candle stuck in wax on my chair, and the brandy I had bought in Veracruz (poisonous stuff), reading Elizabeth Bowen and trying to keep my mind off the rat which moved discontentedly in the shadows. In the *sala* I could hear them jumping on and off the chairs. My second candle lasted till about two and then I lit another – but Elizabeth Bowen was better than candles and bad brandy. She was writing about a familiar and recognisable world, and it was her world, the withered spinsterish world of English people in an Italian hotel, which imposed its acid reality. The rat, the brandy, and the candle, the plank bed in the middle of Chiapas couldn't compete – the rat ceased to bother me; they weren't real, they were fantastic; who could believe in them? I fell asleep at last and found myself in a big Georgian house surrounded by long and unkempt grass. A lady called Madame Talleoni was going to open a school, but how could she do so while her pet bird was loose and wildly angry – a dry twiggy animal with the anatomy of a turkey or a peacock, or a vulture? 'You can't blame it,' she said. 'They sent it to me in a box without shoes.'

MASS BAPTISM

But next night wasn't so good, with only *Kristin Lavransdatter* to fight the rats with. The aeroplane, of course, had not come. They said it would come next day; but as they wouldn't take the fare, I feared the worst. The pedestrian tale of medieval Norway was not so real as Chiapas, though it reminded me a little of Mexico in its casual violence and hard indifferent life. I remembered the story the German had told me of his young sons: how they had gone into the forest near Palenque to kill a stag and one striking the body with his machete felt the axe slip into his brother's leg. Somehow he got home upon his horse, and then came the long wait for the doctor from Montecristo who did not arrive till early morning as he had lost his way in the forest. That was the saga life.

At coffee Fru R told me how a priest had come unobtrusively into Yajalon a month ago from the south. He stayed the night with Señor López, who was a strong Catholic, and held a kind of mass baptism of several hundred children, including the mayor's, at two pesos a head. Fru R, who acted as godmother to some of the children, was present and she heard one woman turned away, because she was fifty centavos short, and told to find the rest. It is a depressing fact that persecution does not necessarily produce Father Pros. Any priests who remained in Chiapas were under no control; the Bishop had been banished; there was no court of appeal against a corrupt priest; and who can judge the temptation to such a priest, living in a Godless state, seeing the world and the flesh grossly triumphant among the swaggering do-nothing *pistoleros* of Tuxtla, to make what money he could while he could? At any moment he might be imprisoned, or banished to join his half-starved brother priests in Mexico City, with nothing to hope for but a good death.

Some time that day a mule team brought in the post with the President's message to the people. It was stuck up on the wall and the mestizo read it out – with great eloquence – to everybody. I was seldom to get away from the oil question after that. Luckily here I had arrived *before* the message; even a Mexican couldn't switch over quickly enough to regard me as the Enemy. For that experience I had to wait for Las Casas. But one had to admire the organisation that enabled the message to be printed, to reach Tabasco on the *Ruiz Cano*, which sailed the day after the expropriation decree, and to penetrate even to this derelict northern territory of Chiapas so promptly.

UNHOLY BIRTH

Next day, of course, no plane. I had arrived on Sunday and now it was Thursday. The telegram from Tuxtla said the plane would arrive on Saturday. Next week was Holy Week and I had promised myself to spend that period in Catholic Las Casas, to see how it was observed in a city where the churches were open – so I was told – but the priests not allowed inside. On Friday the post was to leave, and if they had a spare mule it would be the cheapest way of getting to Las Casas, but it was un-utterably slow: the journey would take four or five days at least. I went to young Gómez and asked him if he could find me a guide and mules to do the journey in three days. He said he'd try, and another long day dragged on – ginger beer at the cantina, the walk up to the edge of town, to the nearly dry *barranca* where the women did their washing, where the butcher's shop stood on piles and the vultures came flapping through the air (I counted twenty-five gathered in his yard).

There was one other gringo I found in town besides Fru R – Herr W, a German, who kept a tiny photo-graphic store. He spoke no English, and we got on as best we could with a little Spanish and French. God knows what had landed him in that village. He was probably agent for something, but I never learned what. The wooden wall of his tiny shack was covered with innocent pictures of naked girls and Plaisirs de Paris torn off the covers of magazines; among them, rigidly, the face of Hitler. Half a dozen books and cardboard boxes of rather bad photographs – that was the rest. Was it he who had written '*Wein, Weib und Gesang*' in the *excusado* of Señor Lopez? He was a small neat man with a little fair moustache, aged about forty-five; I turned over yellowing picture after picture of Yajalon – weddings and funerals and fiestas – the films too badly washed to last, and realised suddenly that I was expected to buy, at an exorbitant price. We agreed that England and Germany together could rule Europe; it didn't seem worth quarrelling in Yajalon about what sort of Europe that was likely to be.

Coffee at the Norwegian's; news from Gómez that there were no mules obtainable, but the aeroplane would almost certainly arrive on Saturday; rats at night: one day was just like another. Reading *Kristin Lavransdatter* by candlelight, reading the account of the primitive birth, I couldn't help thinking of how far worse the horror of birth must be here to Catholics. At least in medieval Norway there was the priest. But in Chiapas now you are robbed of the one blessing granted the parent in return for almost unbearable anxieties – the holiness of the child. You are not allowed to shelter innocence in your house. If you are lucky, the child may be baptised – if it lives – a few years later when a priest visits the village secretly; but that tardy baptism is not the same, after the world has taken its tarnishing account. The children have no bank of sanctity to draw on – the unstained Christian years – and we cannot tell what human nature may owe to that past fund of holiness. It is not inconceivable that the worst evil possible to natural man may be found years hence in Mexico.*

CLAUSTROPHOBIA

Next day the rain woke me. The clouds were right down over the roofs: you couldn't see even the foot of the mountains; there was no hope of an aeroplane reaching

* Of course in the absence of a priest, anybody is allowed to baptise, but I doubt whether in this isolated and ignorant state such baptisms are ever practised.

Yajalon in weather like this. Hunched in the thin rain, the Indians came through – a curious automatic walk, Tibetan rags, creeping by like insects in single file with their long poles. I could hear Señor López, the fanged mestizo, and the schoolmaster joking loudly. It is true what their admirers write of the Mexicans, that they are always cheerful whatever their circumstances; but there is something horribly immature in their cheeriness: no sense of human responsibility; it is all one with the pistol-shot violence.

One got an appalling claustrophobia in this small place wedged in among the mountains round its locked decaying church, and time just going by and the aeroplane always coming tomorrow. At coffee that night young Gómez brought the dreaded telegram from Serrabia, 'Shall not come tomorrow. Will advise you later when I can pick up passengers.' Not even the promise now of any future date. I felt desperate to get away. I implored young Gómez to find me mules and offered him an exorbitant sum if I could start next morning early. He sent me a message that night: all was arranged. The mules would be ready for me at six. I hardly slept at all what with hope, and the rats noisier than they had ever been behind the counter in my room.

THE RAIN

And of course next morning the rain was pouring down, and six-forty-five came and no mules. As soon as the store opened I went to Gómez. He said the mules would come if it stopped raining, but it was impossible to travel in the mountains in this rain. And again, casually, he brought up the aeroplane. It might be here on Monday, and what a lot of time I should have wasted by not stopping for it. They said the same thing at López's, with other arguments. The schoolmaster said I didn't realise how bad the road was; it was precipitous, dreadful; he would never go that way himself. He showed with his hands how narrow the paths were along the mountainside. It would take me four, five days, and the aeroplane would have come in long before that. I began to feel a little scared myself, to be resigned to wait. And then rather terrifyingly everything altered. Fru R's little blonde daughter stood in the dripping rain with a stranger, a small scrubby-bearded man. He would go with me in spite of the rain and for ten pesos less than Gómez's muleteer. He must go up to a *finca* and fetch the mules, but he would be back by midday. He vanished in cloud.

I couldn't help remembering then what people had told me about the roads, remembering too that the other muleteers wouldn't stir in this rain. How long did rain like this usually last? I asked everybody, and all gave the same answer – four days.

To pass the time I went with the schoolmaster to Herr W's to have a game of chess. He checkmated me in six moves. I was distracted by Herr W, who stood just behind me telling me it was quite impossible, it was fantastic, to dream of travelling in this weather. The mountains would be impassable. But the guide, I said. He'd never been to Las Casas, Herr W said. He knows the road only by hearsay. I began to hope that after all he would not return with the mules. Then young Gómez arrived. What was this he had heard, that I was starting without his muleteer? Well, I said, his man had not turned up and the other had said he would go, and now I had sent him for the mules and I could hardly change my mind after putting him to all that trouble. I went on explaining, longing for contradiction. But they wouldn't contradict; they would only go on filling me with misgivings. 'He doesn't know the road,' young Gómez said. 'Wait for the plane, it will come on Monday or Tuesday; I am travelling in it to Las Casas too.' And then the strange muleteer turned up, and there was no more to be said.

9. Across the Mountains
to Las Casas

There was an awful sense of unreality about the start. Fru R packed in my rucksack a bottle of drink – a kind of home-made advocaat, two sausage sandwiches, some candles, a little cheese, a serape, and a great lump, the size of a doll's head, of brown sugar. I left behind with her, a poor return for all her kindness, my hammock and mosquito-net. It was pouring with rain. A few men stood in doorways smiling heartlessly. The rain dripped in under the collar of my mackintosh cape, and the mules stepped gloomily over the cobbles at a funeral pace. It was one o'clock in the afternoon – absurd hour in the tropics to start a journey. I couldn't believe we should reach Las Casas in three days; I couldn't really believe we should ever get away from Yajalon. I was weighed down by a sense of foolishness and impotence as we picked our way through the *barranca* at the edge of the village. In a few hours we should be returning – the gesture of defiance having been made – and I should wait for the aeroplane, reading *Kristin Lavransdatter* and listening to the rats.

There were three mules, one for each of us and one for my suitcase; sometimes the muleteer tried to drag the third mule, sometimes he drove it in front of him; for two hours we proceeded very slowly, step by step through the drenching rain while he lashed and dragged and lashed, calling out in a high hysterical voice, '*Mula.*

O mula.' Then quite suddenly we passed out of the rain (it continued in Yajalon for another two days), but progress was still very slow in water-logged clay; we climbed steeply up and down, with only twenty or thirty yards of level ground to trot on between each climb. I found my stirrups were far too short; it became a painful effort to keep my feet in them. At an ungainly harassed trot we passed through the only Mexican village we were to see till next noon and began seriously to climb, in long spirals, up into the mountains.

On a ridge about a thousand feet above Yajalon the mule with the suitcase ran away. The muleteer had dismounted to adjust the load, and the mule set quietly off at a smart trot down the mountain towards Yajalon about three and a half hours away. My guide lost his head: instead of pursuing on his own mule, he set off on foot, crying and praying hysterically to the Mother of God down the mountainside. Time passed; I saw the mule climbing briskly up the opposite slope, the size of a toy animal, and fifty yards behind it a toy man. Then they both disappeared altogether, and dusk began to fall. I was alone with the two mules – it seemed to be the end of *that* journey.

In the mountains the sun sets early – the horizon is high up the sky. I waited half an hour; the sun dropped out of sight, the forests became black below their gilded tips. The world was all steel and gold, like war. The opposite slope dropped into obscurity, untenanted. It seemed to me that I had better go back too, but I had no experience of driving a spare mule. I tried to drag it, but it dug in its heels and stuck and my mule went on; it was I who was being dragged – backwards out of the saddle, not the mule. Then I tried a little more successfully to drive it in front of me. When the path was sometimes so narrow between the rocky sides that I couldn't keep my feet in the stirrups but had to lift them up behind me, and when at the same time it descended, unevenly, at an angle of forty-five degrees, it wasn't easy to avoid a collision with the loose mule in front. It was easier climbing up the opposite side, and we began to progress slowly and steadily back through the dusk towards Yajalon. We should arrive there, I calculated, if the mules didn't lose the way (I could never find it) before midnight.

But things weren't so bad as that. A quarter of an hour back on the path I found the muleteer with the mule restrapping the suitcase. There was a big bleeding gash in the mule's neck, so I suppose he had taken his revenge, promptly, violently, without sentiment. We had lost nearly an hour, but he still hoped to reach the *finca* of Santa Cruz – a Mexican farm – for the night, but in the dark, in a gloomy Teutonic forest of pines, we lost our way. We went on and on, climbing and descending, the mules slipping on tree-roots, until about seven we mounted to a little windy clearing where three or four mud-and-wattle huts stood black and silent in the moonless dark.

The whole scene – the round huts, a woman passing from one to another carrying fire, the black forest above and below – was African, and so was the courtesy of the old ragged man who came out to greet us. He couldn't give us food, there was no food – his hands were like last year's leaves – but he set a small boy boiling some black thick coffee, and when I asked him if there was a hammock in which I could sleep, he replied with gentle aristocratic courtesy, 'Ah, for a hammock the señor must go to a town. Here he must expect only the luck of the road.'

And the luck of the road was not so bad . . . the rats were there, of course, for the old man's hut was a store-house for corn, but it contained what you seldom find in Mexico, the feel of human goodness. We passed my brandy bottle round and lit one of Fru R's candles – the only other light came from the embers in the centre of the floor. The old man gave up his bed to me, a dais of earth covered with a straw mat set against the mound of corn where the rats were burrowing. It was bitterly cold, too cold even to take off my boots; the door was shut fast, the old man and the guide and the little boy curled up on the floor, and I lay on the hard earth bed almost happy. The fanged mestizo slipped away – reading out the President's message – all the blarney and the evil will of Mexican townsmen, the decaying church, the vul-tures, the rubble in Villahermosa, 'we die like dogs'; all that was left was an old man on the edge of starvation living in a hut with the rats, welcoming the strangers without a word of payment, gossiping gently in the dark. I felt myself back with the population of heaven.

ARCTIC NIGHT

If only Mexicans had been taller! The shortness of the stirrup leathers was torture. We started at six next morning, after a mug of coffee, and before we had been gone an hour my legs ached with the strain. It was after nine before we passed the *finca* where we had been supposed to sleep, but the guide insisted that all the same we must keep to schedule and arrive at Cancuk that night. He painted Cancuk in glowing colours, though he had never been there – there was a Presidencia, so it must be quite a large place where we could get beds, drink in a cantina . . . It was like the promise of Palenque all over again – only much more inaccurate.

We got to a village for food about eleven – a few little dry strips of bacon and tortillas – and my guide tried to lengthen my stirrups with a small scrap of leather he had found. It was no good; after an hour the torture began again. It killed completely what otherwise I might have taken pleasure in – the amazing beauty of nature. The scenery of northern Chiapas is very like that between Veracruz and Orizaba – huge gorges covered with forest, sometimes grey walls of rock falling like a curtain for five hundred feet, trees grasping a foothold in the cracks and growing upwards parallel to the rock. We had to climb seven thousand feet before we reached Las Casas, but for every thousand feet we rose we dropped six hundred. The mules slid down, strained upwards; towards the end of the day we walked for an hour to rest them. After nine hours I began to feel that the words '*Mula. Mula. Echa, mula*' were graven on my brain for ever – that was all this lost magnificent forgotten countryside was to me – '*Mula. Mula. Echa, mula.*'

There were no more villages before Cancuk, only occasional Indian settlements, perched on rocky plateaux above the path, one with a little wattle watch-tower from which an Indian stared down at us as we climbed wearily upwards. After ten hours I began to protest – I didn't mind to a day or so, I said, when we reached Las Casas. Couldn't we stop for the night at one of these Indian villages? I always got the same reply: if we stop we cannot reach Las Casas tomorrow. But that wasn't, I think, the only reason. Indians made my guide uneasy; they were the unpredictable. Little men not much over five feet tall, dressed in long smocks with black mops of hair roughly fringed over the forehead, they came stepping quickly down the rocks more sure-footed than mules, a machete swinging at the hip. Only one man in each village was said to know a little Spanish with which to communicate with the new race; it was forbidden to the others to speak with them. The guide couldn't put up in their presence that Mexican façade of *bonhomie* – the embrace, the spar, the joke – with which they hide from themselves the cruelty and treachery of their life.

And so he persisted that we must reach Cancuk, that fine town with its cantinas and its Presidencia, and at last pointing across the valley to the opposite mountainside he showed me the church: what seemed at that distance a great white cathedral flashed in the late sun out of the dark evergreen trees leagues away. After eleven hours I did begin to get a kind of second wind; it was growing cool, and as we mounted lazily through a pine forest and saw the sun set on our right hand and munched sweet bread out of our saddlebags, I was touched by the faintest feeling of romance. Years ago, I couldn't doubt that, this would have seemed romance to me, to be riding slowly at evening through the mountains, going south towards I didn't know what in an unfamiliar land, the crack and pad of the slow mules' feet on stone and turf, and the immense serrated waste of almost uninhabited country, only an Indian watch-tower leagues away.

We must have risen nearly three thousand feet that day, and at six thousand night fell with bitter cold and wind. And I had lost my serape. It had fallen from my saddle early in the day without my noticing it. But all would be well at Cancuk, the guide said; we could buy a new one in the stores. Stores! We suddenly came round a shoulder of rock on to the church itself. The fireflies moved about us, big and brilliant and close: I could see the light in the tail switched on and off like an electric torch – it was almost the only light in Cancuk. The great cathedral was, after all, nothing but a small square white-washed church, grass-grown and locked and unused, a poor and simple building with two small bell towers and oval plaques below them containing little wreaths, like the plates in Victorian keepsakes where you write the owner's name. And as for Cancuk, the eye could take it in at a glance. It was like a West African village with the tin-roofed verandaed Presidencia taking the place of the chief's hut, standing on the small plateau opposite the church, with the thatched mud huts drifting up and down the mountainside. A big bonfire flared a sort of rough welcome outside the cantina, an icy wind beat the flames; and the cantina was an unwalled shelter filled with men; beds were raised on stakes from the ground and covered with serapes. A tall scarred man like a Moor stalked round the fire with a blanket over his head, and a woman knelt beside a pot making coffee. When we rode up the beds heaved on their piles and rows of eyes peered out of the darkness like a cave of cats: there wasn't an inch of space to spare in the windswept shelter.

We were out of luck. We had overtaken the mail, and there wasn't a bed to be got in Cancuk. There were two beds in the mayor's office and they were both occu-pied. We could choose between the floor and a narrow bench behind the table. I chose the bench, but first I opened my bag and began to dress against the cold – a vest, two shirts, two pairs of pants, my leather jacket.

I was cold even then. But supper tasted good with the heat of the fire on the face – beans and tortillas and admirable coffee, pieces of salt bacon and fried eggs (fried eggs were not easy to eat in the fingers, even with the help of a tortilla). This for the two of us – and corn for the mules – cost eighteen pence.

And then the hard bench wedged between wall and table in the big bare office. The men in the beds breathed heavily, and I slept in fits and starts. About eleven a fist beating on the barred door woke us all. I switched on my torch and saw the doubtful bearded faces lifted from the beds; somebody felt for his revolver holster, and then the password came, '*Con amistad.*' It was the mayor. He showed no surprise at finding four men sleeping in his office. A young brisk man in a wide-awake hat like a western sheriff's, he had been riding hard from Las Casas and had made the journey in twelve hours. A freezing wind blew in with him, and his horse whinnied in the dark.

A GROVE OF CROSSES

I woke the guide at three in the morning; the mules had to be fed, and then I hoped to get away by four. Some people said Las Casas was eleven leagues away and some fourteen – thirty-three or forty-two miles; it doesn't sound very far when you think of cartroads and gentle English hills, but on these rough tracks, climbing and descending, distances are nearly doubled. And we didn't leave at four, for the mules had completely disappeared. The muleteer went wailing through the darkness with my torch; I could see it flash across the bone-white church; he was praying and close to tears, as he had been that first day when the mule ran away. Poor man, he was highly wrought; he wasn't cut out for a muleteer. There was nothing to do but wait for daylight on the mayor's bench. The next time I got up, the stars were still out, but a great fire was blowing beside the eating-hut, playing on the whitewashed ghost of a church. A ghost, indeed, where no Masses had been said these ten years. The guide was still searching and at last in the grey early morning light he found the mules, at the bottom of the *barranca*, at the edge of Cancuk, three or four hundred feet down.

We had breakfast of coffee and fried plantains; the litter on the beds in the eating-hut stirred and became women again; Indians picked their way up the *barranca* and stood silently round the fire watching – little primeval figures of an older day. If Cancuk belonged to the Middle Ages, these belonged to the caves. Then we set out, winding round a huge hairpin bend along the edge of the *barranca*, the path terribly difficult for mules because it was cut in rock; their feet slipped painfully at every step. It took more than two hours to reach the end of that tremendous loop, and there was Cancuk still, just across the gulf. The scenery was magnificent: the great pine forests swept down to where we trudged at a mere six thousand feet, great rocky precipices showed like grey castle walls through breaks in the pines. At one point, aiming at a *finca* which existed, I think, only in the muleteer's imagination, for we never found it, we took an appalling short cut up a foot-wide path at an angle of sixty degrees. It did no good – it only tired the mules – the *finca* wasn't there. After the first three hours the journey became, like all the others, just weariness – a struggle of wills between the guide and me, he determined to reach Las Casas if it took us all day and night, I eager to stop at a village he imprudently mentioned called Tenahape. Of course he won, by-passing Tenahape altogether, so that all I saw of it was a little air-washed toy spread out five hundred feet below our path. Just weariness shot through occasionally with flashes – not exactly of beauty, but of consciousness, consciousness of something simple and strange and uncomplicated, a way of life we have hopelessly lost but can never quite forget. There was a moment at a little brown pebbly river when the guide took a bowl from his saddlebag and filled it with water from the stream and made himself a kind of gruel with a ball of corn – the mules drank and I stood on a stone and washed my face and hands and the shadow played on the stream, and it was like peace and natural happiness. And there was food at a little isolated Mexican farm, the floor strewn with sweet-smelling pine-needles – tortilla and beans and chicken and rice and coffee, the body's needs so easily quieted.

A kind of second wind came, too, with evening and the cool, when we came out of the forest on what seemed to be at last the top of the world nine thousand feet up – a great plateau of yellow grass, across which flocks of sheep and goats came driving together from three-quarters of the globe, a few mud huts, some men on mules cantering bareback by, an Indian herd in his pastoral tunic, a horn winding, and the last pale golden light welling across the plain, dropping down over the ridge which ended it as if over the world's edge, so that you thought of the light going on and on through quiet peaceful uninhabited space. It was like a scene from the past before the human race had bred its millions – England of the Conquest before the forests had been cut, a herd called

Sweyn, the wattle huts, the world of Ivanhoe.

And there was an even older world beyond the ridge; the ground sloped up again to where a grove of tall black crosses stood at all angles like wind-blown trees against the blackened sky. This was the Indian religion – a dark, tormented, magic cult. The old ladies might swing back and forth in the rocking-chairs of Villahermosa, the Catholics might be dying out 'like dogs', but here, in the mountainous strange world of Father Las Casas, Christianity went on its own frightening way. Magic, yes, but we are too apt to minimise the magic element in Christianity – the man raised from the dead, the devils cast out, the water turned into wine. The great crosses leaned there in their black and windy solitude, safe from the *pistoleros* and the politicians, and one thought of the spittle mixed with the clay to heal the blind man, the resurrection of the body, the religion of the earth.

THE HIDDEN CITY

A league and a half to Las Casas, a muleteer had said an hour ago, and again an hour later a horseman overtook us in a forest with the same news – a league and a half. It was seven-thirty, and we had been on the road for nearly twelve hours. The hidden city never came nearer; one simply rode and rode into the gathering night. The horseman knew the proprietor of the Hotel Español in Las Casas and was anxious to lead us there himself, but it is a hard thing at the end of twelve hours to keep up with a horse on a trotting lurching mule. Suddenly we came out of the forest on to the mountain edge, and there below us were the lights of the town – the long lines of streets laid out electrically. It was extraordinarily dramatic to come on a city like this, eight thousand feet up, at the end of a mule track, a city of fourteen thousand inhabitants with a score of churches, after the hairpin bends round the mountainside, after the precipices and the foot-wide tracks, the climbs and the descents. It was like an adventure of Rider Haggard – coming so unexpectedly out of the forest above this city, once the capital of Chiapas and the home of Las Casas, a place with one rough road, impassable in the rains, running down to Tuxtla and the coast, and only a mule track for the traveller from the north.

I couldn't keep up with the horseman's pace any longer and he left us at a canter. The lights were deceptive; we had miles to go yet, edging round a semicircle of mountains before the track went down to the plateau: first a long Indian village with closed doors and shuttered windows, then the white cupola of the church of Guadalupe perched on a hill at the edge of town, and then what seemed an endless cobbled street going interminably on under the clattering hoofs. We had had fourteen hours of riding before we rode into the little flowery patio of the hotel. A room with a bed and sheets, a beautifully cooked meal, steak and greens and sweet bread, a bottle of beer, and the radio playing: I was drunk and dazed with happiness. The neighbours sat round the radio listening to news of Spain, picking out the ravaged villages on a map hung on the wall, marking with enthusiasm Franco's advance. Somebody said, 'Turn on the news from London,' and 'This is London,' they said to me. It was still a Spanish voice speaking in Spanish, but it came from London. It welled out of that solid and complacent building in Portland Place, over the Queen's

Hall and Oxford Circus, over the curve of the world, the Atlantic and the Gulf and the Tropic of Capricorn, over the cemetery with 'SILENCIO' in black letters and the wall where Garrido shot his prisoners, over the swamps and rivers, the mountains and the forests, where the old man slept with the rats beside his corn and the flames beat against the front of the locked-up church. 'This is London,' they assured me again because I doubted it.

10. Holy Week

It was a lovely town to wake to in the early morning light, as the donkeys went plodding round laden with bright chemical gaseosas for the saloons – low single-storey houses with brown-tiled roofs and little flowery patios, the mountains crouched all round like large and friendly dogs; twenty-two churches, of which five were open, but no priest allowed inside.

The finest church is the old colonial church of Santo Domingo sharing a little green square with La Caridad and the prison – once the presbytery. A long flight of steps down into the square, barley-sugar pillars up the façade – the colour of pale terracotta – statues headless where the troops have reached them; inside, flowers and white drapery had been set for Easter, the church was scrupulously clean, a heavy curtain hung before the altar, and Christ lay dead among flowers. The walls were crammed with dark old eighteenth-century portraits of bishops and saints set in heavy and tortuous gilt. It gave an effect of fullness – and of emptiness, like a meeting when the leader has gone. Nothing meant anything any more; it was just sentiment to spread the flowers and drapery; the Host wasn't here. There was no more reason to remove the hat than in a ruin, than in the church on the hill above the city, smashed and shady with love-initialled walls and snaky chambers. Santo Domingo, La Caridad, La Merced with a ruined

cavalry barracks next door in what was once the presbytery, a broken square outside with a rotting bandstand
in the middle of a rubbish dump – well, it was Easter,
we were celebrating the death of God. This emptiness
and desolation was right, in a way.

This was a city of craftsmen. Only one or two stores
in the plaza contained manufactured goods. All up the
mile-long street to Guadalupe were little stores selling
identically the same things – pottery, guitars, serapes,
candles, white linen, shirts, some of it brought in by the
small mute Indians from the hills; the rest woven or
plaited or beaten, as the case might be, in the little rooms
which opened like money-changers' booths upon the
street. Everywhere there were tailors – boys waving open
irons in the street to keep the charcoal burning.

I went into a photographer's to buy some pictures. It
was just a private house with the pictures kept in a
cupboard; I sat on a hard drawing-room chair looking
through them, while a middle-aged lady in a mantilla
made polite conversation. A little image of Christ and
something in the woman's manner of courtesy, gentleness and resignation suggested that I was among friends.
I told her I was a Catholic – it was like opening a strange
door in a foreign town and finding an old friend inside.
I asked her where I could hear Mass, and she sent her
small girl out with me to show me a house where Mass
would be said all through Holy Week: an anonymous
house in a side street, a closed door, nothing to mark the
presence of God. And at intervals all through the day the
bells of Guadalupe rang out – the white soap-bubble
dome upon a rock perched high at the head of sixty-three
steps, each separated by more than a yard of sloping
cobbles, all the symbols of God's presence and nothing

there at all – just flowers and drapery and cardboard angels starting from the wall with trumpets in their hands to blow a trump for nothing. It was sunset; the whole brown town lay flat below; night travelled off the immense hills; tiny bulbs, like fairy lights, came out all down the long street. In the plaza they were selling the Mexican papers four days old; it was bitterly cold when the dark fell, and gusts of icy wind circled round the plaza and the shut cathedral eight thousand odd feet in the air.

THE MASS HOUSE

I got up at a quarter to six. The two little boys who did all the work of the hotel lay asleep in their clothes on benches by the door with only a serape to cover them. A mass of golden clouds lay over Guadalupe. From all directions women moved towards one point in the sleeping town with shawls over their heads. There was no real concealment. The police, I suppose, were bribed; though sometimes, I was told, when money was scarce, a Mass house would be raided, the congregation fined, the priest held for ransom in jail.

Mass was celebrated in a small room hung with white lace. Half the congregation was outside on a balcony a few feet above the small flowery patio. There were about a hundred and fifty people there, but this was only one of several Mass houses in Las Casas. Most were women; there were a few small boys, a few youths, and a number of middle-aged men: a cripple wrapped up to the mouth in his serape leaned against the door.

The priest arrived in a motoring-coat and a tweed cap. His face was hideously disfigured with mauve patches and his eyes were shielded with amber-tinted glasses. Mass was said without the sanctus bell – silence was a relic of the worst penal days when discovery probably meant death; they were days which might at any time return at the whim of some police officer . . . 'I looked about and there was no helper: I fought, and there was none to aid'; 'He was broken for our sins, the discipline of our peace was upon him'; the priest trod carefully between the kneeling women, bringing the Body of God out from the altar on to the balcony, handing Christ across the bowed heads. Afterwards the housewife stood at the door saying good-bye to her guests (there had been no collection: the cost of the Mass was shared among the leading Catholics in the town). You could detect a touch of pride, of condescension, because she had sheltered God in her house. One person at least would feel regret and disappointment if the Mass were ever celebrated again in the churches.

I went into Santo Domingo. An Indian and his woman came in to burn candles before the prostrate crucified Christ. They carried little bouquets of greenery – twigs and leaves from the lemon tree. First they kissed the feet of Christ, then they prayed aloud in a mournful duet, and afterwards the man lit candles and laid the greenery beside the body and touched the wooden thighs with it, to give the lemon leaves virtue as medicine. Then they went gently out, small and black and bowed, and crossed the tiny plaza to La Caridad. They had prayed in Indian, not in Spanish, and I wondered what prayers they had said and what answers they could hope to get in *this* world of mountains, hunger and irresponsibility.

There were only two foreigners beside R's boys in Las Casas – a German bank manager and his wife. I called on them to learn a little of the background to the shut churches and Mass houses and the Indians praying in Santo Domingo. I thought I noticed in the plaza a great many *pistoleros* doing nothing all day between the closed and bolted cathedral and the balconied Goverment office: was it imagination that every morning there seemed to be more men in seedy sun helmets hanging about the Presidencia? There was an air of expectation . . . as if something suddenly was going to go off. Was it simply the effect of the petroleum dispute? England had sent a note to the Mexican Government; a blackboard exhorted in chalk, 'Mexicans! Prepare to give your patriotic mite for the reduction of the Petroleum Debt . . .'; but there was more than the petroleum dispute disturbing Las Casas. Red leaflets were passed from hand to hand and lay like large petals on the paving-stones. Addressed to the workers and peasants and signed by the leaders of the various syndicates, they warned the people that General Pineda was on his way to Las Casas. I remembered that Pineda was the Catholic General who, I had been told in Yajalon, was plotting a revolt from Mexico. That, of course, was rumour; as for the *facts*, they may have been what the German bank manager told me – you cannot tell: it is as if all words and the simplest acts of violence or love get distorted in the sound-box of the great *barrancas*.

Pineda was a conservative rebel; he had held out against Carranza for years in the Chiapas mountains. He couldn't be conquered, though his force was gradually reduced to about four hundred men. Finally he obtained them a free pardon, paid them off, and retired himself across the border into Guatemala. He had never been a regular soldier: he was a brilliant amateur who knew the country he fought in. Later he was allowed to return and was granted the title of General of the Reserve. 'He is just an honest man,' Herr F said, discounting the story of the plot, 'who doesn't like to see people robbed.' He had been elected President of Las Casas and under his administration it had been possible to get a few things done – irrigation, sanitary works – but a month or two ago the *pistoleros* had come from Tuxtla, had driven him from the Presidencia at the point of the gun, and installed in his place a friend of the governor of Chiapas. Pineda had gone to Mexico City and procured an *amparo* allowing him to reoccupy the Presidencia – with the help of Federal troops if necessary – and he had announced a fortnight ago to his friends that he was about to return. He was expected daily, and the *pistoleros* were waiting. Every time an aeroplane was sighted, people looked out for trouble. Perhaps he was saving up a surprise for the Fair which started on Holy Saturday . . . perhaps he would arrive on Holy Thursday or Good Friday when the town was full of Indians from the hills . . . perhaps tonight as I had been told . . . Frau F hated the people here; she and her husband never sat in the plaza these days, they avoided all gatherings in case something started. At any moment a drunken man might fire a gun, and the gringos were unpopular. They had been here twenty years, but they trusted no one. 'Black people', Frau F called the people; they hid themselves, were hypocrites, and all the time watched. Within a few hours of my attending Mass three people had told her that there was a gringo in town who was a Catholic. The trouble was, Chiapas was so poor. All the big estates in the south had been divided up by the *agraristos* and were falling back into desert. Only the farms in the north survived, because the tracks were bad. Chiapas was forgotten in Mexico City; it was so far away Mexicans didn't know that it existed. I had only to see the Spring Fair to know how far Chiapas was ruined. Ten years ago it was a great occasion – oh, the balls and the river parties and the fancy costumes – but now, I should see. She herself wouldn't go near it. You never knew – something might start.

'And the governor,' I said, 'who sent the *pistoleros*? He, I suppose, is a bad man?' You begin to talk in those terms in Mexico – he is good; he is bad – terms as simple as the pistol shot or the act of mercy. Oh, no, they said, he wasn't exactly bad. He was unfortunate. All the responsible people in Las Casas had voted for him. They had great expectations from his rule. But immediately after his election he had to spend three months in Mexico City on business. The result could have been – and probably was – foreseen. They were the important months when the taxes on the coffee crops came in. When the governor returned, the Treasury was bare, and no more revenue would come in for nine months. He had to govern without money, and that meant loans, compromises with all his opponents, with the racketeers who had robbed the state, and nothing was done at all. Now the very people who had elected him considered him the worst governor they had ever had.

That was Mexican politics . . .

Well, the latest news of Pineda was that he would arrive at the Presidencia at six. I left the kindly Germans and went down to the plaza. Other people were waiting too; there were more revolvers about than ever. Every now and then people came on to the balcony of the Presidencia and looked down into the square with what might have been anxiety. A soldier sat on a chair beside the entrance holding a rifle, and a few Indians squatted along the sidewalk selling brown pots. There were more decrepit taxis than usual, and a car or two drove round and round. I sat on a seat, waiting, till seven. Of course he never came, that night or any other. All that happened was that the atmosphere of hostility thickened – and directed itself against me. A drunken group passed and repassed, throwing out gibes; they had revolvers under their waistcoats, so there was nothing to be done but sit, like a prudish maiden lady, pretending not to hear. I was suffering for the ancient wrongdoing of the oil pioneers, the tiresome legal rectitude of the English Government. From that evening the hostility never lifted: I couldn't sit in the plaza for more than a few minutes without a gibe. It preyed on the nerves: it was like being the one unpopular boy at school. I was glad when young Gómez arrived by plane, somebody who didn't mind talking to a gringo, though preferably in private. Incidentally, if I had waited for his plane, I should have had to spend another four days at Yajalon. A strange state where it takes longer and costs less to fly than to travel on mule-back.

HOLY THURSDAY

Because it was a Thursday small boys were everywhere cleaning with knives between the cobbles, scraping up grasses. On Tuesdays and Thursdays it is the householders' responsibility to see that the streets are clean. You can be fined if a single piece of paper is found outside your house, and it is impossible to keep the sidewalks swept, for they are used by the Indians for meals, for cleaning their children . . . There remains the problem of what to do with the rubbish when you do collect it. At one time a municipal garbage truck went round ringing a cowbell, but then the city council ran out of petrol and the service was discontinued.

I went to eight o'clock Mass in the same private house. The altar had been set up in the portico under the veranda; the setting was that of a Christmas crib: Christ in the stable. Roses in flower round the well, the white arch of wall, sunlight and mountains looking in, and open sky. Indian families sat on their haunches among the flowers. The sanctus bell this time rang softly, and a tiny choir sang with reserve to the music of a harmonium. It was too important a feast for many precautions. The priest with the mauve face preached – sacrifice, sacrifice – and the Body of Christ was carried in procession round the well and the flower-beds – the dark Indians bowed among the roses – and up the veranda steps into the room where the Altar of Repose had been set up.

When I came out from Mass it was like an invasion. The Indians were pouring in from the mountains, down the long cobbled street from Guadalupe; they sat on the steps of the locked cathedral eating tortillas; they lined the sidewalks everywhere; they came in thousands to see the crucified Christ. In little straw hats with pointed crowns decorated with streamers of ribbon they plodded in, small and stocky and black-haired; their women had long pigtails and shapeless slum skirts; their faces were hideous and unshaped; but the men were often good-looking in a patient secret way. In Santo Domingo a great green silk hanging hid the empty sanctuary; the altar was covered in flowers and candles. A long train of Indians moved slowly up to the rail carrying little withered bunches, dry brown blossoms from the lemon tree. They handed their bouquets to a half-caste inside the rail, who laid them for a moment on the altar and then gave them back. Then they carried their leaves and blossoms away and stood in the porch of the south door with their backs to the aisle, facing the little plaza and the white cupolaed monument to revolution and the sun climbing the sky, and prayed, crossing themselves in an elaborate mosaic, touching the eyes and nose and mouth and chin. One couple at the altar rail dusted their heads and hands and legs with the greenery they had seen laid on the altar. Mothers sat on the floor with their children under the dark Spanish oil-paintings, the massive gilt walls. Families greeted each other loudly in the aisle and stood laughing and talking with their backs to the altar, the day's magic task done, the medicine blessed, the prayers said. It was an odd mixture of fervour, super-stition, holiday. There wasn't a Mexican to be seen: the churches were given up to the little people from the mountains. And outside small gay stalls were selling candles, fruit, drinks, cakes.

THE BROTHER OF JUDAS

In Guadalupe Christ was led in chains by two tiny soldiers, Indians kissed the rope which bound Him, and up on the roof between the bell towers under the white dome they were hanging Judas on the cross – a hideous figure in a straw sombrero with a paper face like one of

the Ugly Wuglies from Miss Nesbit's *Enchanted Castle*,
those creatures made of paper and old coats and umbrellas who spoke horribly in vowels because they had
no roofs to their mouths. It sagged greyly from the cross,
a figure of unholy despair, and beneath with gross and
horrid jollity sat a stout stuffed figure, in white trousers
and a pink shirt, with a scarlet face; the straw legs
dangled from the ledge under the cross and swayed a
little in the breeze. 'Who was he?' I asked. Oh, he, they
said, was the brother of Judas. They made an awful
family party, there on the church top in their gloom
and their gaiety while the youths on the roof beat a tin
tray and rattled wooden clappers, to tell the town that
Judas and his jolly brother were properly hanged.

Day by day it became more unpleasant to show myself
on the street. I had nothing to do and nothing to read:
I was driven to write an article on Tabasco for *The
Tablet*, sitting in the patio of the Hotel Español. Young
Gómez's presence proved a mixed blessing; true, it was
good to find my ostracism broken, but he insisted on
speaking English, of which he knew even less than I
knew Spanish, and he would answer 'Yes' to all questions
he didn't understand – much as I did in Spanish. Yes,
Pineda was here. Yes, Pineda was coming today, tomorrow . . . Yes.

Beggars were a greater comfort, for to them, too, one
was not a gringo; the blind and halt felt their way every
morning into the patio. They had hope and self-respect
– they gave something in return for what they got; a
prayer in which they believed and in which the donor

217

believed. They had a place in the world, unlike the poor bitter men playing gramophones in London gutters. Every morning the Mother Superior arrived with a basket collecting alms for the hospital. She wore ordinary clothes, of course, and the hospital was called the municipal hospital now – but the nurses were still nuns, and they had still to depend on charity.

I managed to borrow some American women's magazines from Frau F and sat for hours at a time in the patio reading them. It seemed a silly thing to come all this way for that; the awful journey in the *Ruiz Cano*, the weary hours on muleback – to read General Hugh Johnson on Roosevelt and examples of American research. 'This is the conclusion resulting from a study of 242 boys known to their playmates and school companions as sissies. To secure a composite picture of these youngsters, to learn what qualities they had in common, what it is that stamps a boy as a sissy, a series of questions were put to their brothers, sisters, schoolmasters, teachers, and other older persons who knew them well. The answers, tabulated and charted, are revealing.'

Then, when I could bear it no longer, I'd carry the statistics of sissyness in my brain into Santo Domingo or up the long Guadalupe street, stopping for a glass of quince wine or a gaseosa, always moving on to avoid the direct insult to which there was no reply.

Back again to read a 'Diary of Domesticity' by Gladys Taylor. 'Curiously enough, this reminds me of an epitaph I read in a book once, years ago. "They were lovely and pleasant in their lives, and in death they were not divided." That's a better epitaph than Colonel Byrd's in Westover, Virginia, composed by himself and carved on a stone column testifying to a thousand achievements and virtues. Sometimes, in a dark hour, the shortness of life comes into my mind. I wonder about immortality.'

In a book once, years ago . . .

GOOD FRIDAY

It was Good Friday. All day you could see women hurrying with ostrich secrecy towards the house in the side street where the body and blood of Christ was reserved in the little room off the balcony. In Santo Domingo the crucified figure was the centre of a noisy public meeting. Indians shouted and pushed and held animated conversations; babies on their mothers' backs munched tortillas; and in the centre where the soapbox orator should have stood lay the great crucifix. The men brought up more greenery and brushed the wooden loincloth and the thighs with it. What was in those secret minds, with which only priests have ever made real contact? Was it a formal superstition, like not walking under a ladder and throwing salt over the shoulder? Or was there a darker and more passionate idolatry? Now that the Body of God could not be found in any church in Chiapas, was the wooden image taking on a terrible and erroneous importance?

Herr F told me a story of the reopening of the churches in central and southern Chiapas. It happened about six months ago and started in a village called Sinajon. The people had gathered together to kill the tax collector; he was warned and stayed away, and the villagers waited in vain with a dreadful sense of anti-climax. 'We must do something,' they said. 'Let us open our church.' So they fetched their womenfolk and broke open the doors. The news spread so quickly that next day churches were broken open a hundred miles away. In Las Casas the Government put a soldier at every door, but the soldiers acted with great prudence and allowed themselves to be pushed aside without firing a shot. The churches which are open now in Las Casas show the popular choice: Santo Domingo, the most venerated of all; La Caridad, La Merced, Guadalupe, and a little obscure church along the road to Tuxtla with no interest to anyone but the parishioners. I arrived when it was being decorated ready for Holy Thursday. There were few women about; it was being arrayed and guarded by hostile men who watched my movements with suspicion.

And what, I asked a number of people, would happen if next Easter the priests acted with the same suddenness and confidence as the laity – simply walked into Santo Domingo and began to say Mass? Would the Government give way again? Who knows? they said. Perhaps – or perhaps they'd shoot. In Villahermosa one month after my visit the peasants – there were no priests – did act. They had no churches to open, but they set up a rough altar against the back wall of the one ruined church and prayed amongst the rubble. The soldiers came and opened fire and a few were killed – men, women, and children. But then Tabasco has a sterner, more disciplined tradition than Chiapas. I could not help feeling that for a bold priest a great chance was waiting one Holy Thursday when the town was full of Indians.

On Good Friday afternoon the Indians began to evacuate Las Casas. An old Indian sat dead drunk on the pavement near Guadalupe and wouldn't move; with sad dignity he waved his companions away, but they persisted, urging him off to the mountains, taking his load themselves, helping him to his feet, whispering gently, secretly . . . In Santo Domingo a service was held – for Mexicans this time; the Indians had had their hour. The sacristan led the prayers – there was uncertain singing and a wavering organ.

In the plaza the same insolent stares and veiled gibes. I went back to the patio and read the women's magazines. There was an advertisement for a Reference Library for Sub-Debs. 'A date to remember. How to put yourself across so boys will never forget you.' Three cents. 'Tables for Ladies. How do you rate with boys? Here's a talent test for you.' Three cents. 'Rating for Dating. The famous sub-deb chart for getting along with boys.' Three cents.

I loathed Mexico – but there were times when it seemed as if there were worse places. 'In a book once . . .' Here were idolatry and oppression, starvation and casual violence, but you lived under the shadow of religion – of God or the Devil. 'Rating for Dating' – it wasn't evil, it wasn't anything at all, it was just the drugstore and the Coca Cola, the hamburger, the sinless empty graceless chromium world.

SAN MIGUELITO

Herr F led me over the rocks at the edge of town to show me examples of Mexican engineering. First the reservoir, half finished, standing there to crack into ruin in the winter because there was no more money: all money was diverted to Tampico and the oilfields.

The river, a small trickle of water, disappeared into a crack of the mountains; it reappeared again on the other side twelve miles away. But in the rains it became a torrent; a fallen tree trunk, a loose bush could block its escape, and seven years ago there had been a disastrous flood. Herr F had been in charge of the relief operations; he showed me the overgrown neglected canal he had dug at a cost of only two hundred and fifty dollars. Then Cárdenas visited Las Casas; he was not yet President, he was on his electoral tour, and he had promised, if he were elected, men and money. He kept his promise: money poured into Las Casas. Federal engineers began the work all over again, building elaborate showy works. We looked at them: the walls were made of loose rocks stuck in cracking cement; in the next rains the walls themselves would help to block the channel. Then as contrast he showed me what the Spaniards had built eighty years before. The fine masonry of General Utrillo stood intact; only the alteration in the level of the land made his works out of date. A little way above Herr F's canal a house and shed stood on the waste. 'That shed,' he said, 'was a chapel until the Government engineers arrived.' Herr F was not a Catholic, he was a Lutheran, but he spoke with bitterness. The church had been put up by the owners of the house when the father of the family recovered from a sickness. Situated just at the place where the river disappeared into its subterranean bed, at the danger point for Las Casas, the chapel became a place of popular pilgrimage. When the rains came, men, women, and children would go on their knees – some of them carrying the cross – to the river. It must have been a journey of terrible pain – thorn bushes and rocks and steep descents: it was difficult enough for us to keep from falling. When they reached the river they poured water on the cross and carried it back. Herr F in his operations had been very careful of the church, but the Federal engineers threw out the cross and converted the chapel into a shed for their tools.

'Of course,' he said, 'they were afraid of it. The Government, I mean.'

It must have set light to a train of thought, as we scrambled over the rocks and looked down into the dry ten-foot *barranca* where they used to come on their knees, under the cross.

'The Government is very uneasy about San Miguelito,' he suddenly remarked. The mountains of Chiapas stuck sharply up all round the city, perched there on its eight-thousand-foot plateau, parched and chilled alternately each day and night. The twenty-four churches rose like captive balloons above the one-storey houses, the mule tracks descended from the north and the single road ran south – to Tuxtla and the Government offices and the lounging *pistoleros*. It seemed odd that men like that should be troubled about a saint.

'San Miguelito?' I said.

He was astonished that I hadn't heard of San Miguelito. The news had spread as far as Tabasco, a hundred miles away. He had owned a coffee *finca* himself on the borders of Tabasco and Chiapas, and the Indians had daily passed his gate, going to visit San Miguelito. Why, it was causing a religious revival; the Government was so troubled it had sent soldiers to seize the saint, but they hadn't captured him.

'What does he do?' I said.

'He recommends medicines – some of them Indian medicines and some the latest patent medicines from Mexico City.'

'Is he a statue?'

223

'I don't know. I can't make it out – he's very small. Sometimes it sounds as if he's just a picture postcard. Of course they wouldn't let *me* see him.'

The story was this: a poor Mexican farmer had for years kept San Miguelito (whatever he was) in a box. One day, about eighteen months ago, he had opened the box and San Miguelito had spoken to him in a high clear voice. He was so scared he ran all the way into the village of Bochil with the box, and there he had found four friends of his gathered together in a room. He had laid the box on the table and told them his story. Of course they didn't believe him; then one of them opened the box and the thin high voice came out of it. Soon after his astonishing discovery the farmer had died, and now San Miguelito was kept by his wife and his son in the small village of Sanoyo.

This German, as I have said, was a Protestant; he couldn't make head or tail of the thing; he really half believed the story – he knew one of the four men who was in that room when the farmer arrived with his box; he had listened to the pilgrims' tales. It couldn't be self-hypnotism – some of the patent medicines were ones no Indian could have heard of in the Chiapas wilds. There were no wires; apparently you could handle the box while San Miguelito talked. He had the reputation of speaking in German, French, and English, as well as in Spanish and the Indian tongues. A lawyer from Las Casas had visited him and was convinced – but then the lawyer drank. What was one to believe, if one was an engineer, a bank manager, and a Protestant?

We came back into Las Casas and stopped at a cantina for drinks. I couldn't keep my mind off the miracle. I was ready to go to any expense . . . how could

one go on living later with the thought that fifty pesos
had stood between oneself and, well, revelation of some
kind, divine or devilish, if the voice spoke? Then came
the blow. The man in the cantina said San Miguelito was
no longer in Sanoyo: a doctor had been sent from Tuxtla
who put the whole thing down to auto-suggestion and
the saint had been removed to a museum in Mexico City.
But you can never get anything straight in Mexico; in the
hotel the owner, who was a pious Catholic, told me the
saint was still in Sanoyo, and I went out and hired a car.

FERIA DE PRIMAVERA

That afternoon the Fair was due to start – at four
o'clock in the afternoon, if the florid programmes of the
week's festivities were to be believed; but at four there
was no sign of a fair except one shooting-booth and a
children's merry-go-round in the plaza. 'At four of the
afternoon magnificent allegorical cars preceded by bands
of musicians, of enthusiastic students, of athletes, of the
workers' syndicates will tour the principal streets and
avenues of the city to announce the opening of the
festival. At night in El Teatro Zebadua the election of the
Señorita Las Casas 1938 will be declared and a special
programme will be given.' Glancing down the programme one notice in big type 'SELECTA FUNCION
CINEMATOGRAFICA', a gathering of marimba players, a
'sensational encounter at basket-ball', a few dances, a
tennis tournament (*dobles y mixto*), a boxing match.
Certainly the great historic Spring Fair of Las Casas had
fallen on evil times; in the first programmes they had
announced a bull-fight, but they hadn't raised enough
money to attract fighters to this abandoned town.

It was nearly six; people were waiting about in the plaza for Pineda, who didn't come; a few children were shooting in the booth; no other sign of a fair. Then a rocket went off and the procession came into sight – a dingy saloon car with half a dozen young men – students, athletes, workers? – an allegorical car representing spring, and a small open car carrying a big cardboard Kodak carton. Somebody blew a bugle and the rockets went up and the three little motors kept on their sombre, sedate and cheerless round. The Fair had started.

One of the young sons of Herr R from Palenque came to supper with me; his elder brother, he said, had a headache, he regretted . . . but I guessed what that meant. They had had to avoid me already in public. I was a pariah; it wasn't good to be seen about with me. They had probably tossed up to choose the victim, and I felt enormous sympathy for the small fair fifteen-year-old loser. He said the atmosphere at their college was awful: people were polite to your face, but behind your back you became just gringos. A few days ago he and his brother were sent a dollar from America. They were trying to change it at the bank when a man came in. 'He said to the clerk, "I shouldn't take a dirty bit of paper like that, all over germs." And the clerk, he wouldn't give us the proper exchange.'

The drop in the exchange, of course, has increased the hate – as if they believed the difference represented money stolen from them by gringos.

The programme at the cinema was supposed to start at nine, but for half an hour longer than that we were exposed to the unfriendly stare of students in the side boxes. I pitied young R from the bottom of my heart, but how could I tell him so without casting a reflection on his courtesy and courage? He would suffer for this later – to have been seen in the company of a gringo whose presence in town was known to everyone and suspected by most. At last the Queen climbed on to the stage with her maids and courtiers, buxom and brown-eyed and gold-toothed. The girls sat on hard straight chairs in front of an absurd Edwardian drawing-room set of cardboard tables and cut-out ferns, and beside each chair stood a man self-conscious and subfusc. A poet read an ode into the microphone, the brothers Some-thing-or-Other played interminably on the marimba, and somebody made an oration on the petroleum situation. Even foreigners, he said, should contribute to the debt in return for Mexico's hospitality – but where was the hospitality? I wondered, meeting the dark hostile gaze of the students along the wall. Then there was another speech and more marimba playing and a raffle for free cinema seats which went on for half an hour, and at last the great film, specially brought to Las Casas for the Spring Fair: Warner Baxter and Alice Faye in a faded backstage musical. Incomprehensible situations passed across a flickery screen, the lights of Broadway, com-plicated renunciations. They became more fantastic than ever translated into Spanish. The audience sat in silence; they never laughed once. Only the Queen of the Fair sometimes smiled, chin on gloved hand, sophisti-cated and gold-toothed, in mauve. Alice Faye's fair and unformed face was projected in enormous detail weeping enormous tears; her man had failed, taken to drink, while she was featured over Broadway in neon signs and wept for lost love. This was a stigmata they couldn't understand, but I was grateful for the darkness and the torch songs, away from unfriendly eyes.

Next morning we left at six-thirty by the only road. Sanoyo was only fifty kilometres away, but the car took nearly four hours. The road was very bad; it was more a mule track than a road, cut by crevices two feet deep sprinkled with boulders. In the rains it is impassable; only aeroplanes can reach Las Casas then – and, of course, the mules from the north; only necessity at the best of times dictated *that* journey. Yet going to Sanoyo by road was really worse. One dropped six thousand feet, circling the same mountain for forty minutes, bumping slowly round and round on the edge of the precipice, the same scenery on the opposite mountain recurring over and over again, as if one were a needle on a damaged record scraping the same track. A few bright blue birds mocked one with other people's happiness, and the scenery – the great pine forests dropping like curtains – was, I suppose, magnificent, but I was too sick and bruised to care.

It was Easter Sunday, but the only sign of the festival in the little drab village of Sanoyo was at the home of the saint. Some coloured paper streamers hung there, and when we had passed through the yard, a few chickens and pigs stirring the end-of-dry-season dust, we found in the small *sala* a decorated shrine to St Anthony. The old mother slopped about in ancient gym shoes, tying up her white hair in a pink ribbon, and the chauffeur and I sat down on a bench and stared across at another bench where some villagers were patiently waiting. Out from an inner room – through the door I could see the end of a bed, a cheap woman's magazine, and a paper streamer – came a little party of Indian women, tiny and bowed, old and hideous at twenty. With their cave-dwellers' faces and their long staffs they might have been Stone Age people emerging from forgotten caverns to pay their tribute to the Redeemer on Resurrection morning. One of them wept and wept, and a typewriter clattered with curious modernity in the bedroom. A marimba began to play in the yard among the chickens, and a rocket went off at each corner of the house in turn; it was impressive, a little hypnotic, the tinkly pathetic music rising regularly to the explosion and sinking again; it was like the preparation for a great event; I felt my incredulity shaken. Suppose there was a miracle, suppose out of some box a voice did speak . . . it was a horrifying thought that life could never be the same again; one couldn't go on living as one had been living. What happens afterwards to the people who are present at a genuine miracle?

But this wasn't a case like that. The music went on too long; I caught sight in the inner room of little conferences, the old woman slipped in and out weaving the pink ribbon in her hair. There was a young man in the bedroom who filled me with distrust – he had a humorous mouth; he looked more educated than the others, like a garage hand or a man in a radio shop. Radio . . . ?

Then after half an hour the son emerged. He wore a pink shirt which wasn't tucked in; his sleeves flapped clerically when he waved his hands; he had evasive eyes. He said the image wasn't there – it had gone to Villahermosa. We just sat on and took no notice. He asked whether I was a doctor – he hadn't liked doctors since the medical officer of health in Tuxtla had come with soldiers to seize the saint. The saint had hidden in the woods and the disappointed soldiers had fired into the house – he showed the bullet marks on either side of the *sala*. I asked if we could see the saint; he flapped his pink sleeves and said he was in Villahermosa. We sat on. He brought out a visitors' book – there were twelve thousand names recorded; he brought out a pile of certificates of cures. There was always the same formula tapped out on his machine, 'I, Pedro López, certify that I was out of my mind' (or had fits or worms in the head or something) 'and visited two doctors in my native place who said I was incurable. I came to Sanoyo and saw Señor ——' (I've forgotten the name). 'He gave me medicine and now I am quite cured.' Then the signature and the witnesses' signatures and a passport photo of a brutal mestizo face – no mention of the saint.

The chauffeur got up and made a long speech. He said we knew the saint was in the bedroom; the señor lacked confidence in us, and yet how fully worthy we were of his trust. I wasn't a doctor, I was a foreigner who had come from England to see the saint. I was a Catholic and *muy religioso*. It didn't seem to do much good; I caught a small child who came out of the bedroom and presented him with a rosary in a little glass box.

Another hour passed; the music had stopped and the fireworks; an old Indian came in to see the statue of St Anthony and prayed and touched it with lemon leaves and went out. People from the village drifted in and stared at us and looked at the certificates and went out again into the fiery midday sun. A fat woman with a gross spotty face showed us a kind of primitive straitjacket and scars on her wrists – she had been cured of madness. The man in the pink shirt laid in my lap a bottle of maggots which had come out of a man's nose.* The

* These are planted directly – not through eggs – by a large fly which attacks drunks when they lie helpless on the road. The maggots eventually reach the brain; no cure has been discovered.

atmosphere was becoming unbearably clinical.

At last after two hours we wore them down. Resistance suddenly crumbled. The saint couldn't talk because it was Sunday, but we could see him. If we came back on Thursday, then the saint would talk. We went into the bedroom and the son took casually down from a shelf – as if he were handling a grocery and not a miracle – one of those wooden Victorian tea caddies that are divided into two compartments. One compartment was empty; in the other had been glued the fretwork frame of a shrine, and a little picture of St Michael was pasted at the back – the usual picture of the archangel slaying the dragon. Little balls of coloured silver paper filled the caddy, and among these a nail stuck up, and on the nail rested a little hollow head made, I think, of lead like a toy soldier. It certainly wasn't St Michael's head – it was a woman's with crimped Grecian hair, an intaglio head. It was this which would give tongue – not on a Sunday, but next Thursday, though I think, if I had been able to revisit the house, Thursday, too, would have proved an unpropitious day. This wasn't the setting for a miracle; there was something astute and amateurish about the whole thing . . . We put an offering in the box – like the sick people who were not charged a centavo – and said good-bye.

On the way home we stopped for food at an Indian woman's cantina in Istapa and there we heard of a newer San Miguelito, who was also kept in a box, four leagues away by horse; he spoke even on a Sunday – the woman had heard him. So by this time I shouldn't be surprised if there were half a dozen San Miguelitos in Chiapas. The saint is cropping up like boils, and what else can you expect? The Mass is forbidden in the churches; only in the secrecy of a private house can the daily genuine

231

miracle be performed; but religion will out, and when it is suppressed it breaks its way through in strange and sometimes poisonous forms.

The long rough journey from Veracruz was over; tomorrow I was leaving for Tuxtla and Mexico City. Already the capital seemed to me a city of infinite luxury; I thought of going to the Regis and having a Coca Cola highball, the brandy cocktails in Mac's bar, the journalists sitting round drinking coffee in the Café de Paris. But perhaps San Miguelito had been offended by my want of faith. Mexico gave me a back kick.

That evening, describing my visit to Herr F, I nearly fainted, and going back to the inn I was caught in a violent storm. The wet clothes finished me: I could eat no supper. In the night I was feverish. The nights had never seemed colder, as I vomited or struggled across the dripping patio to the choked lavatory. Diarrhoea, vomit, fever, was that what they called dysentery? I had been warned to look out for blood, which was the sign of amoebic dysentery, and sometimes I thought I saw it. And all the time I was haunted by the thought of the next day's journey. The journey to Sanoyo had been bad enough, but that had taken only four hours there and four hours back, and I had had a private car. Tomorrow it was said to be eight hours on end to Tuxtla in a tiny crowded mail bus. It seemed an impossibility – but I had booked my seat on a plane flying the next day from Tuxtla to Oaxaca, and if I missed it, God knew how long I'd have to wait for another. And I was scared. I wanted to be where there were doctors. For the past four or five days I had been drinking water – a stupid thing to do in Las Casas.

And when there's no choice one has to go on. Next day the diarrhoea was as bad as ever, the vomiting had stopped, and the fever a little helped – it took the edge off reality. The bus was old and small, with a wooden roof a few inches above our heads and four wooden benches in front of the mail-bags. Every inch was taken. Three of us sat by the driver where there was really room for one. Two stood on the steps and clung to the windshield. We were like an overgrown fossil as we bumped at seven in the morning along the hideously familiar way to Istapa. At a village called San Lorenzo we stopped for breakfast and unloaded a coffin, and I went up into a stony field to unload my sickness and dysentery. Then on again, that interminable winding descent towards the tropics. We had started in the bitter mountain cold and slowly shed our clothes as we went down. A few miles out of Istapa – five and a half hours by this slow decrepit bus from Las Casas – the road to Tuxtla really began in a wilderness of mud huts and abandoned dredges (everything stopped for the sake of the oil dispute), a good road along which we could scorch at forty miles an hour, dropping down the mountainside towards the Pacific plain. At the edge of a huge precipice above our road, facing the midday sun, a party of Indians stood in prayer, hands raised above their heads, beside a rusting scoop, but when we had mounted to their level they had gone. It was like the boundary of a faith – we were leaving behind that wild region of great crooked crosses, of the cave-dweller faces bowed before the crucified Christ, of the talking saint. We were going back and down to the picturesque Mexico of the *pistolero* and the ruined

233

monastery – through Chiapa de Corzo, all pink wash and palms and tropical fruit and old wounded churches and dusty desolation. This was the tropics and the driver stopped the bus and bought fruit to take back with him to cold Las Casas seven thousand feet above.

Tuxtla is not a place for foreigners – the new ugly capital of Chiapas, without attractions. The railway has not yet reached it, but Serrabia's aeroplanes link it to the rest of Mexico, and there is running water in the hotel and a shower, though the lavatory leaks on the floor and the mosquito-netting stops nearly an inch from the edge of the window, and the door locks won't work and there remain traces of putty along window frames. It is like an unnecessary postscript to Chiapas, which should be all wild mountain and old churches and swallowed ruins and the Indians plodding by or watching from their mud towers the mule tracks from the north. In Tuxtla there are only *pistoleros* – but most of them were in Las Casas waiting for General Pineda – lottery sellers, and hate of the foreigner, and in the market there were hideous impoverished dolls of wood and painted rag, with wicked dowager home-made faces.

11. Return to the City

The dysentery was as bad as ever. I watched anxiously for the blood which would mean hospital and no escape for weeks from this country which I hated. I flew from Tuxtla to Oaxaca in a tiny stuffy Wasp, full of flies which slowly died out against the windows, bumping over the huge brown mountains with a mother and three tiny children and two cocks tied up in straw hats. Sometimes, far below, a church fell into ruin among a few huts in an abandoned plaza, a road snaked for a dozen miles and gave out like a river among rocks.

Serrabia himself was not flying the plane. I was a little disappointed, for I was eager to see a man about whom I had heard so much in Chiapas. He had begun a few years ago on credit with an old machine. The only thing he had owned was the rag he cleaned her with. Now he had a company with a capital of two hundred thousand pesos (say, fifty thousand dollars; it doesn't sound much, but it's a lot for provincial Mexico). One plane flies daily with mail to Mexico City from Tuxtla, on Tuesdays another goes to Oaxaca, and every once in a while a plane visits Las Casas and Yajalon – an old plane which rocks slowly along between, not over, the mountains.

Serrabia himself is a God-made airman. Some people say that the mysterious plane heard at night and supposed to be a German conspirator from Guatemala is really Serrabia just keeping his hand in with a little night flying for fun – fun over the Chiapas mountains. An American flyer once called on Herr F at Las Casas. He was shaken by his trip – he said only a madman or a genius could keep a service going over such a state. Every now and then Serrabia opens a new district. Once he was about to fly Herr F back to Las Casas from Tuxtla when he got the idea of visiting a new village a little out of the way, where the mayor had promised to level a landing-ground. He sent a wire and received a satisfactory reply – the ground was ready. But when they came over the village they could tell the grass had not been cut – impossible to see any obstructions. Nevertheless Serrabia decided to land, cutting a big swathe along the field. The only trouble, he said, was to get up again; he must just taxi back along his tracks. When they were again in the air they began to lurch in a curious way. Herr F took a look behind and saw the tail was loose and flapping. That didn't put Serrabia out: he landed on a river bank and walked up to a *finca* to find some string. They hadn't any string, but he tied up the tail with fishing-line and said he thought perhaps they'd better make for Villahermosa instead of Las Casas – they had workshops there. So they flew right across Chiapas into Tabasco and landed – it was a long way round for Herr F. On that small landing-field another Mexican plane – two-engined – had just come in from Guatemala, all the way with one engine missing. They have as little fear, these pilots, as mechanical sense. I was always glad to arrive somewhere – at Salto, Yajalon, Oaxaca.*

* Since this was written Serrabia has paid the usual penalty of daring in the air.

Oaxaca was lovely in its way, but I was too sick and tired to care for any way, even this way of busy little bosky squares. Hideous peasant pottery in the shops; above the cathedral door a lovely group in stone of the Queen of Heaven crowned. It was odd to go into a church again and see the sanctuary light burning and people kneeling before the Host and notices of Mass and Benediction. An oriental flat-roofed town under the leonine wrinkled hills, with what might be the domes of mosques rising a little way above the even level, from the air it has the appearance of a paved square and life going on subterraneanly. I was back where sometimes I had longed to be – on the tourist track; at any moment I expected to see my old friend from Wisconsin coming round a corner, eager to introduce me to a porter or a waitress who had looked after him. This was a city described in guidebooks where you could hire a taxi and see the sights.

First the cathedral, started in the sixteenth century. The interior seemed curiously small because of the elaborate side-chapels. It was all red velvet and gold: it gave an effect of being padded like some prayer books are. It was a place for prelates, not for prayer. Then the famous Santo Domingo, completed at the end of the seventeenth century. Some people say it is one of the finest churches in the world, but somehow it missed me altogether; I preferred its humbler namesake in Las Casas with the Indians crowding in. They are proud there of the genealogical tree – elaborate foliage spreading across the ceiling in high relief, blossoming into crowned figures, among branches of grapes, reaching at

237

last a pale aristocratic face. But it isn't beautiful; it is too low, too oppressive; suppose a crown should fall? One stoops under the weight of the monstrous Spanish dynasty. The exterior is lovely – all the exteriors in Oaxaca are – solid, simple, blocked out, the carving subordinated to the shape, not as in San Luis Potosí crazily rioting and hiding the form of the church. The convent attached to Santo Domingo is lovely too, what is left of it: the broken patio with a classical fountain, ruined in the time of Juárez, the Indian from this state who conquered Maximilian and first began what he hoped was the destruction and what has proved to be the salvation of the Church. Half of it now is cavalry barracks – a soldier asleep in his leggings, on a fallen stone like a cat, the points of a horse painted upon a wall instead of a Madonna, a bugle blowing. But the most human church to my mind in Oaxaca, unweighted with magnificence, is La Soledad; standing on a little terraced plaza, it contains perhaps the second holiest image in Mexico – that of the Virgin of Soledad (the Lonely), who appeared miraculously. She is the patroness of the state of Oaxaca and of all sailors; the size of a large doll, in a crown and elaborate robes, with a flower in her hand, she stands on the altar above the Host. She is Spanish of the Spanish, a Velázquez Virgin, and the loneliness she solaced, one imagines, was a Spanish loneliness of men heartsick for Castile. She has nothing in common with the wild state behind her, where even that week the Indians of one village staged a minor massacre.

MITLA

I'd had enough; I wanted to get home, not linger in even the most agreeable Mexican town, and Oaxaca was agreeable. The food, for Mexico, was good, but I couldn't eat it; dysentery emptied me; I couldn't remain on my feet for long at a time. I took a car that afternoon to Mitla. It had taken four days on muleback, and complete exhaustion, to see Palenque, if it can be said that I saw it. But it took only six hours' ride on a fairly good road, at a cost of fifteen shillings, to see Mitla, and certainly to the uninstructed these Mixtec ruins are far finer than Palenque's.

One went to them by way of other ruins, the modern ruins of farmsteads. Classical pillars and porticoes were falling back to mud, for they were made of mud just as the houses were, with only a plaster surface. There was no waste and little untidiness; no ugly remains of tile or corrugated iron. Here one was back in cactus land. All the other trees shook refreshingly in the slight afternoon wind, but not these rigid green pipes. Locusts perched on them in the sky-line attitude of horses, the ox-carts trudged by, men winnowed with spades, tossing the yellow seed against the sunset. We stopped at a cantina, and had some mescal – the driver told me it was good for dysentery. I don't think it was, but it was good for our spirits.

The ruins themselves, under the watchful eye of a colonial church, consist mainly of long narrow courts decorated with patterns of tiles, every pattern slightly varied: a kind of cross-stitch in stone. Huxley has aptly described them as 'petrified weaving'. On some walls are the remains of fresco work, like illustrations to a hideous Wells romance: all gas-masks, tanks, and guns of a yet uninvented horror, a mechanistic world. With whatever ferocity the Conquistadores fought, the faith they brought with them – the Virgin of Guadalupe and the Virgin of La Soledad – was more human than this. In the underground burial chambers we held candles to faint traces of blood-red paint. A great pillar, the Columna de la Muerte, supports the roof. The guide asks visitors to embrace it, and from the space left between the fingers, he tells how many years of life remain. It seems favourable – or unkind, as you like to put it – to the long-armed: I had seven more years.

Back to Oaxaca, and as I lay in bed I thought how strange was the sound of taxis at night. I hadn't heard them since Veracruz.

TRAIN JOURNEY

Nor had I been in a train since that previous century, coming down to Veracruz by way of Orizaba. The journey from Oaxaca to Puebla is less agreeable and interminably slow. Nevertheless, I was as happy as dysentery would let me be. Leaving Villahermosa for Palenque, Yajalon for Las Casas, Las Casas for Tuxtla, I had told myself that now at last I was going home, the clock hand was going down, the curve of the globe was turned. But this time, at last, I believed it.

I had nothing to read any more – Cobbett was finished long ago. Nothing to do as the train crawled through the wilderness but jot down notes, the random thoughts of a bored man.

'How one begins to hate these people – the intense slowness of that monolithic black-clothed old woman with the grey straggly hair – removing a tick – blowing her nose – trying to put up a blind or open a lemonade bottle, mooing with her mouth wide, fixing her eyes on people meaninglessly for minutes at a time, slowly revolving her black bulk all of a piece like a mule. And that middle-class child in the black velvet shorts, the striped jersey, and the bright-coloured jockey cap. The hideous inexpressiveness of brown eyes. People never seem to help each other in small ways, removing a parcel from a seat, making room with their legs. They just sit about. If Spain is like this, I can understand the temptation to massacre.

'We have stopped at a dreadful little mining village worse than anything in the Black Country. Mud huts and tin shacks sprawl on top of each other up the same bank, along a tiny polluted stream. One blind beggar makes his way down the train.

'One always hopes for one's children – somehow – a better life. How dreadful to be, like Fru R, an exile with them here!

'The mother of the odious child in the jockey cap knows all the railwaymen along the line. She holds little receptions at each station and even shakes hands with the driver of a passing train. She reads *El Crimen Sexual* and passes it on – to the old slow woman and her younger sister and the child. She has another child coming – or else worms.

'At —— (I have lost my time-table) a whole pack of bitches comes on board, running down the centre of the car picking up the crumbs and bones the passengers have dropped. When they've licked the place clean they leave – with an air of hungry routine. The train goes on.

'The tourist is not encouraged to take this train. There is a quick night service. One begins to understand why.

'The cleanliness and the dirt of these people – always a basin to dip the hands into before a meal and a glass of water to rinse the mouth with after – and then the spittle goes on the floor.

'In Porfirio Díaz's day there may have been atrocities on the haciendas, but one wonders whether their sum of suffering amounted to any more than the bomb in the post at Juárez, the shots in the Opera Cantina, the murders in the papers every day.

'The supporters of the proletarian revolution have staked their lives on a philosophy. It is the only reason they have for going on with the grim job of living. You cannot expect them to admit even to themselves that Russia has proved them wrong – or Mexico – without the comfort of a dramatic conversion to some other faith. Nobody can endure existence without a philosophy.

'Hours before Puebla an awful dusty landscape of whitish grey begins. Flat and uncultivated. Then like an oasis the village of Tehuacán, where the mineral water comes from – Garci Crespo. Bottles of mineral water for sale on the platform before the desert begins again. A consumptive in the car asks to have the window opened. He gestures towards his chest, to explain. He wears a big Mexican hat and a jersey and a scarlet neckerchief – a black Lawrence beard. A little tiny voice comes out – like the noise you get from the whistles in children's crackers. He drinks some water and drops back. There is nothing left of him but the fierce black beard and the big hat. His skin is like paper: his lungs can hardly exist at all.

'The odious child takes all the paper cups from the water-tap by the lavatory and destroys them one by one. Nobody stops him. The white dust from the appalling plain blows against the glass. The heat, with the windows shut, is stifling.

'The plain becomes littered with churches, like pieces

of rock. Dusk drops. Darkness, and eccentric domes
against the black clouds and the stars.'

PUEBLA

Puebla was the only Mexican town in which it seemed to
me possible to live with some happiness. It had more
than the usual wounded beauty: it had grace. Something
French seemed to linger there from Maximilian's time.
You could buy old French glass and portraits of Carlotta
on paper-weights; even the arts and crafts of Puebla
were civilised in a Victorian, European way: glass like
Bristol glass and delicious little sticks of fruit nougat,
toys of straw like the paintings of Tchelichev. And I had
not imagined the tiled churches so delicate in colour, for
tiles can be hideous even in Puebla where the manu-
facturers have presented tiled seats in the public gardens
which advertise in mauve and green majolica their
cigarettes and mineral water. I remember a church
picked out in a thin line of daffodil against the sky. The
air was clear and smokeless, but not so thin as in Mexico
City, and the women were lovely and well dressed. A
kind of social Catholicism lingered here – different from
the faith of San Luis on the edge of violence, the
inanition of Orizaba, the patient carrying-on in the
capital, the wild beliefs of Chiapas. I wanted to return
here when I was well again, but of course I never did.

THE HIDDEN CONVENT

What most interested me in Puebla was the secret
convent of Santa Mónica where the American Rotarian
had been told he would see the bones of the nuns'

babies. It is a grim bizarre place; if it has beauty, it is a beauty which is caviare to the world. The convent was founded in 1678, but in Juárez's day, when the religious persecution began, it slipped quietly out of the knowledge of the world and was only rediscovered by detectives in 1935. For nearly a century it had existed, novices had been admitted and taken their vows and lived and died, without the authorities ever learning they were there. So small a contact has an enclosed convent with the world that it was easy to sever all but one thread which attached them to the life of Puebla. That thread was a servant who quarrelled with her mistress in the private house which formed the convent's façade.

You come to it towards the edge of town in a street that has known better days; tall grey houses slip socially downhill towards the tenement. The door stands always open like that of a shady hotel; stone dormitory stairs run up to a little room where decayed men wait for visitors. They have the plump dominating look of politicians on balconies, but they are shabbier – they are not on to quite such a good thing. The whole place is run now by the Freemasons as a kind of anti-God museum. One guide – as seedy and political in appearance as all the rest – consented to take me round at once and not wait for a party; later, going on hands and knees through a trapdoor, we nearly ran into a party head on, and I caught a few phrases, the regulation sneer against holiness. My guide surprisingly did not sneer; he simply related, leading the way first into the little dining-room where the family who occupied this house had their meals. Here it was that the detectives broke in three years ago on the evidence of the sacked maid. All she could tell them was that the convent was there; food was brought

and went somehow in – but where? – and from the
convent there emerged – but how? – embroideries to be
sold in return. It was a small house just one room deep
in a long street, and this dining-room contained a table
and a vase of flowers, a few hard chairs, two shelves in an
alcove in place of a sideboard, another vase of flowers
upon the floor beside the wall. The detectives had nearly
given the room up, when one of them shifted the flowers
and found a bellpush. He touched it and the whole wall
behind the shelves swung open, and on the other side
steps led straight down into the Mother Superior's
study. They found about forty nuns in the convent,
middle-aged women: there had been no novices for some
years.

'What happened to them?'

'Oh, they were dispersed,' my guide said without
animosity. 'They try to keep up their vocation in private
houses.'

We climbed down into the little hideous pious study:
two glass-fronted bookcases, a table with a dusty cloth,
a hard chair, dark pictures of old saints, an admonitory
Spanish image, a crucifix. Out of the study the Mother
Superior's bedroom – a wooden board to sleep on and
over the bed the ugly wounded face of God. It hadn't
been easy for the detectives even after that entrance;
they found the sleeping-quarters easily enough, but
where was the chapel? They discovered it eventually: a
stone slab was removed from behind the only bath, and
they crawled through – as we did now – into a chapel
lined with stalls. Hanging above each were a rope and
crown of thorns, and a great gilded altar stood at the end.
In a glass case enclosed in a reliquary was the founder's
withered heart, the colour of long-dried blood. There

were more relics in the older chapel behind, where holes in the wall allowed the nuns to watch at Mass the altar of a neighbouring church. Hearts and tongues had been taken out of their cases and lay about, some in chemical jars of spirits and others just piled on a plate like pieces of liver – uninteresting bits and scraps of long-dead people. Who ? No one knew. Another trapdoor led down into a dark retreat, where the nuns could go for contemplation, and to the burial place. The bodies were first bricked up and then when the flesh had fallen the bones were thrown into a common pit; now it was exposed, with a few skulls left for propaganda purposes.

We came upstairs again into a room lined with paintings on velvet – terribly idealised paintings of polite Carlo Dolci agonies. The politicians were very proud of these; they could see no beauty in the dark pit, but these, they were worth a million pesos, the guide said to me. I made some silly flippant remark. He wasn't listening. He said absent-mindedly as we came out, 'Yes, they have stolen everything from the Church.' It astonished me; here indeed was a traitor in the Masonic camp. I told him I was a Catholic, and he said softly and sadly (it came oddly from the seedy political face), 'Then you will sympathise with these poor women and the fight they were putting up.' He led me out, down a wide flight of colonial stairs, under baskets of fern, into the patio, full of trees and roses – one garden for the novices and a larger one for the nuns. They were full of scent and sunlight and quiet and desertion; a cross stood in the centre of a wall and the shrubs climbed up it like ivy. He picked a rose and gave it me – 'to remember those poor women by'. The other day I found it again, stuck at random between the pages of *Barchester Towers*, the potpourri scent creeping up from Mr Arabin's proposal, '"Answer me this," said Mr Arabin, stopping suddenly in his walk, and stepping forward so that he faced his companion. "Answer me this one question. You do not love Mr Slope? You do not intend to be his wife?"' It seems a long way from Barchester to Puebla, to the dark burial place and the pit of skulls where the Masonic guides crawl on hands and knees through the bathroom wall into the deserted chapel, a good deal farther than a few thousand miles, all the immeasurable distance between two human minds.

BACK AGAIN

It is quicker to go from Puebla to Mexico City by motor-coach than by train, and what I wanted above every-thing was speed. For just five weeks I had been out of touch with correspondents; so much can happen, and one never has the expectation of good news. Outside the bus office there was a beggar woman whom some hideous disease had bent double: she could only beg your boots for alms. Sweeping round towards fresh pairs of feet she slipped and fell. She lay there with her mouth and nose pressed on the paving, unable to move and unable to breathe until she was lifted.

I was too sick to appreciate the ride up on to the Mexican plateau – a magnificent road along the moun-tain edge. For the first time since I came to Mexico I could see the great volcano Popocatepetl, a cone of ice bobbing between the woods and peaks, over the decaying churches, like the moon outliving everything. It was beautiful, but I was more concerned with the incom-petence of the driver. These buses go every three hours, every day of the week, from Puebla to Mexico City; and yet before three-quarters of the journey had been done the driver ran out of oil completely. Full of boyishness and amusement, he didn't discover for quite a while what was wrong; it was the biggest joke to him and all the Mexicans, but my nerves could hardly stand it as we sat there by the side of the road waiting for a car with spare oil to pass and the afternoon advanced and I thought how the office where my letters waited closed at six.

In the end we did arrive in time, and I got my letters. As I thought, they weren't so good. A bill from a solicitor's, a lot of newspaper clippings about a lawsuit in London and what Sir Patrick Hastings had said and what the Lord Chief Justice.* It all seemed to me odd, fictitious, and rather silly. I got some medicine and took it and lay down. My room in the dark drab hotel had been moved to another floor, and my luggage was still in the storeroom on the roof and I couldn't find my overcoat. Some proofs of a novel which had been posted to me from New York on April 7 had not arrived, and this was April 21. All the cares and irritations and responsibilities of ordinary life came hurrying back; and I had imagined on that interminable ride to Palenque that once in Mexico City life would become so fine, easy, and luxurious – all brandy cocktails and bourbon and Coca Cola. Well, I had to see about a boat now to England, but I hadn't enough money to pay the fare until I got my deposit back from the immigration office, and of course the value of the peso since I came over the border had slumped. Money cares crowded in, things which had to be seen to . . . and I had been unhappy in Las Casas because there had been nothing to do.

* A libel suit brought against me by Miss Shirley Temple.

I lay on my bed beside the telephone and read again what the counsel and judge had said. There was nothing else to read because my books were in the storeroom on the roof. There seemed to be a threat of further proceedings, I don't know why or on what charge. The whole thing was too bizarre to be true. The telephone leered at me like an idiot with its open mouth. One never gets used to the silence of a telephone in a city where one is a stranger. It adds to loneliness. Perhaps I'd ring somebody up, but whom? In Mexico City there is always the difficulty that there are two telephone services. Unless you telephone by the same kind as the other man's you can't get in touch.

In the end I rang up the secretary of the Legation and went and had some drinks and heard the latest news of Cedillo – how he'd been appointed military commandant of Michoacán and pleaded sickness and lay quiet at Las Palomas. No one yet imagined that he was going to be driven to arms. Then I walked back down the Paseo under the phosphorescent lights of the Reforma. The cars hurtled by and the Indian garage hands in dungarees hugged their girls innocently on the stone seats and some kind of procession of women went by with banners (the oil dispute again); the Avenida Juárez, of course, smelt of sweets. The brandy had made me feel better and I tried to eat some dinner.

There was a new waiter since I'd gone away: thin and dark, with a too confidential smile. He asked me whether I was all alone and I said I was. I thought he wanted to know if I was ready for my dinner or waiting for somebody else. I asked him for a Garci Crespo, to take to my room, and he smiled again confidentially and didn't bring it. I had to ask him several times before I got it, and

every time he nodded more winningly, darkly, knowingly
– as if I were insisting on the letter of a code. When I was
undressing, the glass of the door darkened; somebody
scratched, scratched at the pane: it was the waiter. I
asked him what he wanted; he merely grinned and said
hadn't I asked for a Garci Crespo? I slammed the door
shut and a little while later he came padding up the
passage and scratched again. I shouted to him to go and
turned out the light, but for a long while the small
vicious shadow waited, with the patience of a snake, on
the other side of the glass.

It was a bad night. On the floor below a hysterical
woman screamed and sobbed and a man spoke every way
in vain – patiently, roughly, with love and with hate.
God knows what relationship was breaking up so publicly
in the hotel room. Next day I watched the couples in the
lounge and the elevator, the brown impassive sentimental
Mexican eyes. Surely some mark would be left on a face
by the outrageous night, but none showed. And the
waiter came winningly forward to take my order and
smiled with forgiveness when I said, 'Garci Crespo.' Of
course the woman screaming and the waiter nibbling
outside the door might happen anywhere, but here, in
this city, on the night of what I'd thought would be so
happy a return, they seemed more than usually in the
picture – of a country of disappointment and despair.

OLD THREADS

It was like beginning things all over again. I had forgotten in Chiapas the hatefulness of Mexico City: the
shops full of junk – bad serapes and bad china and
hideous elaborate silver filigree – the taxis tooting all the

time. What had exhausted me in Chiapas was simply physical exertion, unfriendliness, boredom; life among the dark groves of leaning crosses was at any rate concerned with eternal values.

I picked up threads – the dentist first: I couldn't avoid him in the Francisco Madero. He hadn't seen his girl again. He seemed more than ever an awful bore. He couldn't forget that his family had once been rich landowners in Yucatán. He insisted on taking me here and there to see his wife, his mother, an uncle. We walked upstairs and downstairs; he ordered taxis imperiously at my expense. An introduction, and then down the stairs again and another taxi. 'I want you to meet my cousin.'

There were notices stuck up in the streets about an election in Jalisco. 'Four Reasons why we do not support the candidature of Silvano Barbo González. Silvano Barbo González is a fool, an adventurer, an ingrate, a double traitor. He is a fool because . . . an adventurer because . . .'

I hung around the post office waiting for my proofs. I had traced them at last, they were there; but I couldn't have them for another three days. To get a parcel it is first necessary to receive an official notification, which has to be presented between certain hours at a particular window – there is always a queue. Then you are given another paper to sign. This paper has to be carried to another window where you pay an arbitrary charge, said to be calculated by the weight. Then to another window. At a fourth window, I think (memory begins to fail), you receive your parcel. As there is a queue at each window it is impossible to go through the whole routine before the closing hour. You come back and carry on where you left off last time . . .

The medicine did me good. It reduced the dysentery to manageable proportions. Conscience told me that I hadn't visited any of the right places. I took a bus therefore to Taxco, four hours away beyond Cuernavaca.

Taxco is the showplace of the Mexican tourist belt – old Mexico carefully preserved by a society of businessmen and American artists known as 'The Friends of Taxco'. It is the Greenwich Village of Mexico (Mr Spratling makes his silver jewellery there), with a touch of Capri about it, and it is adequately described by Miss Frances Toor in her invaluable guide to the tourist belt, 'Taxco. (Azt. "Ball Game"): A mining town, founded by Borda. Pop., 3500. Alt., 5000. Beautiful and picturesque. Colonial and European in aspect. Even and agreeable climate, crisp nights. Good swimming.'

Taxco, I suppose, would be charming enough, as it clambers up all sides of a steep hill towards a little bosky plaza and a grotesque and lovely church, all crusted ornament and contorted gold, if it had not become an American colony – a colony for escapists with their twisted sexuality and their hopeless freedom. The place has rotted – the soldiers lie about in the streets at night with their women like dogs. All the shops are full of arts and crafts. Directly you get off the bus the children swarm around with a few words of English. 'Shave, sir?' 'Hotel, sir?' 'This is Guadalupe Street, sir.' Nearly all the hotels – from the great luxury barrack on the hilltop downwards – are American managed. The local schoolmaster sat in the plaza having his shoes shined; young and plump and immature with glossy hair, he tried to take on himself the part the priest would have performed in the old days. He was benevolent and patronising, he knew everybody, but unlike the priest he knew nothing. He sat there like a poster advertising something of no value to anyone at all.

Cuernavaca has at any rate what Taxco has not – the interest of history – though not much else except some good hotels, the country homes of diplomats, what was once Cortés's palace (given over to politicians and the sentimental frescoes of Rivera), and little obscene bone figures of men with movable phalli sold secretively by small boys near the bus stop. It is the capital of Morelos, once one of the richest states of Mexico, which was left barren by Zapata's useless rising. A week-end resort for Mexico City, it lies two thousand feet and more below the ridge that separates Morelos from the Mexican plateau, and no one who has read Miss Rosa King's account of her experiences in the Zapata rising can climb that long winding hill, between the scrub and thorn trees to the plateau without remembering the refugees who swarmed up there – women and children crushed together in panic-stricken flight, trampling each other down hour after hour while Zapata's men picked off the rear. That was not much more than twenty years ago; now public taxis will take you from Cuernavaca to the capital – about sixty miles – for two shillings. But history in Mexico has to be very ancient before you feel safe from its influence – any day the new motor-road may hear the shots again, and indeed all the way along from Taxco to Mexico you come on the little military stations which keep the road safe for tourists, or nearly safe. A friend of mine – with her father, an American Senator – was held up by bandits near Taxco only eighteen months ago. The day I passed the poor huts of the soldiers – just twig and mud, like birds' nests, on the bank – were decorated with faded bunting for Soldiers' Day, when the President was to pay special honour to his army, with an eye to Cedillo up in San Luis. The capital was everywhere decorated with posters in honour of the heroic defenders of the Republic, and here along the millionaire's motor-road the heroes looked out of their wretched huts, under the cheap bunting, their overcoats turned up to the ears against the icy evening air.

At the top of the ridge above the Mexican plain one emerged far above the sunset, which poured out between the mountains – a pale green under-water light shading into gold across the Mexican plain towards the volcanic snows, over more churches than you could count of faint pink stone, over haciendas like broken toys, and the wrinkled hills, a hundred luminous miles. On a hilltop a gigantic razor blade, advertising somebody's perfect shave, caught the last light.

ALL QUIET

Father Q came to see me and rang up the Bishop of Tulancingo. Over the telephone he called him Señor – '*Sí, Señor, no, Señor.*' Then we set out together to call on him. He was a different type of man from the Bishop of Chiapas; dark, stout, and young, he reminded me a little of an Indian diplomat. His surroundings seemed more practical and less pious than the old exile's. He wore black lay clothes – only his ring betrayed his rank – and he had an agreeable air of authority and humour. He was like a general in the field, and his field was not his diocese but the whole area of persecution. It was he who, with six girls, had started the training college I have mentioned, in the days of the worst persecution. At the time when Pro was shot he was in prison himself. But Pro was not a solitary victim – he counted over others he had known as we went for a drive together out to Chapultepec, sitting square, talking with immense satisfaction of death. 'The Church needed blood,' he said. 'It always needs blood.' It was the duty of priests and bishops to die; he had no sympathy for complaint and pious horror . . . 'You see the man who is driving us?' he said. 'He is the brother of María de la Luz Camacho, the girl they killed at Coyoacán' (the suburb where Trotsky lived with Rivera in the floodlit villa).

A life – in the worst tradition of uncritical piety – has been written of María de la Luz.* Out of its fervid pages a kind of pathos emerges, the pathos of pious tea parties, study circles, leagues of this and that, matched against the ruthless Garrido. I had seen the results of Garrido's work in Tabasco. Here, when he was Minister of Agriculture, he had organised an attack at the end of 1934 on the Coyoacán church during Mass. Revolvers were distributed to the Red Shirts at the town hall; María Camacho heard of the danger, went to the church – dressed in her best clothes – and waited in the doorway for the attack. Her courage gave others courage, and when the attack came she was the first to fall. Father Dragon with exemplary piety digs up the records of tea parties, amateur dramatics; the fact remains that in Mexico the Catholic societies which we regard in England with such suspicion, with their ribbons and medals and little meetings after Benediction, have been lent the dignity of death.

* *María de la Luz: Protomartyr of Catholic Action*, by Anthony Dragon, S. J.

The Bishop, leaning back in the smooth efficient car driven by the brother of a martyr, said, 'I wish you could have met the Bishop of Veracruz. *There* is a man . . .' In the modern city – among the American teashops, the advertisements for safety razors, the dapper night clubs – there existed, besides medieval violence, this medieval sanctity. The electric-light signs flashed on and off; the Bishop spoke of the other bishop who was dying now in the hospital – his mission in Havana, the most hopeless place in all the Catholic world for missions, where hardened racketeers of the brothel and dance-hall and cocktail lounge wept; how he lay anonymously in bed in a Colombian hospital, crippled with sciatica, next to a dying man who needed a priest – 'I am a priest': his charity. Every week in Mexico City, after he had been expelled from his diocese, he would spend four hundred pesos on food for the poor. He would load the food in a basket and wait until he saw an old decrepit taxi, the kind of taxi which would find it hard to get a fare. Then he would haggle sharply with the driver, driving a hard bargain, and afterwards would ask if he were married and how many children he had and at the end of the drive would give him a peso above the bargain for his wife and one for each child. He would drive into the poorest streets of the city and, choosing what seemed the most hopeless house, he would tell the driver to take the basket. 'Go up to the door and when the woman comes tell her God has sent this . . .'

GOOD-BYE

Next night I went with Father Q to a small private celebration of Archbishop Ruiz y Flores's jubilee – the

256

apostolic delegate who had been expelled from Mexico by Calles, and who was now Archbishop of Morelia. He sat there in the front row of the little hall in the German Club on an uncomfortable drawing-room chair, a small old man with a Pickwickian face, if one can imagine Pickwick a little embittered by the world's violence and injustice – he had seen the worst days of all. Father Q led me up and introduced me. We talked for a little while of Tabasco and Chiapas; he made some infinitely polite remark about England; men in dark suits who might or might not have been priests stood around, with courteous patience. The old man, I remembered, had fought with Calles, bargained, seen his treaties broken, gone patiently on. One was looking at history. I went back to Father Q and my little gilt chair.

It was a very polite gathering, stiff and middle-class and elderly on the hard chairs, there to listen to a programme of music and poetry; it was the end of Mexico for me, my bags packed and my ticket taken. Outside the drums were beating on the eve of Soldiers' Day – the sound of bugles mingled with the gentle decorous professorial music of Debussy. It was like a dream; almost everyone I had met was in this small room. There was the historian Dr C, who had taken me to see the Bishop of Chiapas – oh, years ago. There was the Bishop himself in the front row. And there was the priest from San Luis with the broad gentle face, the air of learning borne quietly for the sake of the humble and the workers. And there was the old aristocratic sceptic I had prayed beside at Guadalupe; but when she turned her head I saw it was another, turned out of the same mould of education and lost possessions and patience. I looked around, half expecting everybody to be here – the dentist with his girl from the Waikiki, the Socialist school teacher from Yajalon, the Norwegian widow with her paralysed mouth and her heavy anxieties, my muleteer, badgered and hysterical, praying to the Mother of God, the American dentist losing the thread of every conversation, spitting and hopeless and thinking of the States, the priest in the tweed cap and motoring-coat and the mauve patch of skin, the old German teacher rattling his umbrella and saying, 'Life is motion', the blind youth Tomás.

'Look, look,' Father Q said excitely, 'he's wearing a Roman collar.' A priest was taking his conductor's baton and arranging the choir – ugly, pious, rather spotty girls most of them, dressed decorously to hide the arms and necks. One didn't wear a Roman collar in Mexico – it entailed a fine of five hundred pesos for the first offence. The bugles and the drums went on outside . . . marching feet . . . the heroic defenders of the Republic preparing to descend on San Luis and Las Palomas. Where was the man who had passed out by the blue soda-water siphon? And the man who had ridden up in the dark as the storm broke near Palenque – '*con amistad*'? And the old hotel-keeper who had regretted the days of Díaz? Then Debussy started, *assez vif et bien rythmé*, and then somebody made a speech – full of tortuous Spanish compliments to the little old man in the front row. People applauded – politely. Of course those others were not there – they were out in the violent world outside; this was headquarters, where they made blueprints – interminably – for a peaceful and holy world.

The '*Regina Cæli*' of Lotti, and then a 'discurso' by a Jesuit – he, too, on this day of jubilee, wore his Roman collar. Fifty years in the priesthood . . . more Debussy, *trés modéré* . . . Señor Alfonso Junco, a leading Catholic poet, read a poem – unrhymed, statuesque, chilly . . . *Ave Maria* . . . it was growing late and rather cold . . . another 'discurso' by a well-known and popular lawyer, full of jokes I couldn't understand. I watched the backs of the bishops – Tulancingo, Chiapas, Mexico, Morelia – and thought of the grave of crosses above Las Casas as the sun went down. It should have been the end of the programme, but another poet – a big, bouncing man in an ill-fitting evening suit and with black curly hair – came on to the platform. He had written something specially for the occasion called 'Night in Michoacán'. He bellowed it out – great rhymed Lepanto stanzas full of fury and drama and sentiment – and the bishops sat on. A last piece of music and the celebration was over. I said good-bye to the historian and Father Q and the priest from San Luis: Mexico, too, was over. The bishops made their way down the stairs in herds; priests turned up the collars of their coats to hide the Roman collars; people genuflected awkwardly on the stairs to the old Arch-bishop, who had worked the miracle of the Eucharist now for fifty years. He came gently down, bitter, kindly, Pickwickian: the dangerous man. They had put him on an aeroplane with detectives in 1932 – he was allowed to take nothing but his breviary – and dumped him across the border.

Here had been, mark, the general-in-chief,
Thro' a whole campaign of the world's life and
    death,
Doing the King's work all the dim day long,
In his old coat and up to his knees in mud . . .

EPILOGUE

(1)

THE BLIND EYE

The way back to Veracruz by the same train: everything repeated. Even the boy singers came on at the same station and sang the same songs and lurched on afterwards towards the same Pullman. The same food and the same tourist trophies at the stations. Only this time the volcanoes were there, moving half submerged like icebergs along the horizon, and this time I didn't get out at Orizaba. Nothing was quite so effective a second time; even the gardenias were a little tarnished.

Next morning the rain came pouring down – the weather was breaking up. There seemed no means of dealing with the rain – the streets flooded immediately. There was no way of getting across from one pavement to another. How does life go on in the rainy season? There was nothing to do but go aboard the German liner in which I had booked a third-class passage, hang over the rail and watch the loading, and wait for the night. The last contact with Mexico was a bribe to the customs man of five pesos to leave my bags unopened – duty is paid on going out of Mexico as well as on going in. There seemed to be a lot of Spaniards on board – one could tell it from the accent – but the stewards carefully segregated them for meals, one service for Latins and one for Nordics. Among the Latins were included a few hawk-like Syrian women on the way to Palestine.

The shadow of the Spanish war stretched across the South Atlantic and the Gulf; it cropped up in Las Casas of an evening round the radio – one couldn't expect to escape it in a German ship calling at Lisbon.

My cabin held six, but at first there were only five of us: an old man who never spoke a word, a fat Mexican who spat all night upon the floor and said, '*No se puede dormir*', because *he* couldn't sleep, and a young Spaniard with a hard handsome idealist's face, and his small son whom he disciplined like a drill-sergeant. There was no doubt at all where he was going, and, when I returned to my cabin just before we sailed, I found a stranger wearing a beret and an old suit which didn't look natural: you felt he was used to a better cut. There were others in the cabin, too; they blocked the door after I got in; they wore their berets like a uniform and each had a little gold chain round his neck with a holy medal dangling under the shirt. At first I couldn't understand their Castilian – they seemed perturbed, they wanted to know who I was. The word '*inglés*' didn't reassure them, but when I said '*Católico*' and showed *my* lucky charm they looked a little easier. The stranger was a stowaway, he was going to 'pay the Reds'; I must promise to tell no one, they said, blocking the door, till we had left Havana. As we sailed out of Veracruz that night we passed a Spanish ship which had been impounded since the war started and the third class emptied on to the deck and gave the dark and silent boat a noisy farewell, '*Arriba España. Viva Franco.*' The stewards smiled gently, bringing round the salad, hearing nothing.

After Havana the volunteers began to disclose themselves, more than two dozen of them. Many of them had their wives and children with them; they wore their uniforms quite openly when we were once at sea, black forage caps and Sam Browne belts, blue shirts with the Falangist fasces embroidered on the pocket. They were very noisy and carefree, without bravado; you felt that going to war was one of the natural functions of man. There was something agreeably amateur, too, about their Fascism. I think the Germans looked a little askance when the arms went up in salute for nothing at all, for a silly old man, for a joke. '*Arriba España's*' and '*Viva Franco's*' burst boisterously out for no reason on the hot unshaded deck, with a hint of mockery. Killing the Reds, that was a man's occupation; but all this dressing up to do it, that was a joke, a game. They enjoyed it, but not in the serious German way. Oh, the consultations on deck, the handing out of envelopes, the open conspiracies. There was one printed form which aroused my curiosity: instructions from Burgos? I learned what it was when Sunday came.

The blind non-intervention eye was very blind indeed, and the German ear was very deaf. On Sunday there was a Church parade; the volunteers marched up to Mass in the first class; twenty-five of them lined the wall in uniform; one man stood at attention on each side of the altar; it was impressive, as a funeral is. A monk preached (I had seen him playing chess, cheery and unshaven in an old striped shirt and no tie). He preached on suffering and sacrifice and offering up your agony to God. After the Mass was over, before the priest had time to leave the altar, the volunteers broke into the Falangist hymn – that was what they had been learning all the week from the printed forms. And then, inevitably, the Fascist salute, '*Arriba España. Viva Franco*'; every arm went up but mine, yet no one minded at all. These were

Spaniards, not Germans.

It was odd comparing them with their German allies – the young German farmer, for instance, from Chiapas, who joined heartily in the right cries and hated Christianity. I tried to involve him in argument in front of the volunteers. 'This,' I wanted to indicate, 'is your ally.' They stood listening with mild astonishment, the holy medals dangling round their necks, while he plunged bull-like at Christianity.

'But you must admit that – so far – nationalism hasn't produced any art, literature, philosophy, to compare with the Christian.'

'I see you do not know the works of Ludendorff. Listen to me. The Christians have only winned because they have killed all not Christian. Once we had nothing to give people, only Religion. Now we give the Nation. But we are not atheists like the Reds. We have a God, one God.'

'The old Jewish Jehovah?'

'No, no. A Force. We do not pretend to know what he is. A Principle.'

The volunteers listened politely to the new Germany, but one of the cooks jumped overboard; he hadn't been home for ten years; perhaps he couldn't stand the prospect.

For more than four hours we sailed in circles looking for him; men were posted inconspicuously about the deck; everybody was seasick. A note of irritation became evident among the Nordics – a kind of faint peevish hatred of the man who had inconvenienced them. As for the Latins, they didn't care at all. Then the ship straightened out and went on. With terrible quickness the drowned desperate man was forgotten – people got their appetites back in time for dinner.

There is something dauntingly world-wide about a ship, when it is free from territorial waters. Every nation has its own private violence, and after a while one can feel at home and sheltered between almost any borders – you grow accustomed to anything. But on a ship the borders drop, the nations mingle – Spanish violence, German stupidity, Anglo-Saxon absurdity – the whole world is exhibited in a kind of crazy montage.

The world – the Syrian woman, for instance. She never washed; her clothes hid dismal secrets of uncleanliness; her sallow beaky face, with grey dusty hair and one false eye, never concealed an envy and hate for all the Western world. When her own meal was finished she would prowl back and forth behind our table watching every mouthful. She stole spoons and there would be sudden hideous scenes between her and the German stewardess, flaring up by the sideboard. She directed her special hatred at a middle-aged American woman, who should have been travelling tourist; on one occasion she came sidling up and spat into the American's open bag, while all her friends laughed.

The German ex-officer: when sober he was charming, small and fair with a secretive rat-like charm. He had been shot in the stomach during the war and now he drank and drank and drank. By night he would become speechless and immobile. In the early hours of the morning he could be seen sitting alone in the dining-room with his head hanging down and a cigarette guttering out between his fingers – like a doll from which the sawdust has run.

Then there was Kruger, a pale big man with clothes loose as though he'd shrunk, who came on board between detectives. He had been in a Mexican prison down at Tapechula in Chiapas, near the Guatemalan border; he had never expected to come out alive and now in his quiet gentle way, playing with the children, urging me not to have another drink, he showed an amazed gratitude for life. He had been looking after a *finca* for a Swede and one day he thought he'd go into town. He took a stroll round a little hot Pacific town, listened to the marimbas, sat down in the plaza. Two plain-clothes men came up and put revolvers to his head. In Tapechula they couldn't bear strangers. He had no papers, so they put him in jail and told him he'd never get out without them. For eight days in the tropical heat he had no food or water; the floor crawled with worms and other things; no exercise but walking up and down the common cell. The other prisoners tried to start a fight – even in prison you are a gringo, but he knocked a man down and that stopped that. He showed me his big mild bandaged hand; he'd broken it. A man who was in for drunkenness said he'd take a letter for Kruger to the German consul, and the consul brought him money for food, but said he could do nothing, because he had no papers. For three months Kruger stayed there in semi-starvation. Most of the people with him were murderers – one man who wasn't exactly a murderer (he had paid someone else to do the murder) suggested to Kruger that he write to the Mexican Government. He smuggled the letter out and the Government sent an agent down to Tapechula and fetched him away to Veracruz. There they kept him another two months in prison – it wasn't much better than Tapechula – and then shipped him on board the German liner for Hamburg. 'And why hadn't you any papers?'

'Oh,' he said, 'they were stolen from me in a hotel. Up by the American border. In Juárez. A bad town. Nothing but murder all the time.'

He leaned interminably over the rail just staring at the sea, being alive, smiling. Juárez was only one stage of a bizarre journey over a quarter of a century; he was what we call now an escapist. It came out in scraps during the fortnight's voyage, in no chronological order, like a Conrad novel, but when you put them together the scraps fitted. An extraordinary sense of goodness surrounded him, this man who had come from one prison and was probably going to another, for he had once deserted from a German ship and he never for a moment disguised his opinion of National Socialism. 'I am not afraid of anything,' he would say gently when you remonstrated – without boasting, just a fact like his broken hand. Even the German ship's officers recognised this quality of goodness, and extended to him the privileges which were allotted only to a chosen few of the third class. And always his random conversation would come back to one ambition – to be settled on the Amazon. He had once spent six months there, far up over the Peruvian border, on a tributary; and he was going back. Nobody could stop him. He'd stow away in one ship, jump another. When he spoke of it he was like a lover, and like a lover he brought the beloved name into every conversation. We would be talking of Hitler or of his other great theme, that money wasn't important, or of books or women, and then an added gentleness would come into his voice and he'd say, 'The Indians, they eat spiders. A great delicacy,' and you knew he was away in a land where a man could live on nothing, without violence or hate, where what you planted always grew and the water was good to drink and the climate was kind – except to fat men – and there was nothing to worry about any more for ever. Of course if you wanted gold, he said with pity, you could get it – from the natives in return for dynamite and cartridges. There were lots of old mines the Indians knew. He never bothered himself, though once he had got a small bottleful worth sixty marks, but it had soon gone in a hotel which charged seven marks a day. How good the natives were, he said with love; not like the Mexicans. (If he ever saw a Mexican again he'd kill him.) They ran away at first, but when they saw you meant no harm, they soon came creeping back . . . Paraguay was good too, good people; a man could have ten wives if he wanted wives. As for himself, he could go ten years without a woman . . . all he needed to be happy was to be back there, on the Amazon . . .

Leaning over the rail, looking at Havana with disapproval – nothing but drink and women – he said, 'You come with me to the Amazon.' I said I would for a few months. 'Oh, no,' he said, 'you will never want to go home – never. You can buy a house for fifty marks. Why, in Iquitos, the city, the Salvation Army bought a whole block in the square, with a cinema, for two thousand marks.' I said I had a wife and children. 'Never mind,' he said; 'you will never want to go home, never. You can get another wife there.'

He had left Germany in 1913, when he was nineteen, because he believed there was going to be a war. He was a sailor and they said to him, 'This is your last voyage. Next time you do naval service.' So he left his ship in New York and got a job as a fireman in an ice factory. Then he helped with row-boats on the Hudson, but his employer wanted him to marry, so he left that job and joined a circus. His job, because he'd been a sailor, was to test 'the big top'. Another time he was sent down to Alabama to work on a construction gang. After the war he shipped on a rotten old British freighter with bad boilers at Norfolk. The crew had all deserted, so they took men off the streets – twenty-five pounds a head to go to Liverpool. It took them fourteen days. At Liverpool the immigration officer repatriated the men, took away Kruger's employment papers, and sent him back to Germany. Then he got a boat, to the East, but the captain was an ex-naval officer and treated his men like dirt. Kruger lost his temper and threatened to kill the captain with a shovel; the captain called the chief, and he threatened to kill the chief too. So they said, 'You wait. We fix you when you get back.' At Alexandria they wouldn't give him any money for shore leave until he threatened to desert, and the same happened at Barcelona. At Barcelona he met a German baker. They went and bought a big cask of wine (he drank in those days); after a while they fell asleep beside the cask and when he woke the boat was gone and he had spent all his money. So he went to the German consul, who said, 'I know all about you, Kruger. You're a mutineer and a deserter. I will not give you a cent.' Kruger said, 'O K,' and enlisted in the Foreign Legion. He served two years – there wasn't a chance of getting away. After that he could choose any town in Spain in which to live and he chose Vigo, he didn't know why. An obscure episode fitted in there, I think, with a German painter who had two wives in different parts of the town. He wanted Kruger to marry too, but instead he got a boat to Lima and so he reached the Amazon. He had a Swedish employer there. 'His first wife,' he said with a gentle laugh at the quaintness of life, 'she was eaten by the Indians.' And so we made a date for Iquitos two years hence – he thought it might take him that long to get back to Paradise. He came gently up behind my chair on the windy third-class deck – the Azores were going by in a thin mist of rain, steep cliffs, a waterfall, the great white church of Flores, and the surf beating up – and he said, 'You worry too much. You don't want to worry. You just want to contemplate.'

'What ?' I said. 'My navel ?'

'No, no,' he said. 'Just think of nothing. Be calm.'

'Perhaps it's easy on the Amazon.'

'That's right,' he said, 'you don't need to bring anything with you. Perhaps a little dynamite. Just a pair of trousers and two shirts and a sunhat. A mosquito-net and a canoe perhaps – but you can get that cheap in Iquitos. You ask for me there. They'll tell you where I am.'

He thought perhaps he'd jump the ship at Lisbon, but they didn't give him a chance. He was carried remorselessly on towards Hamburg and prison. People were kind to him as they are kind to you before an operation, but playing all the afternoons with the children, he wasn't frightened. It was only one more thing to escape from, for escapists get accustomed to prison, hunger, sickness. Sometimes one wonders what it is they do – with so much hardship – escape.

It wasn't a very lucky ship. The day before the cook jumped overboard, an engine broke down and we had to go at half-speed most of the day; and then a woman in the first class fell asleep with a lighted cigarette in her hand and set fire to her bed and herself. It was very hot and then it was very cold, as if we were living through the seasons. Mexico went backwards at twenty knots over the edge of the world. Somewhere, I suppose, the *Ruiz Cano* rolled from Veracruz to Villahermosa and back and the sailors stood about doing up their trousers; the dentist was back at Frontera; and the Norwegian lady waited with hopeless optimism for her son's return. It is awful how things go on when you are not there.

The day before Lisbon silence came down on the third class. There were no '*Arriba España*'s' all the afternoon. The stern father walked up and down, up and down, his child hanging to his arm, up and down, drowned, you could tell, in a sea of unreality: here, for ten days, he had been on a pleasure cruise, there the train for Salamanca left at nine. There was a farewell dinner, perhaps the last good meal before the trenches; '*Auf Wiedersehen*' was printed inside a little scarlet heart on the menus, and there was a speech about 'our great ally' and Austria which had just been annexed – and sacrifice. It wasn't only the Germans who had been turning blind eyes all these days; but the blind eyes of the Spanish volunteers were now beginning to open, like those of new-born children opening on the lunar landscape of the human struggle.

A STATE OF MIND

The ARP posters were new, as one jolted through the hideous iron tunnel at Vauxhall Bridge, under the Nine Elms depot and the sky-sign for Meux's beer. There is always a smell of gas at the traffic junction where the road is up and the trams wait; a Watney's poster, a crime of violence, Captain Coe's Finals. How could a world like this end in anything but war? I wondered why I had disliked Mexico so much: *this* was home. One always expects something different.

> Through winter-time we call on spring,
> And through the spring on summer call,
> And when abounding hedges ring
> Declare that winter's best of all;
> And after that there's nothing good
> Because the spring-time has not come –
> Nor know that what disturbs our blood
> Is but its longing for the tomb.

In the grit of the London afternoon, among the trams, in the long waste of the Clapham Road – a Baptist chapel, Victorian houses falling into decay in their little burial grounds of stone and weed, a coal merchant's window with some fuel arranged in an iron basket, a gas showroom, and a grammar school for girls – I tried to remember my hatred. But a bad time over is always tinged with regret. I could even look back on the dark croquet lawn under the red-brick skyscraper of class-rooms with regret; it is as if everywhere one loses something one had hoped to keep. The young girl and the

Socialist teacher lay on their bunks in the rocking cell of the *Ruiz Cano* and hummed to each other tunes out of a cheap magazine. Why – on the Gulf – had that seemed bad and this good? I couldn't remember.

Mass in Chelsea seemed curiously fictitious; no peon knelt with his arms out in the attitude of the cross, no woman dragged herself up the aisle on her knees. It would have seemed shocking, like the Agony itself. We do not mortify ourselves. Perhaps we are in need of violence.

Violence came nearer – Mexico is a state of mind. One sat in the hideous little convent gymnasium while the rain fell and the bells outside sounded for evensong and a man explained how our children were to be evacuated. An aeroplane flew low overhead and the tradesmen sat in their drab Sunday best and listened, and a woman cried melodramatically. The Mother Superior – with a bone-white face and a twitching upper lip – made notes in pencil. The telephones were cut off, the anti-aircraft guns were set up on the common outside, and the trenches were dug. And then nothing happened at all – the great chance of death was delayed. The motor-cars came cruising back along the Spaniards Road and through Hyde Park; poverty and lust called to each other as usual in the wintertime early dark.

And in Chiapas the white churches fell to ruin staring up at Serrabia's planes flying overhead – like faces the world has corrupted waiting through the dry months and the rains for the footstep, the voice, 'Is it easier to say your sins be forgiven you . . . ?'